SERIOUS DARING

SERIOUS DARING

The Fiction and Photography of Eudora Welty and Rosamond Purcell

Susan Letzler Cole

The University of Arkansas Press
Fayetteville • 2016

Manufactured in Korea
ISBN: 978-1-68226-011-1
e-ISBN: 978-1-61075-595-5
20 19 18 17 16 5 4 3 2 1
Text design by Ellen Beeler
∞The paper used in this publication meets the minimum requirements of the American National Standard for Permanence of Paper for Printed Library Materials Z39.48-1984.
Library of Congress Control Number: 2016936801

To Meg Gertmenian
And in memory of Andrew DeShong

Contents

Preface

Oddly, this book began with a famous missing photograph. In *Camera Lucida: Reflections on Photography*, Roland Barthes discusses the "essence" of photographs and reproduces a large number of them but refuses to reproduce a precious 1898 Winter Garden photograph of his mother as a child. Alone in the apartment where she had died, he looks at images of his mother, seeking "the truth of the face I had loved," and when he finds it, he will not show it to us: "For you, it would be nothing but an indifferent picture, one of the thousand manifestations of the 'ordinary.'" Barthes recreates the non-reproduced image as text. In the end, what we know of Barthes's beloved mother comes to us from his writing about her photograph. "Such is the Photograph: it cannot *say* what it lets us see."[1]

Thus began my obsessive interest in photography and in the relation between the photographer's eye and what Eudora Welty calls "the visualizing mind,"[2] between seeing and saying, and in how one mode of artistic "vision" might refract or rehabilitate another.

Barthes tells us of "that rather terrible thing which is there in every photograph: the return of the dead. . . . Photography has something to do with resurrection." Susan Sontag makes a similar claim: "Photography is an elegiac art, a twilight art. . . . All photographs are *memento mori*. A photograph is both a pseudo-presence and a token of absence."[3] A photograph is a material presence, inanimate yet animating in us a recognizable terror: the dead can and cannot return. Like writing, it calls our attention to the power of the image, ever more problematic in the contemporary world of digital technology.

In my exploration of the photographic eye and visualizing mind, the interdisciplinary art of ekphrasis seems of particular relevance. It has as its root the Greek verb that means "to recount," and it refers to a written account of a visual scene, literal or imaginary. In studies of visual images, including photographs, ekphrasis can be used to portray in words what one is actually seeing. In the description of Achilles's shield in Homer's *Iliad* or in the description of a Greek urn in John Keats's ode, it can be used to portray an already fictional object.[4] But the distinction is not so clear-cut as it seems. Ekphrasis is a doubling of images: one "images" in words what one is "seeing" or what one wants someone else to see, already an interpretation by the visualizing mind.[5] In this doubling of vision, an image becomes sealed in language from which it once again escapes as each new reader looks at the text.

American photographer-writers Eudora Welty and Rosamond Wolff Purcell are well aware of the problematic nature of both photographic and literary work.

What the camera "sees" is not what the photographer sees looking through the lens of a camera. Language is slippery, offering double or triple versions of its meaning even to the most vigilant reader. Shifting light, inversion, unexpected angles of vision, differences in depth of field, framing, convergence as vanishing point inside or outside the frame, blurring or ambiguity in the final developed form, boundary-crossing—these aspects of photography have their literary counterparts in the writing of Welty and Purcell. The question I wish to explore in particular is simply this: What happens when a would-be photographer becomes a celebrated writer and a would-be writer becomes a celebrated photographer?

One possible account of these contrasting trajectories would be that each artist gives up what the other artist brings to perfection. But Eudora Welty and Rosamond Purcell offer a more complicated story. Each paradoxically seems to give up, early in her life, interest in a mode of art that returns, resuscitated or refracted in a new form, like Shakespeare's Hermione, coming back from death as a statue that lives, in *The Winter's Tale*. The recovery of what seemed left behind, gone forever, represents a refusal to turn one's back on the past, allowing it to become a haunting presence in one's life and art.

Acknowledgments

This book would not have been possible without the generosity and kindness of many people who offered valuable assistance of different kinds during the periods of research and writing that produced *Serious Daring*: Justin Ardito, Jillian Bedell, Peggy Blumenthal, Pierre Bourgeois, Robert Bourgeois, Marya Bradley, Mary Baine Campbell, Alexandra Cannon, Christina Carew, Julia Coash, Sean Corcoran, Garrett Dell, Eric Donelson, Heather Dubrow, Deborah Frattini, Forrest Galey, William Germano, Elizabeth Gilliam, Robert Hubbard, Jeanette Huettner, Amie Keddy, Greg Knobelsdorff, Julie Lee, Ben Letzler, Joyce Letzler, Robert Letzler, Pearl McHaney, Jen Martin, Matthew Martin, Suzanne Marrs, Kelly Matera, Natalie Miller, Sean O'Connell, Dennis Purcell, Sylvia Shuey, Carol Stockton, Todd Swatling, Jeff Tillbrook, Alan Trachtenberg, Michael Witmore, and Pat Yeaman.

Andrew DeShong and Meg Gertmenian read anew all of Eudora Welty's fiction as they offered invaluable counsel on my discussions of her writing. Kenneth Letzler graciously bestowed time and expertise on matters legal and technological during every stage in the completion of this book. Jerome Nevins with infinite patience taught me the intricacies of accessing, reproducing, and placing each image in *Serious Daring* and, along with others, never stopped believing that the book would find its proper home. *Serious Daring* is seriously enriched by the photographs provided by the Mississippi Department of Archives and History and by Rosamond Purcell.

I deeply appreciate Dr. Julia M. McNamara's continual support of my research and writing as well as Albertus Magnus College's granting a sabbatical leave, 2009–2010, during which I completed the first draft of this book.

I am especially grateful to David Scott Cunningham and Deena Owens at the University of Arkansas Press for their strong support and careful shepherding of the manuscript through its various stages of preparation for publication, as well as to the staff at the press, who have been helpful at each stage: Brian King, Melissa Ann King, and Charlie Shields.

One nearly inexpressible acknowledgment remains. I want to thank my husband, David Cole, whose unwavering support, capacious wisdom, and ever-deepening love so beautifully accompany my life and my writing.

Introduction

So I do not give up the camera eye when I am writing—merely the camera.

—Wright Morris, *Time Pieces: Photographs, Writing, and Memory*

The photographer-writer Wright Morris seems to have settled a question raised by this book. In fact, he seems to settle it even more decisively when he adds: "I would say that the people who can write, and want to write novels, are offered few choices and have no options. They must become writers. They will bring their camera eye into their books. . . . I use the same eyes to type the pages of a novel and to focus the image on the ground glass." Well and good, but the eyes that serve in typing a page (such as this one) are not the same eyes that see life into a work of fiction. In a lecture given three years later, however, Morris qualifies his earlier statements: "Through writing, through the effort to visualize, I became a photographer, and through my experience as a photographer, I became more of a writer. . . . I would make one crucial distinction. What I *see* as a writer is on my mind's eye, not a photograph. Although a remarkable composite of impressions, the mind does not mirror a photographic likeness. To my knowledge I have never incorporated into my fiction details made available through photographs. . . . The mind is its own place, the visible world is another."[1] In revisiting his view of the relation between the writer's eye and the "camera eye," Morris clarifies the difference between them.

In this book, I bring together two women, American photographer-writers Eudora Welty and Rosamond Purcell, who seem worlds apart. *Serious Daring* travels along the roads taken by artists who find a kind of productive ambivalence in the desire to pursue one path after seeming to have forsaken another. The resolution of the tension underlying their different choices is illuminated by an examination of how, for each, the forsaken art stubbornly accompanies the chosen art.

Eudora Welty, born and bred in the American South, living in Jackson, Mississippi, for most of her life, had just published what may be her finest novel, *Losing Battles* (1970), at the time when Rosamond Wolff Purcell, born and bred in the Boston area, where she has lived for most of her life, began to take her first tentative photographs.

Eudora Welty's father, Christian Welty, was from rural Ohio; her mother, Chestina Andrews, from the mountains of West Virginia. Rosamond Purcell's father,

Robert Lee Wolff, was born in New York City; her mother, Mary Andrews, in Boston. (Curiously, Rosamond Wolff Purcell and Eudora Welty were both named after their maternal grandmothers, who themselves had the same maiden names: Rosamond Capen Andrews and Eudora Carden Andrews.) Welty's family settled in Jackson, Mississippi, where Christian Welty found lifelong work as one of the directors of the Lamar Life Insurance Company. The Wolff family settled in Cambridge, Massachusetts, where Robert Wolff taught courses in Byzantine and Russian history as well as in Victorian literature at Harvard University. Born in 1909, Eudora Welty remained unmarried and childless during her long life. Rosamond Wolff Purcell, born in 1942, has been married for more than four decades to photographer and optical engineer Dennis Purcell, with whom she has two sons, Andrew and John.

Early in her life, Eudora Welty wished to be taken seriously as a photographer. She is celebrated today as a short-story writer, novelist, essayist, lecturer, memoirist, and, finally, photographer. At the age of ninety, Welty "was interested in a new publishing venture": a book of photographs of Mississippi cemeteries, titled *Country Churchyards*. "A year later," Suzanne Marrs tells us, "[her] health and memory were precipitously failing." Eudora Welty died on July 23, 2001, at the age of ninety-two, and was buried, "within sight of the house where she had been born," in Jackson's Greenwood Cemetery—the very cemetery she had photographed first, and often, almost seventy years earlier.[2]

Rosamond Wolff Purcell, who early in her life wished to be taken seriously as a writer of fiction, has become an internationally acclaimed photographer as well as an author and memoirist. At the time of this writing, Purcell was at work on "a new publishing venture" of her own: producing visual images of particular passages in Shakespeare's plays, using, "as my stage—my only stage," photographs of reflections from mirrored apothecary jars.[3] Rosamond Wolff Purcell has said, "Once a photographer . . . always."[4] Perhaps the ninety-year-old Eudora Welty would have agreed.

In his famous essay, "The Work of Art in the Age of Mechanical Reproduction," Walter Benjamin both celebrates and limits the role of photography. He asserts, problematically, that photography was "the first truly revolutionary means of reproduction. . . . [F]or the first time in world history, mechanical reproduction emancipates the work of art from its parasitical dependence on ritual."[5] In this context, as Richard Wolin points out, Benjamin seems to view as necessary the sacrifice of "a unique, non-mechanically reproduced auratic art."[6] In "Some Motifs in Baudelaire," Benjamin defines his concept of aura: "Experience of the aura . . . rests on the transposition of a response common in human relationships to the relationship between the inanimate or natural object and man. The person we look at, or who feels he is being looked at, looks at us in turn. To perceive the aura of an object we look at means to invest it with the ability to look at us in return."[7] Benjamin sees the photograph as "eminently non-auratic: it lacks the all-important capacity to return the gaze." Thus, while he sees photography as "decisively implicated in the phenomenon of the 'decline of the aura,'"[8] Benjamin believes that words "can have an aura of their own. This is how Karl Kraus described it: 'The closer the look one takes at a word, the greater the distance from which it looks back.'"[9] On the other hand, Mary Price offers a strong rebuttal: "I now wish to claim boldly that aura is a concept applicable, despite Benjamin, to photography." She adds that "although Benjamin denies aura to the photograph, the language of his description of actual photography tends to supply it."[10] Marianne Moore (like many of us) imagines a photograph returning one's gaze. In her poem "Blue Bug: Upon seeing Dr. Raworth Williams' Blue Bug with seven other ponies, photographed by Thomas McAvoy: *Sports Illustrated*," she addresses the subject: "In this camera shot, / . . . you seem to recognize / a recognizing eye."[11] In a poem addressed to Nadar's celebrated photograph of the French poet Charles Baudelaire, Richard Howard writes: "If we look hard / at things they seem to look back; / out of a writhing greatcoat you stare at us."[12]

Eudora Welty famously "look[s] hard / at things . . . [that] seem to look back," both as writer and photographer. At about the age of six, she stood alone in her front yard, "just at that hour in a late summer day when the sun is already below the horizon and the risen full moon in the visible sky stops being chalky and begins to take on light. There comes the moment, and I saw it then, when the moon goes from flat to round. For the first time it met my eyes as a globe." These sentences appear near the beginning of Welty's 1984 memoir, *One Writer's Beginnings*, but her delicate response to the effects of light suggests that this might also be the story of one photographer's beginnings and the presence of Benjamin's aura. The moon returns her gaze ("it met my eyes as a globe"), and then the auratic moon invites itself into language, tactile and nourishing: "The word 'moon' came into my mouth as though fed to me out of a silver spoon. Held in my mouth the moon became a word. It had the roundness of a Concord grape."[13] Eudora Welty's extraordinary "beginnings" are indelibly imprinted here, and they are connected with her sensitivity to light. Her imagination responds to, and stretches beyond, the merely visual; in saying what she sees, she is becoming a writer.

René Paul Barilleaux sees a strong connection between Welty's literary and visual art: "Both a compassionate observer of the world and a passionate image maker, [she] was a visual artist who used the camera much . . . [as] she used language when working as a writer."[14] I think the relationship of the visual artist using the camera and the writer using language is more complicated and, ultimately, more mysterious. What Barilleaux frames as a statement, I wish to reframe as a question: what *do* we find when we seek connections between the photographic eye and the visualizing mind in the work of two photographer-writers?

One may ask: Why focus on these two artists among the many who practice more than one art? There are, of course, numerous writers who practice photography and not a few photographers who write. The chapters that follow are not offered as an argument with which the reader is asked or obligated to agree or disagree. They are rather an invitation to explore the possibilities of affinities in unlikely places. While Eudora Welty and Rosamond Wolff Purcell represent very different generational, geographical, cultural, and familial worlds, the career of each is a mirror image of the other. In the course of time, their artistic journeys converge, circling back toward their beginnings.

Rosamond Purcell prefers to photograph books with problems: they are rotting, decomposing, with pages that cannot be opened. She resuscitates these books in her startling visual images of them and then writes her own book: a memoir about gathering materials for her work as a photographer. Purcell finds her way back to writing by becoming a photographer.

Eudora Welty abandons and dismisses her early practice of taking what she calls "snapshots," including her magnificent black-and-white photographs of small-town and rural Mississippi, yet returns to photography in the eventual publication of four volumes of these snapshots as well as in the key roles photographic images play in her fiction.

Serious Daring looks at the inverse trajectories of two women who make compelling art out of the tension between literary and visual cultures. In each case, the art that is ultimately pursued is full of traces of the seemingly abandoned art. Welty's fiction offers abundant images of photographs, photographers, photography; Purcell's photographs are filled with images of books, texts, writing. Looking at these two artists in conjunction may illuminate each in new ways.

"It is literally impossible to photograph what is not there," Mary Price tells us.[15] For this kind of vision, Welty turns to writing. For Purcell, what is "not there" is impossibly present in the life her uncanny photographs bestow on inanimate objects. Each in her own way, Eudora Welty and Rosamond Purcell return the dead to the world of the living.

W.J.T. Mitchell has well argued that "[we] need to account for not just the power of images, but their powerlessness, their impotence, their abjection. We need, in other words, to grasp *both* sides of the paradox of the image: that it is alive—but also dead; powerful—but also weak; meaningful—but also meaningless."[16] Eudora Welty and Rosamond Purcell are paradoxical representatives of Mitchell's "paradox of the image." Welty as a fiction writer presents what for her is the "impotence" of the photographic image, while Purcell in her full engagement with art photography celebrates its power. At the same time, Welty and Purcell represent "*both* sides of the paradox" by giving life to the visual/verbal imagery they seemed to have disowned.

* * *

The first chapter of *Serious Daring* presents nine visual images in which conversation is the central focus. The talking implicit in Welty's pictures will find a new home in the masterful dialogue of her novels and stories. Chapter 2 briefly surveys the appearance of diverse photographers, photographs, and photographic implications in the language of Welty's fiction.[17] Through a detailed study of two of her stories, one early and one late, chapter 3 shows how the writer's eye may share what Welty calls "a kindred impulse" with that of the photographer.[18] In these stories, "A Memory" and "The Burning," the protagonists' journeys from one mode of vision to another parallel Welty's own journey from the photographic eye to the visionary imagination. Chapter 4 explores the implications of Welty's description of the author as "always seeing double, two pictures at once in [her] frame."[19] The double focus of this chapter is on Welty's characteristic use of simile rather than metaphor, as illustrated in *Losing Battles*, and her reliance on the dual voice of free indirect discourse in *Delta Wedding*. Chapter 5 looks at deeper reverberations of ekphrasis, memory, and angles of vision in Welty's last two novels, *Losing Battles* and *The Optimist's Daughter.*

Chapter 6 introduces the counterposed journey of Rosamond Wolff Purcell from writer to photographer as a continuing dialogue between observer's eye and visualizing mind. Chapter 7 situates Purcell's earliest published book, *A Matter of Time*, her collection of black-and-white photographs, in relation to Eudora Welty's black-and-white snapshots and what they both call the "alchemy" of art making. Chapter 8 identifies in Purcell's later photographic work a plurality of views, a double vision that recasts Welty's use of free indirect discourse in her fiction. Purcell's extended ekphrasis of visual images relies on arresting similes that, like Welty's, become a new way of seeing. Chapter 9 connects Purcell's interest in curiosities, fossils, and junk with her emergence as a writer of memoir, *Owls Head*. Like Welty in her memoir, *One Writer's Beginnings*, Purcell offers a glimpse of her "beginnings" in the innocent, sensuous discoveries of a six-year-old child who will become a visionary artist. Welty's experience as photographer finds ambivalent expression in her fiction; Purcell's complicated attitude toward writing makes a similarly ambivalent appearance in her photography. Chapter 10 explores the diverse (and surprising) ways in which Purcell's relation to writing continues to accompany her photographic work in *Bookworm*, a collection of beautiful, transformative images of dying books and barely readable words. The final chapter focuses on Purcell's "coming home," the photographer's return to the art of writing, in allusive images that resonate with the life of Shakespeare's plays.

When I spoke with Purcell about her book *Landscapes of the Passing Strange: Reflections from Shakespeare*, she said: "There are certain projects where I feel I'm coming home. And I don't always get to do them. And this is one. This suits me to a T. This *is* coming home."[20] I myself began this project some years ago as a Shakespeare scholar daring to enter upon foreign ground. In my study of Purcell's *Landscapes of the Passing Strange*, I, too, come home.

It is time to enter the work of the photographic eye and the visualizing mind.

1

Eudora Welty

Nine Photographs of Talking

A picture of someone talking is to me an elemental example of the problem of the outside and the threshold. . . . [E]very viewer of the picture can "hear" something different. Talking escapes, and so it is itself an image of what is both included and never included in a picture.

—Jeff Wall, *Jeff Wall: Selected Essays and Interviews*

The Canadian photographer Jeff Wall offers an illuminating version of W. J. T. Mitchell's "paradox of the image."[1] The "talking" that is so firmly embedded in Eudora Welty's fiction is both "included" and at the same time "never included" in her snapshots. This chapter will look at visual images of conversation Welty may have heard as she was taking the pictures from which it escapes.

In her twenties, Eudora Welty traveled across Mississippi, working as a Works Progress Administration (WPA) junior publicity agent and taking photographs on her own, eventually amassing "a collection of three hundred unposed studies"[2] of African Americans. Doris Ulmann had published *Roll, Jordan, Roll* in 1933, with its "romanticized, staged photographs of African Americans." The photojournalist Margaret Bourke-White, like the photographer Dorothea Lange, also carefully arranged the poses of her subjects. Erskine Caldwell, Bourke-White's collaborator and later her husband, said of her technique as a photographer: "'She was in charge of everything, manipulating people and telling them where to sit and where to look. . . . She was almost like a motion picture director.'"[3] In contrast, Welty says of her photographic subjects: "I would never have dared to interfere with the poses."[4]

Welty was interested in the work of Berenice Abbott, to whom she had written in 1934, applying, unsuccessfully, for admission to Abbott's photography class at the New School for Social Research in New York. Undaunted, Welty continued actively to pursue a career in photography even while she was writing her early fiction.[5] In 1935 she attempted to publish *Black Saturday*, a book that included a collection of her photographs, and was rejected by Smith and Hass in New York.[6] In 1936, Eudora Welty sprang into public view as both photographer and writer. She had a one-woman show of black-and-white photographs at the Lugene Galleries in New York City from March 31 to April 15, 1936.[7] In June of that year, the first short story she had ever submitted for publication, "Death of a Traveling Salesman," was published in *Manuscript* magazine.[8] In the same month, her short story "The Doll," was published in *The Tanager*, a Grinnell College magazine; that fall, *Manuscript* published another story, "Magic." In November, The Camera House announced that it would exhibit her photographs in New York the following year.[9]

Thus began the two vocations of Eudora Welty, one far overshadowing the other. Four collections of forty-one stories and five novels, along with essays, book reviews, and a remarkable memoir, were eventually joined by four collections of her photographs, beginning with *One Time, One Place: Mississippi in the Depression, A Snapshot Album* in 1971.[10] "What [Welty] the photographer recorded on film," Suzanne Marrs points out, "the writer recorded in memory. . . . [Welty] did not, as she later told interviewers, consult her photographs when writing, but the memories of those photographic occasions stood her in good stead and would frequently appear in her fiction."[11] Memory is an increasingly pervasive theme in Welty's writing. Her "memories of . . . [certain] photographic occasions" inform both her stories and her novels, as will be seen in the next chapter.

The following snapshots of people talking show particularities of dress (worn, torn, soiled, missing buttons) as distinctive markers of social and economic status; facial expressions and telling gestures; physical postures that represent individual character or relationships: people standing upright, bent forward, sitting in groups, squatting on the ground; occasional cityscapes; a background of trees, grass, sky; the play of light and shadows; pieces of paper (content unknown); the presentation of a scene from changing angles and distance; and, above all, conversation. However, as Alan Trachtenberg has rightly observed, one "cannot rely on the viewer's understanding of a picture as if it were a voice, a word in a story."[12] Welty does not bring voice to her visual images; she brings voice to the people who populate her writing.

The black-and-white snapshots discussed in this chapter segregate blacks and whites, who do not appear together in any of these pictures, as would generally be true of the Mississippi Welty inhabited and photographed.[13] Her photographic practice both discloses the reality of racism in the South and defies it by allowing a white woman to witness and share intimate moments in the lives of the black community. As Welty said in an interview, "my pictures were made in sympathy, not exploitation. If I had felt that way, I would not have taken the pictures. . . . Human feeling for human beings was a response to what I saw."[14]

In the introduction to her photographs in *One Time, One Place*, Welty says that the majority of her photographs were taken either without the knowledge of the subjects or with "only their peripheral awareness. . . . The snapshots made with people's awareness are, for the most part, just as unposed; I simply asked people if they would mind going on with what they were doing and letting me take a picture. I can't remember ever being met with a demurrer stronger than amusement."[15] In perhaps another variation on Mitchell's paradox of the image—or rather the paradox of Welty's photographic practice—Timothy Dow Adams makes the intriguing suggestion that in "many of [Welty's] group pictures, the people . . . , either because of the novelty of having their picture taken or because of the complicated familiarity combined with distance that characterized black and white relations of the time, often seem to see her and not notice her at the same time."[16] Several group snapshots reproduced here may illustrate this noticing and not noticing of the photographer: *Making a date/Grenada/1935*, *Saturday trip to town/Hinds County/1939*, and *Union Square/New York City/1930s*.

Eudora Welty never shied away from taking pictures of the talking that escapes. While the captions[17] of the following images do not always focus on conversation, the composition of the photographs does.

Tall story/Utica/1930s (Plate 1)[18] captures two black farmers, side by side, their forearms touching. Each wears a somewhat worn hat. The face of the larger man is in three-quarters view, the brim of his hat tipped up, his eyes downcast; his lips, slightly apart, begin a sweet or cautious smile. He is listening. The hat of the thinner man to his right is pulled down over his partly shadowed profile; his eyes are cast downward across the bulk of the man next to him, as if he is inwardly assessing the effect of his "tall story" on his companion. His mouth is open, his upper teeth visible; a gesturing right hand is raised in illustration or emphasis. He is talking. We are invited to look, not listen.

The two men wear denim or cotton jackets, the shirts beneath buttoned to the neck. The larger man wears a sweater with large checks. As I look more closely, I am moved by a large, square-shaped hole near the bottom of his sweater, just above the waist. The camera has caught marks of poverty without eclipsing the dignity of the black farmer.

In the background are trees and buildings, slightly blurred, and grass. Behind and to the right of the larger farmer is a small figure with a sack over his shoulder, his face turned away. In the midground behind the men stands a telephone pole.

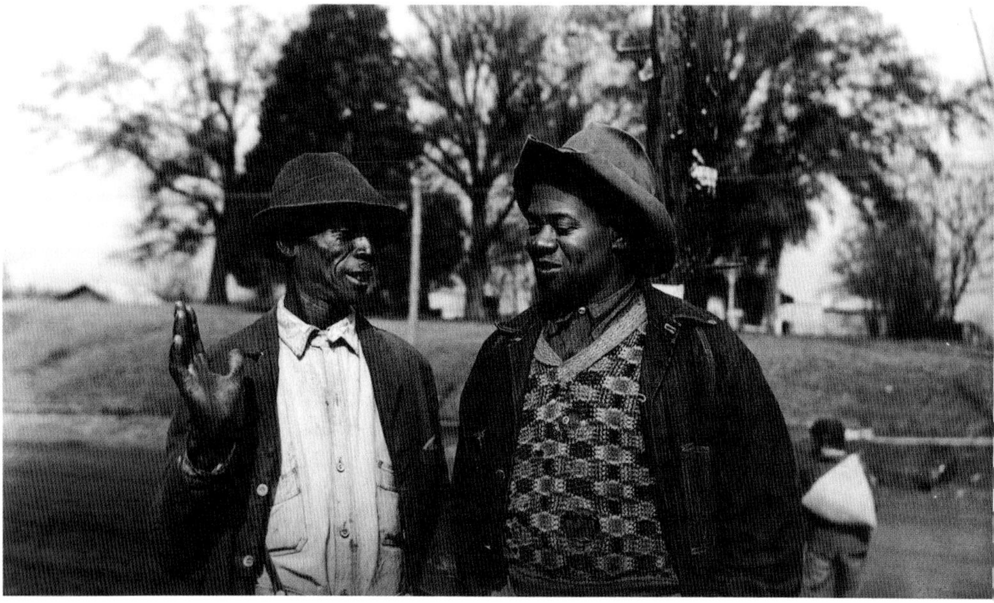

PLATE 1. Tall story.

A horizontal line suggestive of a telephone wire seems to connect the heads of those in conversation. Foregrounded is the talking that escapes.

Farmers in Town/Crystal Spring/1930s (Plate 2) shows three white men, all wearing less worn, somewhat more expensive hats than those of the two farmers in *Tall Story*. The large central figure in overalls has his back, crisscrossed by suspenders, to the camera, his right hand pressed against his right hip with thumb pointing upward toward his waist, his left hand digging into a back pocket, his sleeves rolled up to the elbow. The thinner man to his right, seen in profile, stands, bent slightly forward, with hands neatly folded behind his back, the ends of the fingers of his right hand stretching out beyond the frame of the picture. His slightly shadowed gaze is focused intently on the face of the farmer to the far left, whose bushy white mustache covers lips that seem to have just finished speaking, as if they are for a moment in silent communion. The upper bodies of the two men to the left and right of the picture are partly concealed by the jutting arms of the bulky farmer who stands between them.

It is impossible to know what is being discussed or what the photographer might have heard, if anything. The casual intensity of the figure to the right and

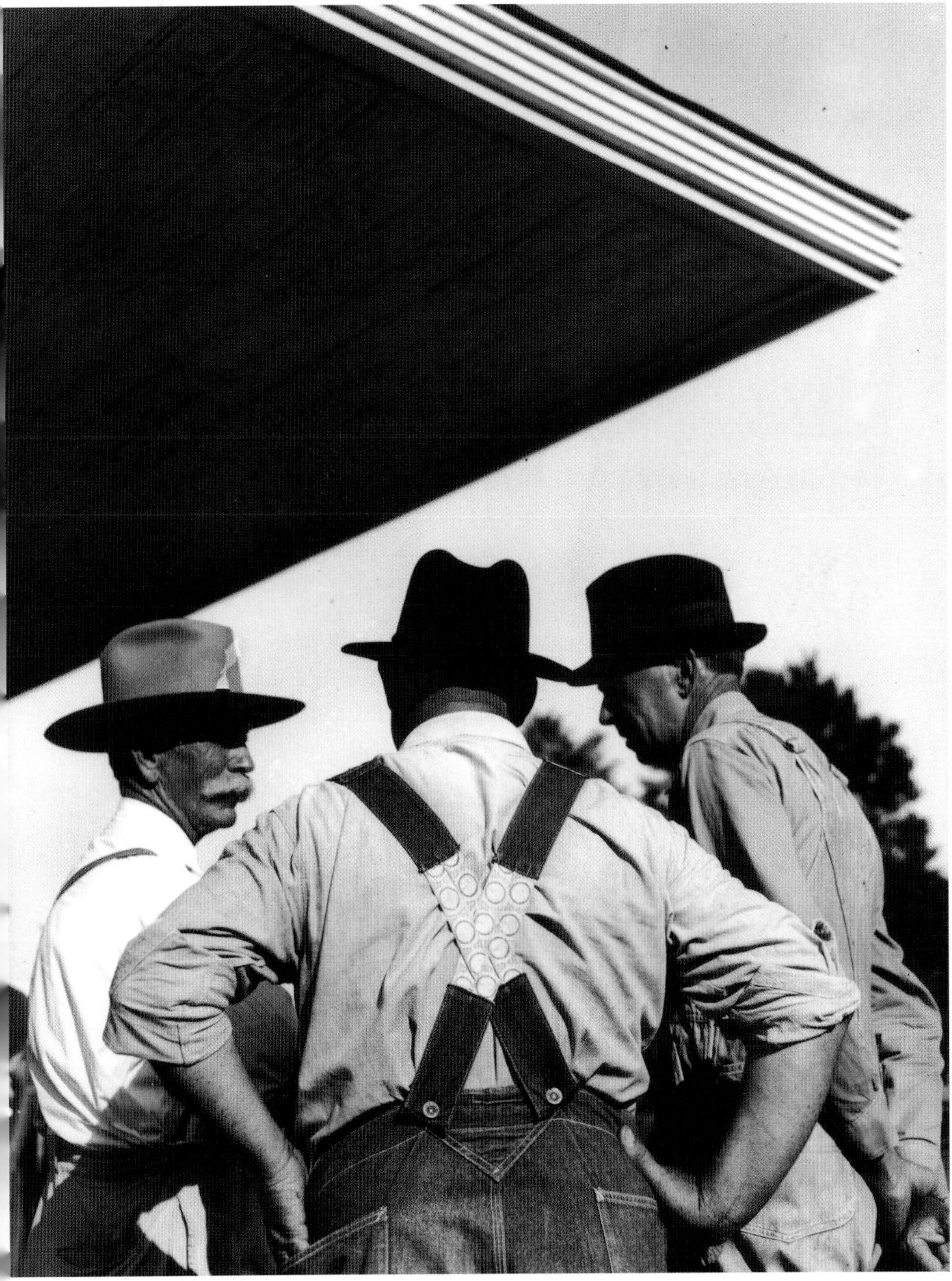

PLATE 2. Farmers in town.

the somewhat stoic expression of the man who meets his gaze contrast with the slightly tense, seemingly overbearing posture of the central figure, whose face we cannot see; even the back of his head, just below the brim of his hat, is in shadow. The act of talking, like its content, is hidden from the viewer even as it controls the scene.

Political rally on the courthouse grounds/Pontotoc/1930s (Plate 3) presents a much larger group of white people: in the foreground are three figures, two men and a woman, squatting on the ground, while two others, a man and a woman, stand, bending forward. In the middle background are at least four men, all hatted, in light slacks and shirts; beyond them, in the far distance, are more figures, smaller and indistinct. The main conversation occurs in the foreground. To the left of center squats a man, wearing glasses, a white shirt, striped slacks with cuffs, and black hat with an elegantly elongated brim, his mouth slightly open and his head tilted upward to meet the intently focused eyes of a thin man to his right, bending toward him with hands on knees. Both men are seen in profile. Their hats, one lower than the other, form a diagonal axis reaching upward to the sharply focused leaves of what seems to be a white ash tree in the upper right of the frame. The unbuttoned, partly soiled left sleeve of the man bending forward and the creased, perspiration-soaked back of his white shirt beneath light-colored overalls suggest some time spent toiling in the sun, presumably in a common cause. A third man in dark overalls, squatting just behind him and to his right, is gazing downward at something, possibly a note, in his hands; his lips are pursed, perhaps in response to what he looks at or in response to the courthouse rally. To the far left, an extremely thin woman in a polka-dotted dress squats on the ground, her dark hair in a bun, her taut, wrinkled face half hidden by the black hat of the man squatting next to her. Part of her torso disappears outside the frame. She seems to be gazing upward at the man bending forward: it is not clear if he is still talking or listening. The other woman in the foreground, wearing a light-colored, open-necked dress, her hair pulled sharply back from her face, stands slightly left of center, bending forward toward the space between the two squatting men. Her face is fully visible, and yet it is not possible to say exactly what she is looking at or reaching toward—perhaps the hollowed-out watermelon halves lying on the ground.

Clearly, an important event in which people with a shared interest have participated has occurred or is about to occur. The camera focuses on talk, the kind of talk that may follow or precede a political rally. The squatting and bending figures are all in slightly uncomfortable positions, positions that we know will have to change at some point—perhaps an image of the need for, and inevitability of, change. The talking we do not hear will be followed by action we do not see.

In a picture titled *Conversation/Grenada/1935* (Plate 4), no one at the moment the snapshot was taken seems to be talking to anyone. In the background, against

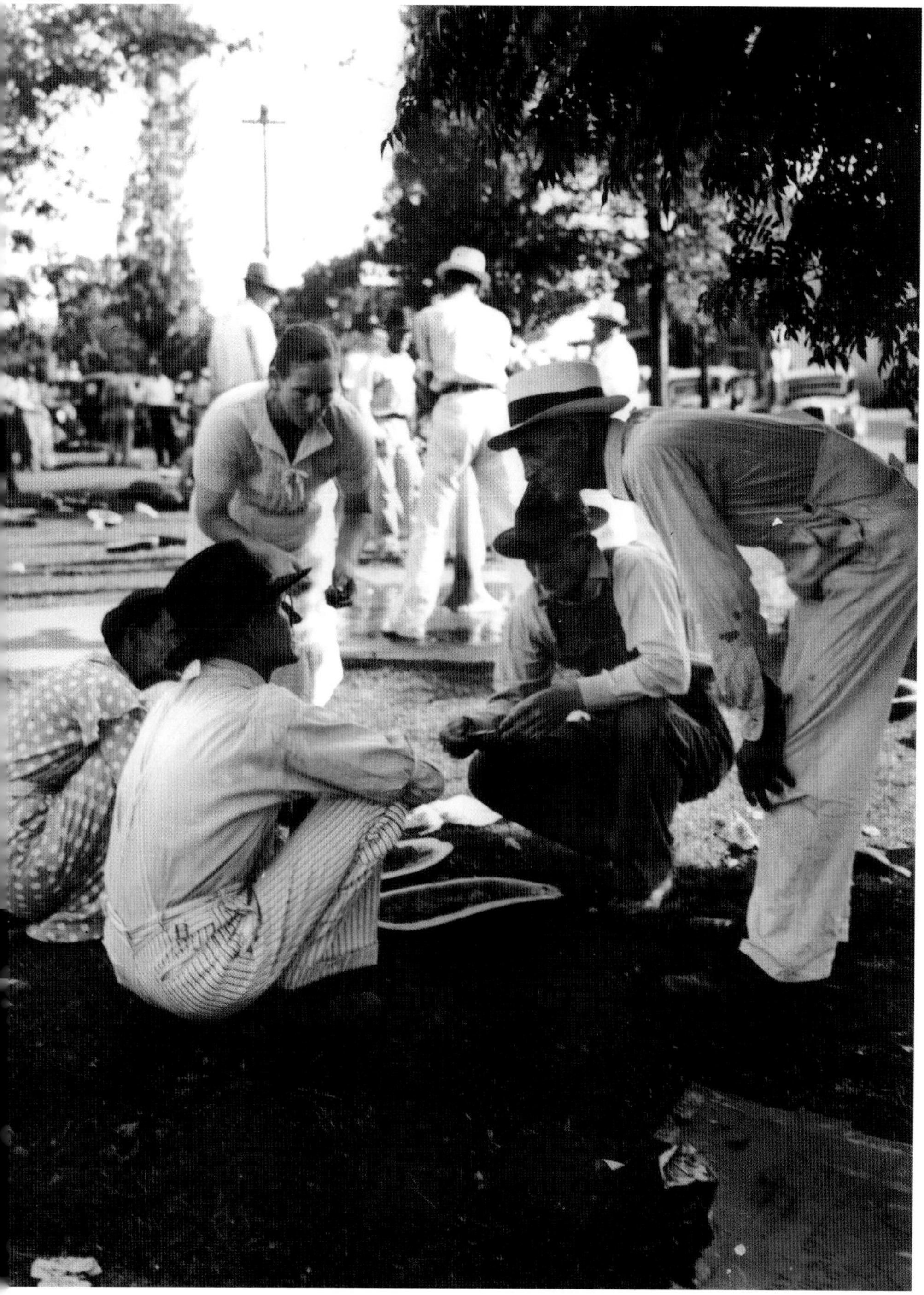

PLATE 3. Political rally on the courthouse grounds.

a bare white sky, are a tall, dark, deciduous tree, blurred city buildings, and two parked cars. To the right is the rear of what seems to be a delivery truck with a few letters visible ("JAS").

In the foreground are three figures. Two young black women, wearing somewhat similar light-colored, wrinkled dresses and heels, with hair straightened and neatly arranged, stand on the sidewalk near a young black man whose face is angled away from them, either in contemplation or perhaps distracted by something he sees just outside the frame of the picture. One woman has her back to the camera, her face almost in profile, her gaze seemingly directed at the young man; the other woman is seen in profile, her eyes angled toward the face of the young man who does not return the gaze of either woman. All three figures stand with arms akimbo, the pose of the woman in profile more nearly resembling that of the young man.

The man wears dark slacks, a short-sleeved shirt open at the collar, suspenders, and a jaunty cap shading one eye. His mouth is slightly open as if he might be about to speak, after further thought, or as if he is in the middle of having nothing more to say. Peeking out of the pocket of his shirt is a white piece of paper, pressing against one of his suspenders. In the midst of this scene, the small square of paper catches the light, its contents unknown, like the writing disappearing outside the right frame of the picture. What is both included and not included is undecipherable, a mystery escaping, like talk in a photograph.

In the foreground of *Making a date/Grenada/1935* (Plate 5), a young black man in profile, wearing torn, striped pants, his semi-crushed hat protruding from a back pocket, stands near a young black woman. His mouth is slightly open as if in speech. He does not look directly at the woman, but his somewhat foreshortened left arm seems to reach toward her. In the far background are a blurry car, a few buildings, and some trees. Just behind the couple, a store window reflects the back of a man facing the street.

The woman's gaze is directed toward the camera, as if she suddenly catches herself being photographed in the midst of a private conversation. She wears a simple, sleeveless dress. We see her worn, soiled, white shoes with laces undone. Her right arm is bent at the elbow, the forearm across her waist, the right hand supporting the left elbow. Her left forearm stretches upward, making the third side of a slightly crooked figure of a box with a missing top. The pinky of her left hand points diagonally upward above her partly open lips, pressing against her right nostril. It is as if that tiny gesture, along with her posture, registers the camera's violation of an intimate moment. The young man, interpreted by Welty's caption as making a date, seems oblivious to the camera's eye. The wide-open, wary eyes of the young woman stare at us as if we were trying, impossibly, to enter the conversation, to make a date with the photograph.

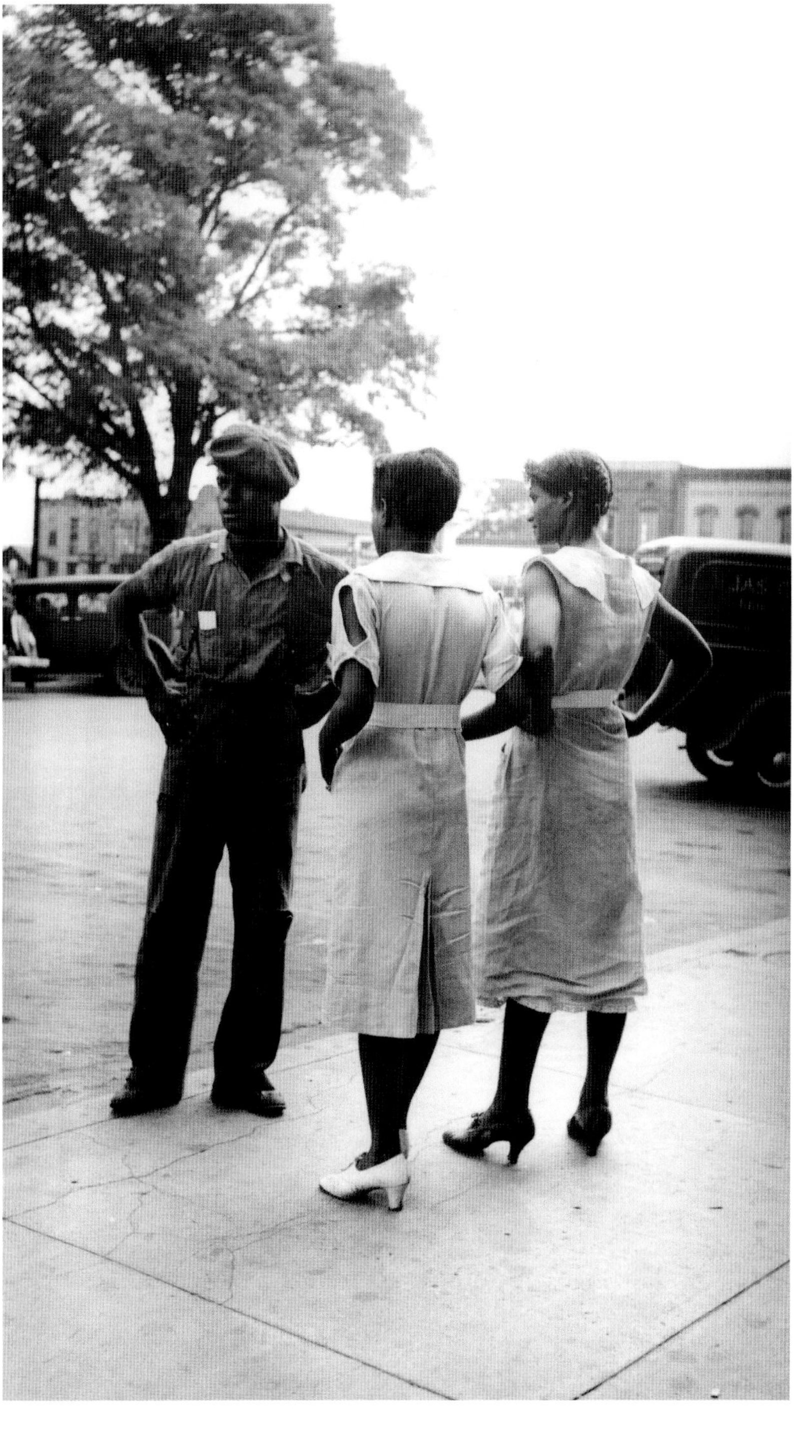

PLATE 4. Conversation.

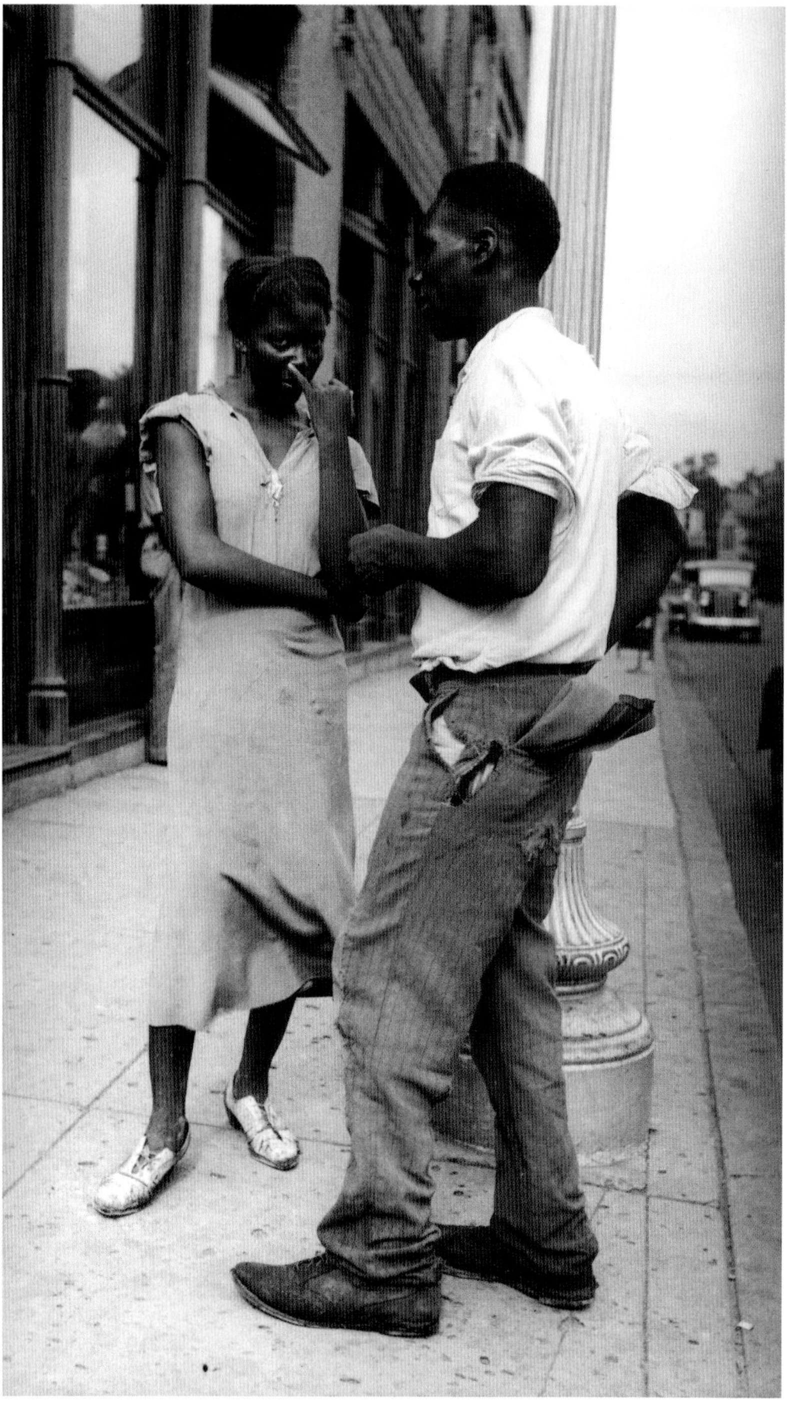

PLATE 5. Making a date.

In *Saturday trip to town/Hinds County/1939* (Plate 6), a handmade wooden truck, with no sides, no top and the steering wheel on the right side, is parked in front of what appears to be a gas station. The words "U.S. Government Motor Gasoline," seen in the background, tell us little of significance in the visual scene. In the foreground, seated on the truck, are ten black country people: young girls, young women and men, and an older man and woman. The women wear dresses; all but one wear hats of various shapes and styles. The men wear white shirts, long pants, and caps or hats. The faces of the passengers on the far side of the truck are in profile, their backs to the camera; only their white hats and upper bodies are visible. A young woman, wearing a printed dress, white heels, and rolled-up socks, sits in the front seat, her head angled toward the driver, who has turned his face to the camera with a careful, inquiring gaze. Only one other person seems to notice the photographer: a young girl with hands clasped in her lap looks directly at the camera, perhaps with some apprehension, certainly with interest.

Amid this large group, one person is talking. A middle-aged woman, in a spotless white dress with open collar and a wide-brimmed straw hat, her left hand on her knee, her head in profile, is speaking to the man seated next to her at the back of the open truck. He wears a clean long-sleeved white shirt, suspenders, dark-colored pants, and a hat with a small but well-formed brim; his hands, like those of two of the young girls, are folded in his lap as he gazes back appreciatively at the woman speaking to him alone. Under his white mustache his lips are closed, but he is listening intently to the animated woman by his side. He sits somewhat perilously above the back wheel of the vehicle, his right leg hanging down; his left leg is missing, the bottom half of his trousers crumpled up on his thigh. He seems calm and ready for the trip to town. There is no visible cane or pair of crutches to aid him. Nothing in the photograph suggests how he can remain safely balanced on the truck once it begins to move. One mystery begets another: the talking that escapes is what secures him in the scene.

In *Back street/New Orleans/1930s* (Plate 7), a lot is going on and it takes scrutiny to find the crucial conversation. A group of seven children, all white, play in a yard. High above their heads laundry billows on lines stretched between buildings. In the far left lower corner of the photograph, a boy with one leg angled backward at the knee and arms raised seems to be playing ball by himself. He is seen in profile, his head tossed back as he gazes upward. The leaves of a tree form a canopy far above him.

To his right, in the center foreground, a small child sitting bent forward on a tricycle watches him intently. Two other children, a boy and a girl, standing in the middle distance, also gaze at him; a third boy moves between them, his face and one hand turned toward the child to his right.

In the far background, a man in a suit, with his back to the camera, stands on a porch, possibly conversing with the unseen occupant(s) of a house with many

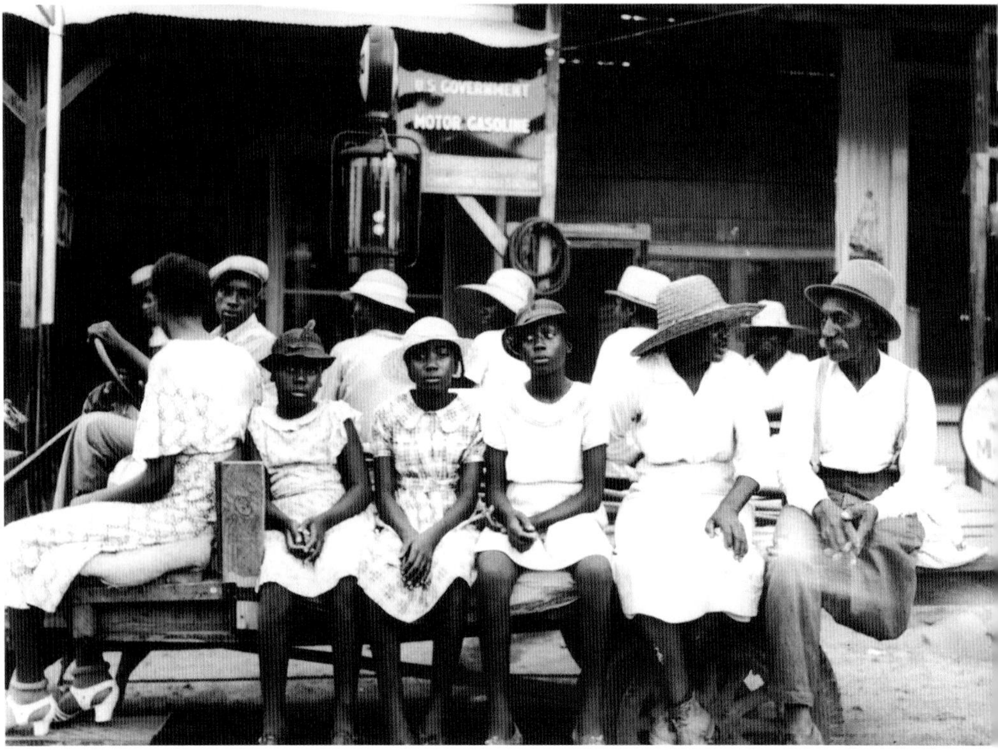

PLATE 6. Saturday trip to town.

door-like windows. More laundry hangs across the upper and lower balconies of the two-story building. Two figures with their backs to the camera stand on or near slanted stairs leading to the upper balcony.

Two children of almost equal height, a very young boy and girl in the middle distance, stand to the right of three taller children. The boy, in dark overalls and white shirt, his head in deeply shadowed profile, is facing a blond-haired girl, her light summer dress blown forward slightly by the wind. The little girl's left arm reaches diagonally toward the face of her small companion as he bends toward her. His right arm, white sleeve rolled up, stretches in her direction.

Two tiny figures are talking together, completely oblivious to all else in the scene. Their intense concentration on conversation becomes the central focus for the viewer just as it is for those talking.

Royal Street/New Orleans (Plate 8) shows three white women in casual summer dress standing together on a second-floor New Orleans balcony. The angled perspective of the camera draws the viewer's eye upward toward the backs of two of the women. Both are dark-haired with arms akimbo, facing a third white-haired woman who leans on the balcony's wrought-iron railing with one hand, as if to gain added support in this conversation. Though her face is visible, it is hard to tell if her expression is truculent or sad; the mouth is a bit blurred, perhaps caught in the very act of responding to the two women confronting her. On the street beneath the balcony, a small boy, in dark overalls and white shirt, walks by unnoticed, unmindful of the conversation taking place above his head.

In an article accompanying this picture, published in *Vogue* in August of 1944, Welty writes:

> I took this snapshot in New Orleans on Royal Street one day, and the next minute a chorus of three old ladies on a balcony muttered—the same as asked me why. It is hard to guess why the act of taking a picture with a camera is always suspect. You can do all kinds of other things in public without a question being

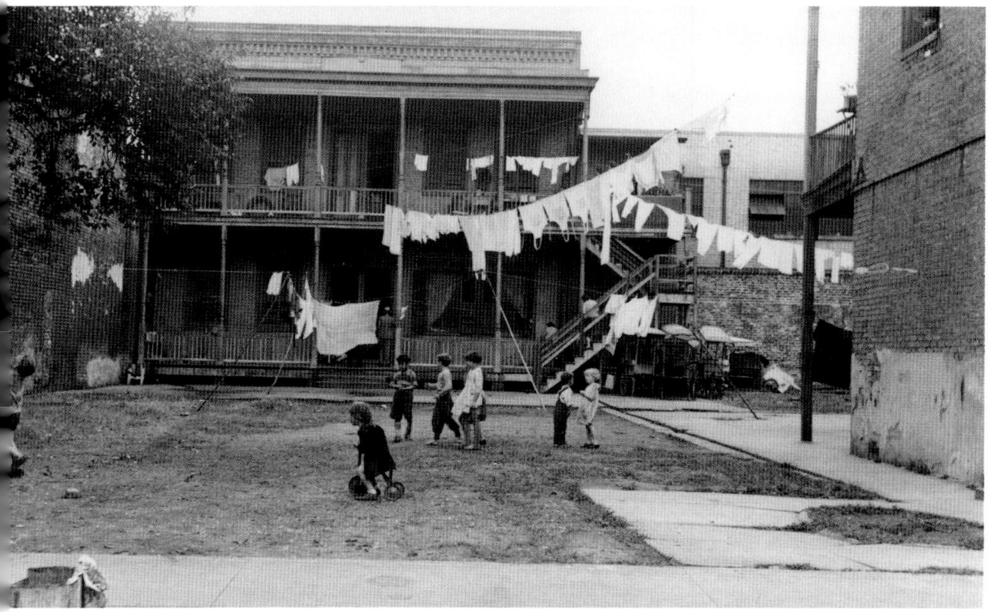

PLATE 7. Back street/New Orleans.

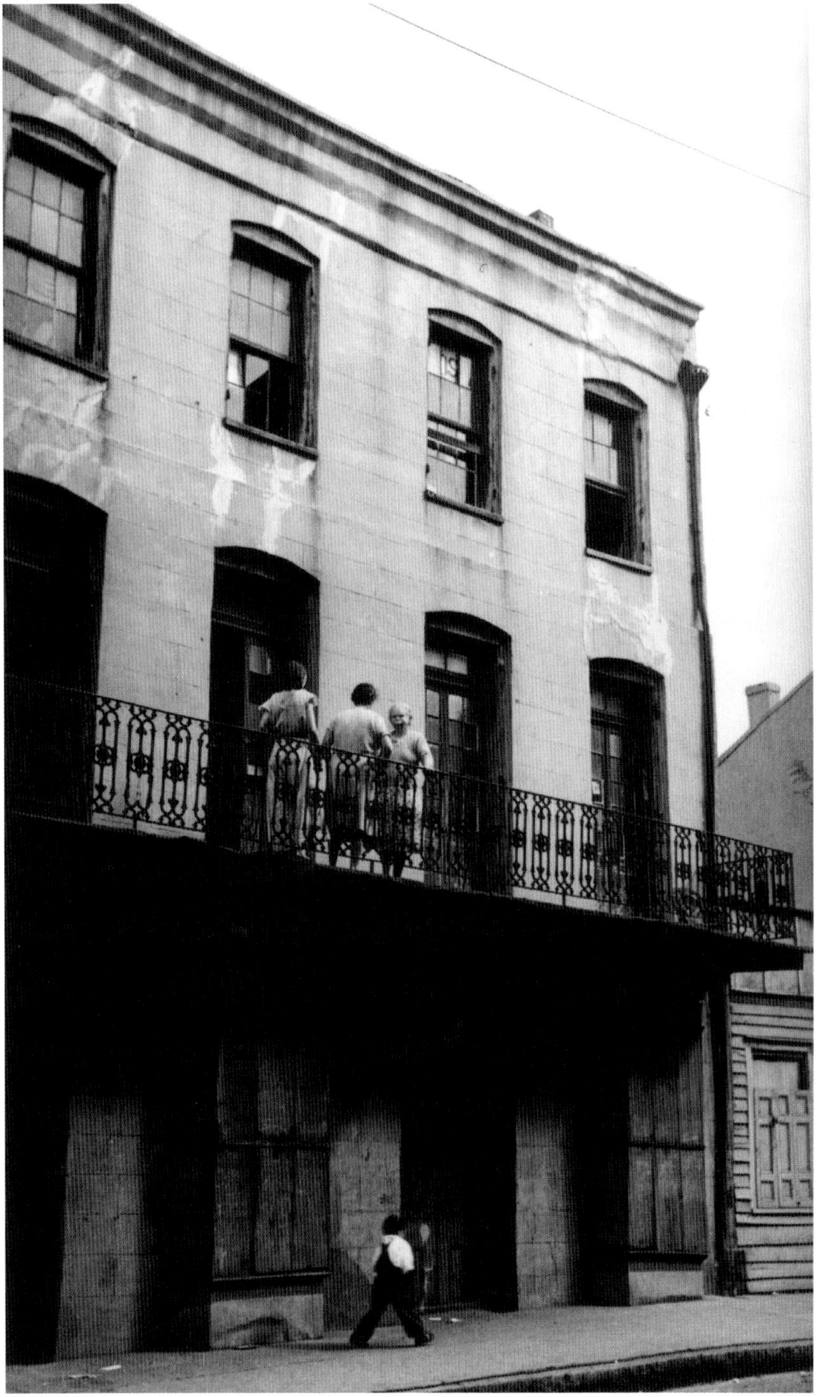

PLATE 8. Royal Street/New Orleans.

> asked—but if you click your camera at something people from nowhere run up and ask, "Why did you take that?"
>
> Perhaps it goes back to atavistic beliefs that to carry off an image of something, or its picture, means you want to steal its soul.

"It is clear," she writes, "that the fascination of a photograph of anything is that it imprisons a moment in time—and is that really different from stealing its spirit, its soul? . . . Yet this must be, in a sense, the purpose of nearly everything we do—certainly in the arts, painting, and writing, we steal spirits and souls if we can, and in love and devotion, what do we do but pray: Keep this as it is, hold this moment safe?"

> So in the lowly photograph we can do this to anything—a little boy walking fast in a shuttered street—with a little machine and the slightest motion of the finger. Photography is crude in itself, but the act of photographing is kin to something better when we look at the little prints that come of it, we get a fine, unproportional satisfaction, as if we had netted a prize.[19]

Welty discloses her own sense of the problematic nature of photography, "crude in itself" yet "kin to something better." The "something better" for Welty is her celebrated fiction.

Union Square/New York City/1930s (Plate 9) presents six men, in hats and winter coats, standing or sitting on a bench in one of Manhattan's most famous downtown parks. In the background are city buildings of various heights and open sky. It is daylight, during the Great Depression; the men are well-dressed and seemingly out of work. Hands are stuffed into coat pockets and the tree behind the men is bare of leaves. The picture, a familiar image of Depression-era New York City, offers glimpses of many stories, all untold.

Only one figure faces the camera, the upper half of his face shaded by the brim of his hat. His right hand, resting on what could be a folded newspaper, holds the remains of a half-smoked cigarette; his left hand is hidden inside his coat pocket. His mouth is partly open, as if gaping at the photographer . The man sitting next to him glances away, his eyes and upper right cheek in shadow; his overcoat is buttoned up to the neck, his lips pressed closed, his look slightly downcast, pensive.

In the center foreground stand two figures. The man closer to the bench is wearing a light-colored coat, his hands stuffed in its pockets and his collar pulled up. His lips are a thin line under shadowed eyes. The man standing beside him wears dark slacks and an overcoat, his right hand hidden in his pocket, his coat collar turned up. His mouth is slightly open as if he might have been speaking, has paused, and is about to begin again. The somber expressions of the two men suggest a shared discontent.

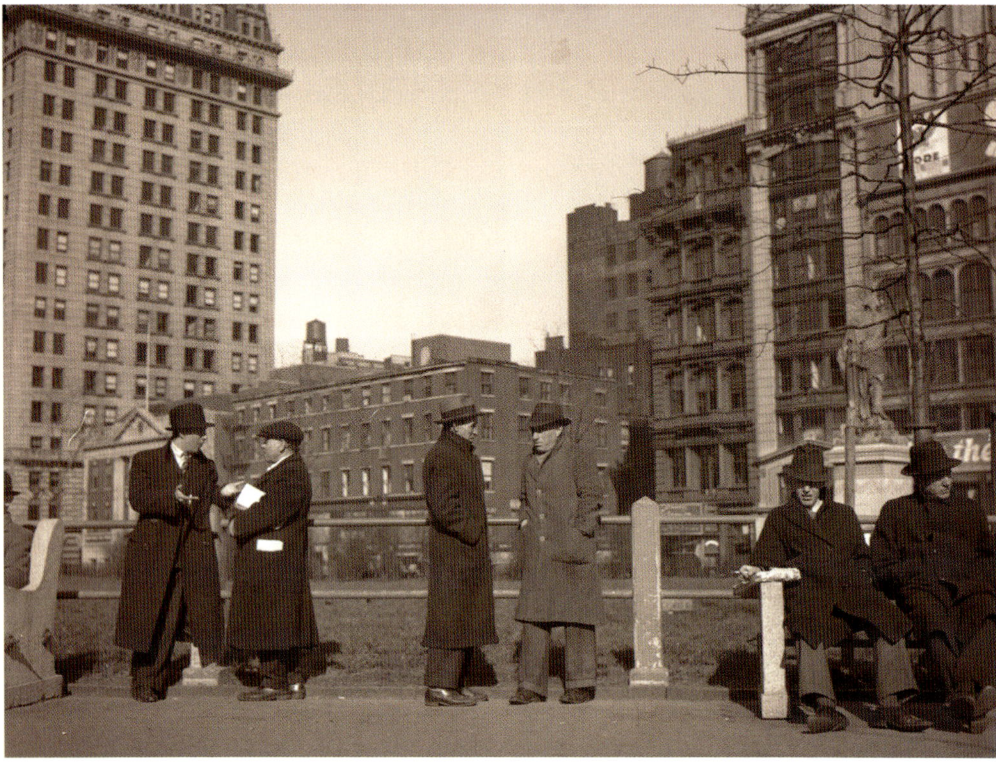

PLATE 9. Union Square / New York City.

In the left foreground, two men stand in front of a park railing, facing each other. Here is the mutual gaze of speaker and listener. One man, wearing black slacks, white shirt, tie, and black hat, his coat open and unbuttoned, holds a cigarette gracefully in his ungloved right hand. His eyes are shadowed by the brim of his elegant hat. His mouth forms words as he gestures. The stockier man beside him, seen entirely in profile, wears a dark cap, dark slacks, and overcoat. From his left coat pocket peeks a white object; under his left arm we see a larger white rectangle, possibly a newspaper whose ads he has been searching. He seems to be relaxed, interested, clearly taking in the words of the man whose gesturing left hand almost touches his coat.

To the far left, almost outside the frame of the photograph, part of a stone bench and the left arm and shoulder of a seventh man are visible. His head, of which we see only a sliver, is turned toward the other figures in the scene. I imagine his coat tightly buttoned, his collar turned up, his hands in his pockets.

Only the two men talking seem unaffected by the cold.

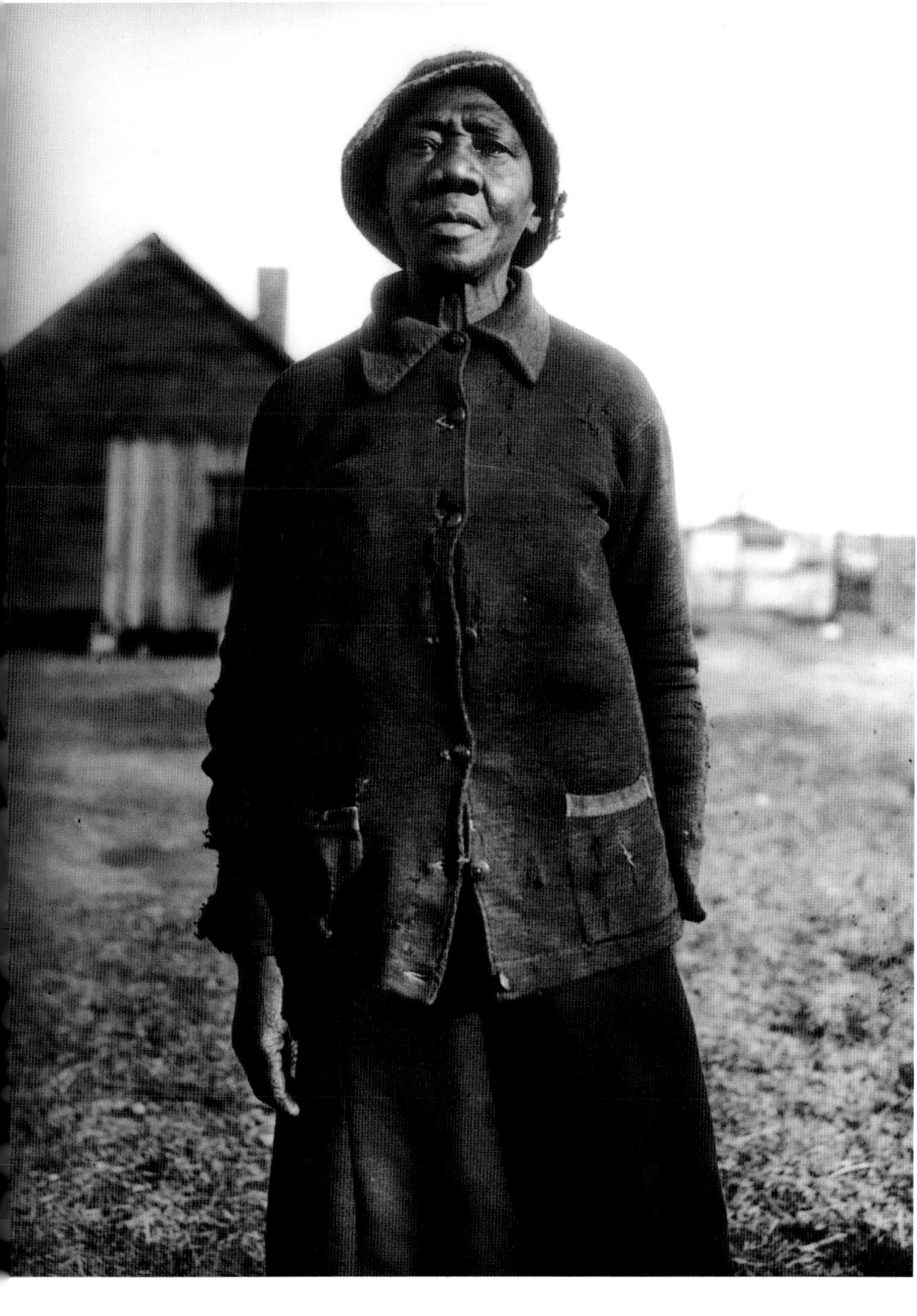

PLATE 10. A woman of the 'thirties/Hinds County.

Welty's captions and occasional remarks on her own photographs rarely offer detailed commentary for the viewer-reader. An exception is a picture described by an interviewer in January of 1989 as one of Welty's "most poignant photographs": *A woman of the 'thirties/Hinds County/1935* (Plate 10). When she is asked what happened to the woman portrayed, Welty replies:

> "I don't know. I think she lived on the road between here [Jackson, Mississippi] and Utica, where I used to go quite a bit, and where I took a lot of pictures. And I think I did see her a time or two after that. She has a sensitive face, as you can see; she was well aware of her predicament in poverty, and had good reasons for hopelessness. Well, she *wasn't* hopeless. That was the point. She was courageous. She thought it was a hopeless situation, but she was tackling it."[20]

This chapter ends with a photograph that depicts no conversation. A solitary black woman stands erect, her head raised slightly. We see the veins stand out in her throat. Beneath the tattered sleeve of a torn sweater buttoned up to her neck, her right arm hangs down close by her dark, pleated skirt, the left hand hidden behind her back. Her hair is completely covered by a worn, closely fitted cap. Behind her are several blurred buildings.

The woman is neither smiling nor dejected. Her full lips seem to offer something in silence to the viewer even while her eyes, gazing into an indeterminate space, do not meet your eyes, however you look at her. And you cannot stop looking at her, at her strength and dignity and stance, alone in a field, almost filling the whole picture. She speaks to no one, but "every viewer of the picture," as Jeff Wall has said, "can 'hear' something different."[21]

When I first saw this picture, what moved me, unaccountably, was a button left unbuttoned in the middle of that worn and torn sweater. It is what Barthes has called the *punctum* (a particular, often accidental detail in the scene of the photograph). The *punctum* "rises from the scene, shoots out of it like an arrow, and pierces me," Barthes says. He describes the *punctum* as "sting, speck, cut, little hole—and also a cast of the dice. A photograph's *punctum* is that accident which pricks me (but also bruises me, is poignant to me)."[22]

What arises from the visual details of Welty's snapshot is not a voice but the beginning of a story—a story of a situation where there is good reason for hopelessness, and hopelessness is refused. The auratic photograph returns the photographer-writer's gaze:

> When a heroic face like that of the woman in the buttoned sweater—who I think must come first in this book—*looks back at me from her picture*, what I respond to now, just as I did the first time, is not the Depression, not the Black, not the South, not even the perennially sorry state of the whole world, but *the story of her life in her face* [italics mine].[23]

2

Photography in Fiction

I learned quickly enough when to click the shutter, but what I was becoming aware of more slowly was a story-writer's truth.

—Eudora Welty, *One Time, One Place*

Reynolds Price suggests that Eudora Welty's snapshots of "rural and smalltown Mississippi were among the forces that brought her to the realization that her prime compulsion was to push beyond the silent voice of image to the stronger but slower voice of words. . . . [S]ome steady mystery in the world before her . . . was moving her [beyond "the frozen moment" of the snapshot] toward another angle of vision as her ultimate foothold."[1]

In the introduction to her first published collection of pictures, *One Time, One Place: Mississippi in the Depression, A Snapshot Album*, Welty stakes her claim for writing over photography: "Insight doesn't happen often on the click of the moment, like a lucky snapshot, but comes in its own time and more slowly and *from nowhere but within*" (italics mine). "In my own case, a fuller awareness of what I needed to find out about people and their lives had to be sought for through another way, through writing stories."[2]

In Welty's writing, photography appears in diverse and quite often discredited ways. Frequently, fictional characters are photographers; often photographs themselves play key roles. The language itself has photographic implications in the absence of either a photographer or a photograph. Welty's fiction offers abundant images of photographs and photography, but they are everywhere problematic.

In discussing Welty's fiction, I follow neither a strictly chronological nor rigidly thematic order but, rather, attempt to bring out what seem to me the shifting patterns of her preoccupation with photography. In "Hello and Goodbye," set in Jackson, Mississippi, the narrator recalls taking publicity pictures as part of a new part-time job. At first, she simply asks her two subjects, beauty contestants identified only as the Queen and the Hostess, "Are you ready?," allowing them to assume their own poses. In contrast with Welty's usual practice, the photographer then suggests a particular location and pose. The Hostess encourages the photographer to give further suggestions to her subjects, even providing the very language with which to do so. "'Give?' asked the Hostess, pursing her lips. 'Sure,' I said."[3]

The story "The Whistle" presents Jason and Sara Morton lying between quilts beside their fireplace. Later, Mr. Perkins's whistle will blow, as it always does when there is a severe freeze in Dexter, and the Mortons will hurry outdoors to cover their young tomato plants with their quilts and clothing. Before the whistle is sounded, Sara lies awake, "trembling with cold." She recalls the May sun shining on ripening tomatoes ready for shipping in Dexter. In her dreamlike memory, a traveling photographer appears, lame and odd, selling posed pictures of couples: a crippled man who "walked like a duck was back taking poses for a dime of the young people with their heads together." At the end of the story, husband and wife wait silently for morning, "[holding] very still, . . . with bent heads,"[4] as if they are one of the couples in the photographer's posed photographs, but returned to life.

In *Delta Wedding*, an itinerant photographer takes a wedding picture of the Fairchild family, "generally smiling," in a pose arranged by the bride's father. One child's hand salutes just as the flash goes off. Before the photographer reshoots the same group pose, he casually announces that he has in his satchel a photograph he took of a young woman killed by the train on which he was riding. In referring to this horrid event as he pats his satchel to get everyone's attention, his phrasing eerily seems to suggest that the still photo in his satchel collaborates with what has destroyed her life: "I got a girl killed on the I.C. railroad."[5]

In *Losing Battles*, there is a three-page choric ekphrasis of an old photograph taken at the wedding of Beulah Beecham and Ralph Renfro, discussed in detail in chapter 5.

The short story "Kin," narrated by Miss Dicey Hastings while visiting her relatives in Mississippi, includes another itinerant photographer, Mr. Alf J. Puryear. In Great-uncle Felix's parlor at Mingo, Mr. Puryear shakes out "a big piece of scenery, . . . hook[s] it to the wall," and photographs his assembled customers, one by one, against it. Dicey, who resists having her picture taken in this way, believes that what would appear in the photograph would be "none of Mingo at all, but the itinerant backdrop . . . a scene that never was, a black and white and gray blur."

Dicey's great-uncle Felix also does not have his picture taken. In fact, he is not even aware of the presence of the itinerant photographer, invited into his house by a distant kinswoman. Old and unwell, left alone in his featherbed, Felix is, instead, interested in writing. He makes Dicey hand him a pencil and laboriously writes on the flyleaf of an old hymnbook. While he writes, Dicey remembers past summers, sitting beside Felix on the front porch steps, silently looking at pictures in a stereopticon, a kind of slide projector designed to allow one view to fade out while the next faded in. Her great-uncle's absorption in the dissolving views produced by this magic lantern was absolute. When he put the stereopticon to his eye, he seemed, to the children gathering around him, to be invisible.

In that long-ago summer, Dicey could not yet read. Now Felix wordlessly hands her the folded page of his writing. When the torn page from the hymnbook is later unfolded, Kate and Dicey see: "'River—Daisy—Midnight—Please.'" The two cousins try to decipher the story hidden in these four words. Kate connects the first two (river daisy); Dicey takes "Daisy" to be a woman's name, though it was not the name of Felix's wife, Beck. Kate refuses to believe there could be a mysterious woman in her great-uncle's past, argues away "Midnight" because the family had gone to bed at dark, and finally declares that "Daisy" must be some kind of mistake. "'Daisy was Daisy,'" Dicey says to Kate; then she thinks to herself: "It was the 'please' that had hurt me."

The meaning hidden in four labored-over words is never revealed. Dicey, who can read now, has been given the kernel of a story, its secrets unknown. As she leaves Mingo, she looks at the faces of the country people still grouped on the porch after the photographer has left, "posed there" as if on a ship just embarked. "Their faces were like dark boxes of secrets and desires to me, but locked safely, like old-fashioned caskets for the safe conduct of jewels on a voyage."[6]

What is precious and voyage-like, for Welty, is a vision of mystery transacted in writing. "The mystery lies in the use of language to express human life," Welty has said. "In writing, do we try to solve this mystery? No. . . . In very practical ways, we rediscover the mystery. We even, I might say, take advantage of it."[7]

"Going to Naples" features a mother and her eighteen-year-old daughter, Gabriella Serto, who join other passengers aboard the *Pomona*, sailing from New York to Palermo and Naples. At one point, Gabriella's mother, "smiling as at a little foundling," looks at a tiny, ragged photograph of her daughter as a baby and then announces that Gabriella is no longer a child. The simile of the foundling suggests the distance between the visual image and the daughter it would portray. In fact, the photograph later falls into the ocean and is never referred to again.

An eager young man named Poldy attempts to display a snapshot of his bride-to-be, whom he has never met. Waiting for the priest to begin a shipboard Mass, he tries to show the picture to the other passengers, who yawn or look elsewhere. Gabriella, encouraged by her mother to pay attention, says simply, "'You can't hardly see her.'" Poldy snatches back the picture and passes it to a widower,

Mr. Ambrogio, who remarks politely, "She knows how to pose." Aldo Scampo, with whom Gabriella is having a small shipboard romance, arrives and the snapshot is immediately pressed upon him. The priest enters and Poldy retrieves his snapshot, "kissing his bride and snapping her back under the elastic band" that held together his personal papers. The photograph, unremarkable to those who are forced to view it, substitutes for the woman he expects to marry when Poldy "kiss[es] his bride," but then it is immediately restored to its status as one object among many, "snapp[ed] . . . back under the elastic band."

On their last night aboard the ship, a group of passengers sit on the deck while old Papa sings. The listeners become a chorus, moving close together, "as if for some strange, starlit group-photograph, to be found years later in a trunk." The reference to the starlit photograph illuminates no particular person in it. The discovery of its hypothetical existence is located far in the future, in a confined space, where its context would likely be entirely lost.

A final photo fails to prepare its viewer for the actual appearance of its subject. As the *Pomona* nears Naples, Gabriella remembers one of the photographs that hung "over the dining-room mantel at home, . . . the yellow one of Nonna with the startled eyes under a mound of black hair." After they disembark, Mama responds to her mother with wild excitement: "'*Ecco*! *Ecco*! . . . *Mamma mia*!'" Gabriella's response is a startled cry: "But she doesn't look like her picture!" Nothing in the photograph has prepared the granddaughter for the small figure dressed in black, waiting quietly, her face wrinkled, her hair white. And nothing has prepared Gabriella for the sound of her Nonna's voice, "so beautiful and without reproach." In the presence of this voice, speaking words she could not understand, Gabriella's "gaze wavered and fell."

Gabriella's mother smiled at the photograph of her baby as if it were of unknown parentage. Gabriella causes the baby picture to fall into the sea never to be seen again. Passengers assembled for singing are re-imagined as a group photograph destined to be hidden for years in a trunk. Gabriella can hardly see Poldy's bride-to-be in the snapshot he shows her. Nonna, waiting in Naples for her daughter and granddaughter, "doesn't look like her picture!"

Photographs in "Going to Naples" are not associated with accuracy of representation or even careful attention. They do not prepare one for the human voice or for the passage of time. Even Poldy's bride-to-be doesn't show up when the ship arrives in Naples. All he is left with is his snapshot, snapped back under an elastic band.

There is one passage at the end of the story that, if it were attached to a photograph, might redeem the failures of the pictures that preceded it. As she sets forth with her mother and grandmother, Gabriella remembers "the golden moment of touch" in her goodbye to Aldo. "The moment—bright and effortless of making, in the end, as a bubble—seemed to go ahead of them as they walked, to tap without sound across the dust of the emptying courtyard, and alight in the grandmother's homely buggy, filling it."[8] The just-past moment becomes the future, already seeming to move ahead of the present, crossing dust and emptiness to fill the space of a new vehicle for a new journey, as if the story of what took place aboard the *Pomona* will find its place in the land voyage of a grandmother's homely buggy. A memory, not a photographic image, will carry the past into the future.

Eugene MacLain, the protagonist of "Music from Spain," walks out of the San Francisco apartment he shares with his wife after slapping her in the face during breakfast.[9] On Market Street, he sees the girlfriend of a sailor having her photograph taken in the arms of a stuffed gorilla in a penny arcade. In the window of a bookstore, he sees a "dark photograph" that looks like the image of his wife, Emma, but turns out, when he reads the caption, to be that of the occultist Madame Blavatsky. Later, walking with a Spanish guitarist whom he has befriended, MacLain sees a large photograph of a sideshow woman also named Emma, whose huge countenance seems to be looking at him with accusation. In the photograph, the sideshow Emma is wearing lace panties; nearby, a real pair of faded red panties without lace is exhibited, "vast and sagging, limp with dust and travel," as if in mockery of the photographic image. MacLain puts on the hat of the Spaniard and arranges its brim as if he were looking at himself in Emma's mirror with "the little snapshot stuck in the corner."[10] Photographic images in "Music from Spain" are accusatorial, mocked, and marginalized.

Welty's well-known story "Why I Live at the P.O." includes a photographer who takes "pose-yourself"[11] photos and has married the female narrator's sister, Stella-Rondo. Mr. Whitaker had taken dozens of photographs of his bride in a flesh-colored kimono, a part of her trousseau which her uncle is now wearing in the front yard. Stella-Rondo, viewing this scene, says, "'I simply declare that Uncle Rondo looks like a fool in it, that's all.'"[12] Imitating a photograph of his niece, the uncle becomes ridiculous.

"The Key" focuses on Albert and Ellie Morgan, a middle-aged, married couple from Yellow Leaf, Mississippi, as they wait in a railroad station. Deaf-mutes, they miss the announcement of the departure of the train to Niagara Falls, a place they had hoped might bring love and happiness into their lives. Albert now places hope in a key he has found on the floor: "happiness, Albert knew, is something that appears to you suddenly, that is meant for you, . . . a shiny thing that reminds you of something alive and leaping."

Ellie takes out of her purse a little card with a photograph of Niagara Falls, and Albert, looking at it, tells her that if you lean against the little rail pictured there, you will hear the waterfall: "'You listen with your arms and your legs and your whole body. You'll never forget what hearing is, after that.'" Ellie smiles and stares "deep, deep into the tinted picture of the waterfall." Then she signs to Albert that they might be there even now if they hadn't missed their train. The tiny photo invites the imagining of sound that, in turn, encourages the mistaken notion of an impossibly rapid arrival at the scene imaged. For Albert, hope resides not in a tinted picture but in a small key dropped by a red-haired stranger. Value is placed not on a visual image but on what one makes of an ordinary thing in one's midst, a "shiny thing that reminds you of something alive and leaping,"[13] on imagination itself.

In "The Winds," Josie, awakened in a night of fierce wind accompanied by persistent lightning, is brought downstairs to wait out a severe equinoctial storm with her parents and brother. She drifts off into a long reverie about another girl, then opens her eyes: "The lightning was flowing like the sea. . . . Her parents' faces were made up of hundreds of very still moments."[14] The faces of Josie's parents, illumined by the repeated flashes of lightning, are presented as if created by a series of photographic stills converging. The real danger and severity of the storm are deflected by these "very still moments."

Katherine Henninger points out a crucial role photography played for black southerners in "making visible what white southerners had carefully, violently, rendered invisible," alluding to "the walls of photographs often found in blacks' homes in the South."[15] The short story "Livvie" includes photograph after photograph, an incremental parade. Livvie is sixteen when Solomon, an old black man who owns his own land and house, marries her. For nine years, she lives with him in forced seclusion, Solomon growing older and frailer, finally dying in his own bed on the very day Livvie has kissed a young black field hand, who will replace him as his wife's lover.

In the front room of Solomon's house, on the mantel, are photographs of either old or very young men, "printed in faint yellow—Solomon's people." On the wall of the bedroom are two calendars, somebody's diploma, and, beneath that, Livvie's only possession: a photograph of the baby of the white family she had once worked for, before her marriage. The photographic images of the old and the very young represent the extremes, and unresolvable tension, of Livvie's life with Solomon. Livvie's sole possession is a photograph of someone she is not related to and could never have been: a white child. Solomon's photographs are of his own kin, people Livvie doesn't know and will never meet.

On the wall over Solomon's bed is a photograph of him with hair "like a king's crown"; now "the spring had gone out of it." The photo of her old husband as a young man is foreign to his wife: "she would forget who it was."

When a certain light hits his face, Livvie sees the sleeping man as baby-like, "new, . . . smooth and clear." The changes in the appearance of her husband's face recall the baby Livvie once cared for and anticipate the coming of youth into her life. Finally, it is her imagination alone that allows Livvie to "see" Solomon as he lies dying: "she could almost look through his forehead and see what he thought."

Among the photographs in this house, none reveals what is hidden in the old man's face. "It was an old and strict face, a frail face, but behind it, like a covered light, came an animation that could play hide and seek, that would dart and escape, had always escaped. The mystery flickered in him, and invited from his eyes. . . . Then he took hold of the quilt; then he was dead."[16] What is alive and mysterious in Solomon animates his old, worn face. What a photograph could not capture dies with him.

A photograph earns Mrs. Pike a cash reward[17] for identifying a rapist in "Petrified Man." Mrs. Pike is "very observant," so observant that she notices the three-month pregnancy of a stranger before anyone else does, but it is a photograph in an old magazine that reveals the identity of Mr. Petrie, now masquerading as a petrified man in a traveling freak show. Leota, working in a beauty salon, tells the story: "'So when she seen the photo, . . . it all came to her. Like a flash.'" When Mrs. Pike first saw the petrified man, he looked familiar, but "'lots of people look familiar.'"[18] What she recognizes in the photograph is the way Mr. Petrie, her former neighbor in New Orleans, turned his head and looked at her when she brought him breakfast. A past action is petrified in a visual image. For perhaps the only time in Welty's fiction, a photograph seems to trump life—and Mrs. Pike gets her five hundred dollars cash.

"At the Landing" presents the secluded life of an elderly man and his young granddaughter, Jenny. The single photograph in the story is a "little picture on the wall of . . . [Jenny's] mother with upturned eyes." The upturned eyes of her mother cannot meet Jenny's gaze.

At sunset, grandfather and granddaughter eat their supper served by the cook in a pavilion outside the house: "A little picture might be preserved then in all their heads." When the old man looks at his granddaughter across the table, "the gaze that went so fondly between them held and stretched tight the memory of Jenny's mother."[19] A mutual gaze, denied by the upturned eyes in the photograph, prolongs and tightens the memory of a mother who had died raving. After her grandfather's death, Jenny loses even that.

"The Bride of Innisfallen" includes allusions to photography but no actual photographs. A group of strangers meet and share stories on an English train before boarding the *Innisfallen* for Ireland. After their arrival in Cork, one of the passengers, identified only as "the American girl," sees a chalk mark, made by customs on her luggage, become auratic: "it stared at her from the sensitized optic dark, and she felt exposed—as if, in spite of herself, when she didn't know it, something had been told of her." The "sensitized optic dark" and the experience of being "exposed" suggest the imagery of photography, but the language in the final clause makes a claim for the writer's voice: "something had been told of her."

When the *Innisfallen* had first arrived at Cork, it was greeted with the shout: "'There's a bride aboard! Look at her, look!'" The bride, who until now has not appeared in public, smiles but does not look at those who gaze at her. We are told that when the bride smiled, "it might almost have been for her photograph; but still she did not look up—as though if even her picture were taken, she would vanish. And now she has vanished."[20] There is no photographer and no photo, only the feared effect: the subject vanishes.

Photographs in Welty's stories turn out to be deferred, abandoned, inadequate, enigmatic. The pictures may be posed (as in "Hello and Goodbye," "Going to Naples," "Music from Spain," and "Why I Live at the P.O."); they may appear on little yellow cards ("The Key"), in faded yellow on a mantel ("Livvie"), or miniaturized on a wall ("At the Landing"). Itinerant photographers find their way into Welty's stories (e.g., "The Whistle" and "Kin") and her novels, *Delta Wedding* and *Losing Battles*. Suggestive references to photography abound in Welty's fiction, but ultimately what Reynolds Price calls "the silent voice of image"[21] gives way to "a story-writer's truth."[22]

* * *

It is clear that photographs and photography continue to interest Welty in her writing life. It is also clear that the practice of photography alone is not enough for her.

3

The Visualizing Mind

If she closed her eyes she might see something.

—Samuel Beckett, *More Pricks Than Kicks*

Roland Barthes has said that a photograph touches him if he "shut[s] . . . [his] eyes, to allow the detail to rise of its own accord into affective consciousness."[1] When pressed to say whether she has relied on her photographs "for a scene or an element in a story . . . [she] has written," Eudora Welty replies, simply: "No. The memory is far better."[2]

Photography and writing for Welty are "two unrelated things," which "perhaps a kindred impulse made [her] attempt," and she names that kindred impulse: "an inquiring nature, and a wish to respond to what I saw, and to what I felt about things, by something I produced or did."[3] Welty both links and distinguishes between what happens when she takes a photograph and when she "sees" through the lens of the writer's visualizing mind.

In his review of Jane Campion's film, *Bright Star*, Christopher Ricks makes an important distinction between visualizing and seeing:

> To visualize is not the same as to see; more, it is incompatible with seeing. It is to form a mental picture of something not visible, perhaps not present, perhaps even not possible.[4]

This is another way of arguing that taking photographs and writing stories are "two unrelated things." Ricks's distinction is made explicit in the short story "The Wanderers": "Miss Katie couldn't spare her good hand to put up and shade her eyes; yet after you had passed, you saw her in that position, in your vision if not in your sight."[5] Welty writes of her first published story, *Death of a Traveling Salesman*, "As my work would continue to be, 'Salesman' was visual in texture;

but I had not taught myself in time for the first story to see in the specific detail and selectively."[6] To "see in" for Welty is insight that clearly calls for "vision," not "sight."

If photography and writing are "two unrelated things" connected for Welty by "a kindred impulse," is it possible to find traces of the journey from one mode to another, from seeing to visualizing? In two of Welty's stories, "A Memory" and "The Burning," one early and one late, there is neither photographer nor camera. Here, Welty's way of showing the limits of photography is to leave photography out of the story.[7] The protagonist's journey echoes the author's journey from the photographic eye to the visionary imagination.

"A Memory," told in the first person, offers a reading of the figures of would-be photographer and image-making dreamer. The narrator recalls a time when, as a child, she used "[her] hands squared over her eyes, finger tips touching," as frames for her view of everything she wished to look at in the world around her.

One summer morning, lying on a beach by a lake, the water shining "like steel" beneath a noonday sun, the child sees an auratic "rectangle brightly lit, actually glaring at [her], with sun, sand, water, a little pavilion, a few solitary people in fixed attitudes, and around it all a border of dark rounded oak trees, like the engraved thunderclouds surrounding illustrations in the Bible." Nature is visualized as both steel and holy text. As Welty has noted, a frame is fundamental to both photography and fiction: "I was conscious of that when I was getting my pictures, at least when I was printing the results. . . . [W]hen I took art [lessons in Jackson, Mississippi] from Mrs. Hull, she taught us that device: framing with your fingers. Studying drawing and painting made me aware in writing a story of framing your *vision*, as a way toward capturing it."[8]

The child in "A Memory" sees, framed by her fingers, a rectangle with a dark border, within which people are frozen in fixed attitudes, as if in a group picture. In fact, everything she sees that summer by the lake appears "as a kind of projection," a phrase poised between the discourses of photography and imagination. Ultimately, the visionary triumphs over the visible: "from any observation I would conclude that a secret of life had been nearly revealed to me."

The narrator holds in her memory a precious moment when she touched the wrist of a young boy as they passed each other on the stairs at school. Now, on the beach, she watches the crude activities of a man, two women, and two young boys who have arrived together. The man pours sand into the bathing suit of the older woman, who pulls down the top of her bathing suit, exposing her large breasts as lumps of sand empty out. The events the child witnesses dispel her memory of touching the wrist of a boy she loved, a boy whose innocence contrasts with the playful adult sexuality of the man and woman on the beach. She closes her eyes but "could see them still, large and almost metallic, with painted smiles, in the sun." In the word "still," Welty offers a double meaning: the child continues to see the other figures on the beach while her eyes are closed and she also sees them as if stilled in a posed photographic image.

The child can no longer recover her memory of the boy on the stairs. She feels "the heavy weight of sweetness" which had accompanied it, "but the memory itself did not come to me." In an anti-Proustian moment, the triggering sensation is felt but the memory fails to occur: "the story of my love, the long narrative of the incident on the stairs, had vanished." She opens her eyes and sees the "blur of an empty beach."[9] The little pavilion by the lake "met [her] eye"; suddenly pitying it, she wept. The eye met by the pavilion is singular, as in the practice of a photographer. The beach becomes a photographic blur, its former human figures missing in the foreground.

The people in Welty's snapshots are, in a sense, no longer "there" (whether or not they are blurred or disappearing within the frame). The characters in her stories are always there: that's where they live. At the end of "A Memory," the narrator remembers lying on the beach, once again "squaring . . . [her] vision with . . . [her] hands"; now she gives a future to the photograph-like, squared image. She imagines herself watching the boy walking into a classroom, "with this hour on the beach . . . added to my love." Her imagination takes her further into the scene. She foresees the boy silently staring back, "his unconscious eyes looking beyond me and out the window, solitary and unprotected."[10] The narrator is no longer seeing through the frame of her fingers. She sees herself seeing, and seen beyond, her vision amplified by experience and the visualizing mind.

The movement from photographic eye to visionary imagination, only hinted at in "A Memory," is fully and dramatically realized in Welty's "The Burning," published over a decade later. The story has as its occasion the burning, twice, of Jackson, Mississippi, a rare use of Civil War events in Welty's fiction. After a white horse walks through the front door of Miss Theo and Miss Myra's house, the two sisters do not look directly at the horse. Instead, they lift their eyes to the Venetian mirror over the fireplace in their parlor and see "a white silhouette, like something cut out of the room's dark."

The horse has arrived with two Northern soldiers, one riding and the other walking by its side. Ordered by one soldier to hold the horse's bridle, the slave Delilah looks in the mirror. She sees the horse looming and, in the "more blurred" background, the other soldier pushing aside tables and chairs. "There in the mirror the parlor remained, filled up with dusted pictures." Miss Theo half-carries her sister "to the chair in the mirror, and put[s] her down."

Allusions to black-and-white photography appear throughout the opening scene. The white silhouette in the mirror is like something cut out of the dark. The white horse looms in the foreground while the soldier in the background is blurred. The slightly disorienting phrase "the chair in the mirror" seems to reverse the literal and the imaged scene. All that we have viewed we have viewed through a mirror's reflections, which, like the upside-down images formed on film by the glass lens of a camera, give a reversed picture of the subjects portrayed. What is literally visible is quietly put in doubt.

The sisters leave the house wearing their crushed dresses and jewelry. They pause under a tree, "without any despising left in their faces which were the same as one, as one face that didn't belong to anybody. This one clarified face, looking both left and right, could make out every one of those men [who will torch their house] . . . and mark every looting slave also, as all stood . . . fixed like serenaders by the light of the moon." Those who stand fixed before the final looting and burning seem arranged for the camera's eye, and yet the combining of the sisters' faces into "one clarified face" that looks to left and right simultaneously defeats and replaces the photographer who must shoot first from one angle of view and then from another. John P. Schaefer notes that "the lens of the human eye has an angle of view (that is, the angle of what you can see to the left and right of center as you look straight ahead) of about 50 to 55 degrees. . . . *[T]he angle of view for every normal* [camera] *lens is the same* (approximately 50 to 55 degrees)."[11] Here is the co-presence of Welty's "two unrelated things," yoked by "a kindred impulse." The stillness of subjects fixed by the photographic eye and the impossible simultaneity of opposite angles of vision performed by the doubled eyes of one face compose a scene that is itself almost unbelievable.

After the house has been burned, the two sisters and Delilah walk together, holding hands, looking at the ruins of Jackson, "all chimneys, all scooped out." Henri Cartier-Bresson has said: "We photographers deal in things which are continually vanishing, and when they have vanished, there is no contrivance on earth which can make them come back again. We cannot develop and print a memory."[12] Welty as photographer took poignant snapshots of Mississippi chimneys and the remains of abandoned houses,[13] but none of those visual images represents what she imagines here.

The three women discuss a baby, Phinny, fathered by the sisters' brother, Benton. Amid a yard "charged with" butterflies, they find a silver Jubilee cup lying in someone's hammock. Miss Theo extracts from the hammock two long cotton ropes, which are made into nooses and hung from the branches of a nearby tree. After Delilah is forced to assist in her mistresses' deaths, she hides in "the jungly grass . . . , with cauldrons of ants, with butterflies riding them, grasshoppers hopping them," mosquitoes stinging her. She asks Miss Theo what to do, but Miss Theo's open eyes don't tell her. Eventually, she finds her way back to what is left of the burned house: "she knew it by the chimneys." There is no further attempt to present these chimneys, lone survivors of losses.

Inside the house, Delilah finds in the ashes a burned book, an image that will appear hauntingly in Purcell's photographs. As Delilah begins to imitate Miss Theo reading aloud from a book that she probably could never read and that can't be read at all now, she sees the Venetian mirror, face-up, in the "craw" of the chimney. Again she is uncertain what to do; again, there is no one to ask. Crouched low to the ground, she hears the noise of cannon, horses running fast, things burning. She crawls to her only companion, the mirror. She cleans the glass with her spit and sees "a face all neck and ears, then gone." No longer able to give reflections of what is in that house, the mirror "did not know Delilah"; its "gleam was addled."

In the mirror, Delilah sees intimations of a new mode of seeing. Gold and honey gather and flow in water, then are "twisted up into houses." People, in fantastic and festive array, walk "in early light with hives of houses on their heads." The photographic language of light and shadow is now part of a visionary scene. The mirror sends up "minnows of light" where an unidentified face is floating, "pure as a water-lily shadow." The minnows now leap into life, "fighting, aping old things Delilah had seen done in this world already, . . . and what anybody now could do to anybody." Then, as the July sun blazes down on the roofless house, "the mirror fell[s] her flat."

In the most spectacular visionary moment in all of Welty's work, Delilah becomes her own image-maker. Her earlier experience of hiding in jungly grass is transformed into an apocalyptic scene, with echoes of the last book of the New Testament,[14] as Delilah waits for what will gather beneath and above her: "bees saddled like horses out of the air, butterflies harnessed to one another, bats with masks on, birds together, all with their weapons bared . . . that whole army of wings . . . all this world that was flying, striking, stricken, falling, gilded or blackened, mortally splitting and falling apart, . . . spiraling down to bottomless ash."

> She dreaded the fury of all the butterflies and dragonflies in the world riding, blades unconcealed and at point—descending, and rising again from the waters below, down under, one whale made of his own grave, opening his mouth to swallow Jonah one more time.[15]

Earlier, Delilah had entered a yard "charged with" butterflies; now, part of an army of winged fury, butterflies charge her. The heightened language portraying what is mortally splitting and falling apart cannot be considered excessive, given the horrors Delilah has witnessed in the human world.

The weirdness of the vision comes partly from the role played by insects, particularly the butterfly, which appears frequently in various—usually more benign and beautiful—incarnations in Welty's fiction.[16] Metamorphosis, central to the insect's natural life cycle as it transforms from egg to caterpillar to chrysalis to butterfly, is central to Delilah's vision of a world changed utterly.

The metamorphoses here are uncanny: bees saddled like horses, bats with masks, dragonflies and butterflies with unconcealed blades—falling and rising from water where a whale is made out of his own grave.[17] The whale opening his mouth to swallow Jonah a second time rewrites the biblical story of the prophet swallowed by a great fish but disgorged later unharmed. Jonah metamorphoses into Delilah's child, Phinny, swallowed by the fire that twice burned Jackson.

In the mirror, Delilah sees a "motherly image" of herself as a warrior-animal. She bares her teeth, looks in the ashes, and finds Phinny's bones.

Wearing Miss Myra's shoes, with Miss Theo's shoes tied around her neck, she follows the road to the river. She carries the bones of her dead child, wrapped in a square of material from her skirt. On her head rests the silver Jubilee cup the three women found in a hammock that provided nooses for the two sisters. All that is menacing and destructive she has survived.[18]

Delilah enters the waters of the Big Black, "her treasure stacked on the roof of her head, hands laced upon it."[19] It is not clear whether her "treasure" is the cloth holding Phinny's bones or the Jubilee cup, with its possible allusion to a year of rest in ancient Israel when slaves were to be freed and property restored. Welty gives life to the mirror's image of people walking with "hives of houses on their heads." Amid roofless buildings burned to the ground, Delilah makes a roof of her own head and a treasure upon it that will not fall, spiraling down to bottomless ash.

Just before their deaths, Delilah had confidently announced to Miss Myra and Miss Theo that it would not rain until Saturday. Now, submerged to the chest in the Big Black, she knows, but does not remember how she knows, that the river will not rise to swallow her. Harold Bloom, for whom "The Burning" is "perhaps the most formidable of all Welty's stories, with the kind of rhetorical and allusive difficulties we expect to encounter more frequently in modern poetry than in modern short stories," says of Delilah at the close of the story: "she marches on to what is presented ambiguously either as her own freedom, or her death, or perhaps both together."[20] A black slave, no longer relying on images reflected in framed glass, has become a prophet and a visionary.

* * *

In Tennyson's "The Lady of Shalott," a mysterious lady, high in a tower above a river that flows to Camelot, sits weaving "a magic web," using the reversed images of her "mirror's magic sights." An unknown curse will fall on her if she pauses to look directly at the world. When the image of Sir Lancelot flashes into her mirror, she looks down from her tower and the mirror cracks. On the river in a small boat, "like some bold seer in a trance," she looks again at Camelot with a "glassy countenance" and dies.[21] In Tennyson's poem, the mirror imagery —"glassy countenance"—is transferred to the face of the female visionary. The Lady of Shalott, isolated from direct experience of the world and then unable to survive without her magic mirror, may be in the background of Welty's "The Burning," whose female protagonist will also go out on the river at the end, but as a fierce survivor of both her experience and a new mode of vision.

4

Doubling

[The writer] is always seeing double, two pictures at once in his frame, his and the world's, . . . and he works best in a state of constant and subtle and unfooled reference between the two.

—Eudora Welty, "Place in Fiction"

Writing about writing, Eudora Welty uses the language of the photographer: the frame, the double seeing of images (the first reversed), the keen recognition of two kinds of pictures while holding both in view. Reynolds Price has praised Welty's extraordinary "skill at pictorial precision in words," particularly her "yoking of disparate sights in a single image of startling freshness."[1] John F. Fleischauer also notes the "ingenious appropriateness" of Welty's imagery, carefully adding his useful distinction between simile and metaphor: "although Alfred Apple calls . . . [her images] metaphors, in fact they never are. Virtually all of Eudora Welty's imagery occurs in similes or in simile-like, hyphenated adjectives."[2] Welty's "always seeing double" produces abundant, precise, beautifully placed similes that give a sense of unexpected but utterly convincing convergence. The two affiliated elements of a simile are each present while joined, like two partners in conversation with each other—a conversation perhaps like that between the photographer's eye and the writer's visualizing mind.

In Welty's snapshots, there is only one angle of vision. In her fiction, a plurality of views, in a variety of ways, shifts perspective from one character to the next, changing and expanding the "camera angle" within a single work. This chapter will focus first on the use of multiple perspectives in Welty's novels *Delta Wedding* and *Losing Battles* and then on Welty's characteristic use of simile to produce two pictures at once in the frame.

It is important to note that not everything we want to see occurs within Welty's narrative frame. The imagined vanishing point of a photograph has a counterpart in what lies just outside the author's narrative frame. What Diane Arbus has said about a photograph—"[it] is a secret about a secret. The more it tells you, the less you know"[3]—can also be said of Welty's fiction. The death of R. J. Bowman, the title character in her first published story, "Death of a Traveling Salesman," occurs just outside the frame of the narrative: "He covered his heart with both hands to keep anyone from hearing the noise it made. But nobody heard it."[4] Like the fate of Delilah after she crosses the river with Phinny's bones, the marital happiness of the bride in *Delta Wedding* is left in doubt. All we know is the mother's worry for her daughter: "'Sometimes I'm so afraid when Dabney marries she won't be happy in her life.'"[5]

Losing Battles presents a family reunion celebrating the ninetieth birthday of Elvira Jordan Vaughn ("Granny"), in which the intermingling of voices exchanging stories begins to resemble scenes from a play. By contrast, *Delta Wedding* relies on free indirect discourse, a mode of narration that "combines elements of direct discourse and indirect discourse . . . , [creating a] 'dual voice' that may interweave or even merge the voices of narrator and character."[6] Welty's "always seeing double" is, in this case, represented by the interweaving of two modes of telling a story.

In *Delta Wedding*, nine-year-old Laura McRaven has traveled by train from Jackson to attend her cousin Dabney's wedding at Shellmound, the family plantation in Fairchilds, Mississippi. Ellen and Battle Fairchild, the parents of the bride (and of eight other children, with another baby on the way), have not seen their niece Laura since the funeral of her mother the previous winter.

In the course of preparations for Dabney's marriage to Troy Flavin, the overseer of the Fairchild estate, stories are told and retold, secrets are kept, mysteries remain. In an astonishing feat of multiple framing, almost everything we know is conveyed through the free indirect discourse of many characters. There are at least forty-seven different shifts in free indirect discourse,[7] shared among nine characters, all female: Laura, Ellen, Dabney, Shelley and India (Dabney's sisters), Robbie (the estranged wife of Laura's Uncle George), Aunt Tempe, Aunt Jim Allen (a deaf aunt), and Roxie (a black servant). Of these, Ellen Fairchild has the most instances, at least thirteen; Laura and Dabney have six each. Laura's free indirect discourse is the first and the last in the novel.

In addition to its inherent dual voice, free indirect discourse in *Delta Wedding* at times offers a further doubling, complicating the multiple angles of vision already in the novel. For example, India, one of Ellen's four daughters, sits on the floor, gazing at Aunt Tempe: "India could read her mind. The table lamp provoked Aunt Tempe." A little later, "Aunt Tempe closed her eyes," and "India followed her gaze." Then they sigh together.[8] In the doubling of the point of view within the dual voice of free indirect discourse, the imagination of India enters the mind of Aunt Tempe, who sees with eyes closed.

Another variation on the use of free indirect discourse is simultaneity, as when Robbie's and Ellen's perspectives converge suddenly after Great-aunt Mac accuses Robbie of marrying George for his money. Robbie replies, "'No, ma'am. I married him because he begged me!'" The free indirect discourse of Robbie joins that of Ellen: "To be begged to give love was something that . . . for a moment . . . struck Robbie and also Ellen humbly to earth, for it implied a magnitude, a bounty, that could leave people helpless."[9] Bringing together the views of characters so different in social status and temperament has an affinity with what Reynolds Price calls Welty's "yoking of disparate sights in a single image."[10]

At times, blurring occurs in the novel as it does in some of Welty's black-and-white snapshots.[11] In her nightgown, Laura stands at the door of Shelley's bedroom, observing her cousin write in her diary. Laura's glance takes in almost everything in the room, but there are various items of jewelry inside a little box, jewelry that Laura cannot possibly see. "Shelley would not be caught dead wearing any of them." The point of view seems indeterminately presented by Laura's gaze, the authorial third-person narrator, and Shelley's free indirect discourse, which controls the scene after she says: "'Go away, Laura! . . . You aren't supposed to watch us every minute!'"[12] In Welty's snapshots, blurring occurs in the background; what is foregrounded is more clearly focused. When Shelley is foregrounded, her point of view becomes more clearly focused as Laura disappears.

After Dabney's wedding and honeymoon, the family assembles at Shellmound. "One great golden star went through the night falling." First Laura, then India, then Dabney cry out at its beauty. India, criticized by Dabney for not dressing properly, runs off to look at the river. "She stood showily, hands on hips, as if she saw some certain thing, neither marvelous nor terrible, but simply certain, come by in the Yazoo River."[13]

In Welty's fiction, what is "simply certain" is rarely found. What *is* found are angles of vision, doubled or tripled; what is seen is always seen from within a particular point of view. Welty, however, imagines the ultimate vanishing point. "Even we [readers]," she says, "shall lie enfolded in perspective one day."[14] For Welty, the perspective vanishing in the distance is "the true one to hold in mind."[15]

At the end of *Delta Wedding*, an unidentified voice says, "'Oh, beautiful!,'" after another star falls in the sky. Laura says, "'I saw that one too. . . . I saw where it fell.'"

> She turned again to them, both arms held out to the radiant night.[16]

Louise Westling notes that "Laura has the final word in the novel."[17] It is true that Laura speaks last. In the novel's final one-sentence paragraph, however, the angle of vision is indeterminate. It is not clear whether this vision of radiance in the night sky is that of the third-person narrator or of Laura alone or is third-person narration and free indirect discourse inflected by Laura, India, and Dabney. The only "certain thing" is light seen at a great distance, falling yet beautiful in its fall.

Eudora Welty has described how she printed her snapshots at night in a darkroom she had set up in her kitchen: "the negatives were lovely to work with. . . . I like showing background, a long perspective, in the kind of portraits I attempt. I wanted to set people in their context. . . . I just wanted to get the subject and play with it afterwards; cutting and enlarging and so on, I find my composition."[18] Cutting and enlarging, presenting a long perspective, a background, and a context, Welty finds her composition in her fiction. In *Delta Wedding* and *Losing Battles*, a primary mode of "showing . . . a long perspective" is the retelling of stories, with their inevitable perspectival shifts.

A crucial story told and retold, meditated on and mentioned, at least sixteen times in *Delta Wedding*,[19] has to do with an event that occurs just before the novel opens, i.e., outside the frame. Uncle George has risked his own life to save his mentally challenged niece, Maureen, from being hit by an oncoming train. George had tried, and failed, to loosen Maureen's foot, caught on the track where she had been dancing. The other family members jump off the trestle as the train approaches, but George remains there with the girl. The Yellow Dog, the same train that brought Laura to Fairchilds, miraculously stops just before it would certainly have killed George and Maureen.

The train episode, related to Laura shortly after her arrival at Shellmound, is revisited by nine different characters until, near the end of the novel, after an unidentified girl has actually been killed on the railroad track by the Yellow Dog, it becomes "just a little story in the family."[20] Enlarging and then cutting, Welty composes a *mise en abîme* in which many narrations—with multiple angles of vision, varied perspectives—become, finally, one "little story" inside the frame of a larger narrative.

At one point, Shelley reenacts the experience of George and Maureen on the trestle. With three passengers, including Maureen, in her car, she suddenly drives across the railroad tracks just ahead of the Yellow Dog. She performs the mad risking of life that was, up to now, George's, and then makes her passengers promise never to reveal what has happened. Shelley takes over George's story but refuses to make it her own. Earlier, Robbie senses that George feels that "old stories, family stories, Mississippi stories, were the same as very holy or very passionate [*sic*], if stories could be those things."[21] Those "things" *are* the stories Welty writes but Shelley is not yet ready to tell.

Shelley is the figure of the future writer in the novel. She "rewrites" the train story, putting four lives at risk and then saving them. She takes command of the action and forbids the others to speak of it, preventing the event from becoming just another little family story. Instead, she hoards it in memory, as a writer will, as Welty does, all the while waiting, as she has learned to do, for "what you can't see . . . now." She "[thinks] to herself, . . . as though she read it in her diary":

> If Shellmound were a little bigger, it would be the same as the world entirely. . . . Perhaps that was the real truth.

Shelley, like Welty, discovers that a particular place in Mississippi could be the same as the world, if enlarged by the writer's imagination playing over memory. She is willing to "live in waiting, sometimes in terror," so as not to diminish a mysterious event to an anecdote comfortably retold by a family, but instead to reside in a place of beauty and change, weathering it all. It is a "vision of choice," one Welty made and Shelley has before her.[22]

In contrast, Shelley's mother, Ellen, says, "in her Virginia accent, 'I never rate [write].'" Ellen is a seer who makes us partners in her seeing: "What would happen to everything if she were not here to watch it, she thought." Ellen eventually invites her niece Laura to stay with the Fairchilds because Laura's father, Mr. McRaven, while decent and devoted, has "*no imagination*" (emphasis Ellen's). After Dabney's wedding, looking at her daughters dancing, seeing them all alike, suddenly "as if a bar of light had broken a glass into a rainbow she saw . . . each different face bright and burning as sparks of fire to her now, more different and further apart than the stars."[23] The fire, the burning, and the glass, along with the sheer force of light breaking upon the scene like the July blaze of the sun in "The Burning," are reminiscent of the black slave Delilah's role as prophet and visionary.

In *Delta Wedding*, Ellen represents both the photographer's eye and the possibility of visionary imagination. She sees the evanescence of the moment's truth, caught in the present-fast-becoming-the-past and the present-simultaneously-becoming-the-future:

> Though by another hour the fields would seem to jump in the sight with heat, now there was over them . . . the distance and clarity of fall, out of which came a breath of cool. Ellen took it.[24]

Ellen "took" it the way Welty as photographer took the moment that would seem to jump in her sight. In her fiction, Welty animates the breath of life arrested in her snapshots.

* * *

Losing Battles appeared more than two decades after *Delta Wedding*.[25] In his recently published collection of essays, Christopher Benfey is not much taken with either novel: "the longer performances, *Delta Wedding* and *Losing Battles*, go on and on, with short story characters who try and fail to take on the depth and complexity of novel characters." He has further criticism of *Losing Battles*:

> The title comes to seem like an admission of narrative exhaustion. Welty allows herself no internal description of her characters. . . . But she indulges in the most baroque efflorescence of metaphor in describing settings and props, and these, finally, are the true pleasures of the novel.[26]

Allowing herself "no internal description of her characters," Welty knew exactly what she was doing in *Losing Battles*. She set the novel in Tishomingo County, Mississippi:

> It appealed to me as a stage to put *Losing Battles* on because life there had been so whittled down to the bare bones of existence. No history but the struggle to keep alive. What was life but family? I was trying to describe what the characters' lives were like without benefit of any editorial comment at all, or any interior description. I wanted things shown by speech, by action, and by setting, location. And characters to reveal themselves and each other by conversation—action and conversation. I confined it all within a big family reunion, to a time length of two days and the night between. Plus the essential flashback.

She adds:

> My usual method of narration is more introspective; I am in the characters' minds all the time. So I was trying to see if I could do without any of it. It proved to be the most difficult novel I think I ever wrote.[27]

Welty's polyphonic novel could not be contained within the frame made by hands squared over a single narrator's eyes, as in the early story "A Memory." *Losing Battles* clearly veers toward a dramatic structure with its cast list, its somewhat confined time (two days and one night) and place (Tishomingo County), its emphasis on conversation, and its ironic anagnorisis (the foiled discovery of Gloria Renfro's true father) and peripetia (the rescue of Judge Oscar Moody by Jack Renfro).

The action of the novel concerns Jack Renfro's escape from the state penitentiary, one day before his official release, in order to attend a family reunion in honor of Granny's ninetieth birthday. He meets his baby daughter for the first time, rescues and reconciles with the judge who had sent him to prison for two years, and, at the end, attends the funeral of Miss Julia Mortimer, the legendary teacher at Banner School, who had warned Gloria not to marry him. The reunion both widens in its scope and threatens to unravel, but, on the way to Miss Julia's funeral, Judge Moody says to Jack: "You kept hold of us all for a pretty good little while there this morning."[28] That is what Jack has done, literally and metaphorically.

Welty's snapshots of conversation are mobilized and transformed into a "dialogic text" in which "a multiplicity of voices . . . interact and compete."[29] The choric voices provide multiple, shifting frames for the story of an extended family that includes Granny's great-great-grandchild. "What was life but family?" Welty says of the part of Mississippi she chose as her setting. "If Shellmound were a little bigger," Shelley Fairchild says, "it would be the same as the world entirely." Life "whittled down to the bare bones of existence" at Granny's house in *Losing Battles* is very different from life at the Fairchilds' plantation in *Delta Wedding*, but in each case what for Benfey goes "on and on" is the life of a novel whose multiplicity of characters and points of view make up a whole world. For Benfey, the title *Losing Battles* "comes to seem like an admission of narrative exhaustion." The title *Losing Battles* could, in fact, be read as suggesting the failure of any literary work, however exhaustive, to encompass the ever-vanishing, vanishing point of ongoing life.[30]

If one keeps track of *Losing Battle's* thirty-five named characters, living and dead, most of those foregrounded will take on appropriate novelistic detail and depth, conveyed through their conversation and action. There is also a slightly blurred background, as in Welty's snapshots, of various "descendants and cousins and married kin of the Beechams."[31] As for "the baroque efflorescence of metaphor" that provides "the true pleasures of the novel" for Benfey, the figure of speech that most clearly invites pleasure is the simile.

Losing Battles's extraordinary similes discourage an automatic leap to symbolism on the part of the reader, offering correspondence rather than the implied equivalence of metaphor. Welty has said that her fiction is "visual in texture."[32] Her similes are literary parallels to the startling images of visual convergence to be discussed later in Rosamond Purcell's photographs.

"Discovery," for Welty, "is a matter of vision." The transfer of the writer's "lonely, unremitting, unaided, unaidable vision . . . without distortion . . . onto the pages of a novel," and from there to the reader, is "alchemy."[33] Welty describes the unified awareness of two characters in one of her stories as "my third character, the straining, hallucinatory eyes and ears, the roused-up sentient being of that place."[34] These straining, hallucinatory eyes and ears are apparent in Delilah's visionary imagery at the end of "The Burning." In a novel mainly told in dialogue and by a chorus of voices, Welty's "third character" manifests itself in her similes.

In *Losing Battles* there are, of course, many non-hallucinatory similes in which the visible simply calls up the visible. Jack and his wife, Gloria, with their baby, Lady May Renfro, come to a bank overlooking a road that "dropped away on both sides below them, like a sash picked up in the middle on a stick." A buzzard comes by, "flying slow as a fence-walker." A few sentences later, Welty writes: "Presently there came a sound from the road itself, thin as that of a veil being parted." After Jack's friend, Aycock Comfort, says that he hears gravel, "thoughts seemed to chase one another up and down his forehead, rippling it like a squirrel's tail."[35] The first two similes find correspondences between objects that are visible to the eye (road and sash on a stick; buzzard and fence-walker). There is a slight straining toward "hallucinatory eyes and ears" in the third simile which connects an auditory experience, invisible to the eye (a sound from the road), with an image that is partly visual (the veil) and perhaps partly aural (the sound of the veil being parted). The fourth simile strains to make what is invisible (thoughts) visible (the rippling of a squirrel's tail, replayed on Aycock's forehead).

Similes associated with light and shadow are often poised between the visible and the visualized, as Christopher Ricks has distinguished these terms. When Granny's family sings, "the tree over them, . . . with its ever-spinning leaves all light-points at this hour, look[s] bright as a river." The image of spinning leaves as light-points is characteristic of Welty's photographic eye, her close attention to the effects of natural light, but the tree that looks as bright as a river is not easily seen, though quite easily imagined. In the evening, Jack and Gloria lie on the floor of Granny's porch, atop a faded quilt: "blanched again tonight by moonlight, it showed a pattern as faint as one laid by wind over a field of broomsedge. . . . A female voice, superfine, . . . thin as a moonbeam, strung itself out into the night."[36] One can see the effects of wind on a field of broomsedge, once one knows what broomsedge is.[37] A female voice thin as a moonbeam is sheer alchemy.

After Jack's younger brother, Vaughn, has rescued the Banner School bus from a ditch, the "moon, like an eye turned up in a trance, filmed over and seemed . . . to float sight-less. . . . Lightning branched and ran over the world with an insect lightness." In a complicated interplay of the visible and the visualized, the moon is given an eye, or rather is likened to the eye of someone in a trance; "filmed over" and "float[ing]," it becomes "sightless." The image of lightning running over the world "with an insect lightness," combined with the word play on "lightning" and "lightness," seems meant to be visual but, in fact, is visionary, like the insect imagery in "The Burning." There is thunder; a cloud passes in front of the moon: it "was round for a minute longer, like a berry in the open beak of a bird, then it was swallowed."[38] The perfectly ordinary image of a berry in a bird's open beak is followed by the hallucinatory swallowing of the moon.

Earlier, Vaughn,[39] driving the school bus back to Granny's house, "could feel that bus on its own wheels rolling on his tongue, like a word of his own ready to be spoken, then swallowed back into his throat, going down, inside and inside. And at the same time, the sky that he could see went on performing—more stars fell, like a breaking chain."[40] In her memoir, *One Writer's Beginnings*, the moon met the eyes of the six-year-old Eudora Welty as a globe, and its name entered her mouth. In *Losing Battles*, the round wheels of a bus roll on a young boy's tongue like his own word ready to be uttered. We are not told what that word is, only that it is swallowed whole. When Vaughn looks up at the night sky, he sees stars falling, like young Laura at the end of *Delta Wedding*. The simile of the breaking chain is beautiful, but what is most mysterious in this scene is the unnamed word that stays far down, "inside and inside," even as the visible world goes on performing.

As the novel ends, "the sycamore trees in the school yard [are] tinged on top with yellow, as though acid had been spilled on them from some travelling spoon."[41] The image of a surreal spoon that spills acid as it passes over the sycamores in the Banner schoolyard shows that serious whimsy can accompany "serious daring"[42] for Eudora Welty, perhaps more often in her writing than in her snapshots.

* * *

Describing the origin of her story "A Worn Path," Welty says that she "saw a solitary old woman like Phoenix [Jackson]. She was walking; I saw her, at middle distance, in a winter country landscape, and watched her slowly make her way across my line of vision. The sight of her made me write the story. I invented an errand for her. I brought her up close enough, by imagination, to describe her face, make her present to the eyes."

> But the full-length figure moving across the winter fields was the indelible one and the image to keep, and the perspective extending into the vanishing distance the true one to hold in mind.[43]

Here is a perfect portrayal of the interplay of photographer's eye and writer's visualizing mind. Welty observes a figure walking in the middle distance; she allows the figure to move undisturbed across her "line of vision," as if seen in the lens of her hand-held camera. Then her imagination not only invents an errand for the journey she is watching but acts like a photographer, refocusing the camera to bring the face "up close enough," so that it can be viewed and described in detail. But it is the whole figure moving slowly across the winter fields, something her snapshot could never capture, that is the indelible image, the one to keep, like a photograph, but not *as* a photograph. She has said, "I felt the need to hold transient life in *words*—there's so much more of life that only words can convey—strongly enough to last me as long as I lived."[44] The "perspective extending into the vanishing distance" is the one Welty chooses as visionary writer.

5

Reverberations

"Beulah, this picture's filling up with the dead," said Aunt Beck.
"After this year, let's not try taking it off its shelf any more."
—Eudora Welty, *Losing Battles*

During the ninetieth birthday celebration for her grandmother, Jack Renfro's mother, Beulah, suddenly says, "I think it's about time for us to take a little prettier view of ourselves." "Go bring out my wedding," she tells her daughter, Elvie. "Stand on a chair and reach carefully." The "wedding" that comes out carefully is the largest photograph in Eudora Welty's fiction, almost two feet long and at least seven inches high. "'The only picture that ever was made of our whole family,' Miss Beulah said, while a crowd gathered behind her shoulders."[1]

The ambiguous phrasing, "bring out my wedding," as if the photograph *is* the event, gives poignancy both to the care taken in bringing it out and to its unique character as the only representation of Beulah's entire family. For more than three pages in *Losing Battles*, there is a choric ekphrasis of an old photograph taken at the wedding of Beulah Beecham and Ralph Renfro, when all six of Beulah's siblings and their grandfather were still alive.

Granny's assembled family gazes at "a little prettier view" of themselves, taken by an itinerant photographer, "one of life's wayfarers, a picture-taker," and sent back a month later rolled up so tightly that it has sat on a shelf, held down by two flatirons, for twenty-five years. Welty presents a portrait of a family looking at its own, long-ago portrait.

The wedding photograph is first described in terms of light and darkness, foreground and background: "The earlier company had lined up three deep that day on the front porch and steps of this house where they themselves were now. They stood then in April light; the house stood dark, roof and all, as a woodsy mountain behind the water-splash of the bride." The photograph is then re-presented in the polyphonic mode of the novel, one voice following another, filling in its "story," identifying the living and the dead, supplemented by third-person narration.

> At the apex of the group stood a medium-tall, upright lady with black hair showing under her hat, with her hand over the arm of the man standing in a preacher's stance. . . . The old lady didn't say a word.[2]

On the lighted porch[3] of Granny's house at nightfall, the first Sunday of August, the present family looks at the past family, seen in April daylight against a darkened house. The image of her younger self standing next to her deceased husband leaves Granny speechless, as if, like Gabriella Serto's grandmother in "Going to Naples," she "doesn't look like her picture."[4]

Welty's intimate relation to photography informs this scene. Beulah's daughter Etoyle notices that her uncle, Sam Dale Beecham, now deceased, is somehow in the photo twice. The third-person narrator explains this (pre-digital) mystery: "Evidently by racing the crank of the camera and running behind backs, Sam Dale had got in on both ends of the panorama, putting his face smack and smack again into the face of oblivion."

> Though too young and smooth to print itself dark enough not to fade, his face could not be mistaken.

Welty's phrasing gives agency to Sam Dale as printing his own unmistakable yet faded photographic image, even as the young man futilely attempts to double his odds against oblivion. The picture filling up with the dead is a comic critique of photographic representation, an ironic illustration of Welty's statement about developing and printing a snapshot in her darkroom at home: "Let it show what was inherent in it."[5]

Aunt Nanny flattens her finger on a blur in the photograph "where someone had moved." Beulah, looking at the blur, identified as Rachel Sojourner, asks: "But what's she doing hiding in my wedding picture, and I never saw her before?" The blur is a key figure in the quest to solve the mystery of Gloria Renfro's true parentage. "'She's been in the company room with you all this time, Gloria,'" said Aunt Beck. "'Your mother.'"

> "I can't see what this girl looked like," said Gloria, coming at last to look at the picture with them.

Rachel Sojourner is nearly invisible in the blurred photographic image. Beulah never saw her in the picture before and Gloria can't see her now. And yet "she's been in the . . . room" with Gloria all this time, as if the image *is* the dead mother's presence. Just after this exchange, Aunt Beck says: "'Beulah, this picture's filling up with the dead. . . . After this year, let's not try taking it off its shelf any more.'"[6]

Shifting points of view form the choric examination of an old family photograph. Figures in the "prettier view" are doubled, blurred, deceased, or disfigured. Beulah, ready to share Aunt Beck's perspective, asks that the picture be returned to its shelf. But Aunt Cleo is not through with her examination. A new member of the family (by marriage), who does not know the family stories, Aunt Cleo serves as interrogator. She moves her finger slowly across the photograph and pauses to point to someone unknown to her.

The image that receives the most detailed attention in this scene is neither kin nor welcome: Miss Julia Percival Mortimer, the dreaded and heroic Banner schoolteacher, who no more wished to be in the photograph than the family wished to have her there. "She was standing, . . . ignoring the camera, looking off . . . as from her own promontory to survey the world. The . . . long-focused eye, . . . the very way the head was held, all said that the prospect was serious."[7] The person who ignores the camera is, significantly, the one with the "long-focused eye." Julia Percival Mortimer, like the author, surveys a world beyond what a photograph can frame.[8]

Beulah's little daughter Elvie asks where she was. "'Lucky for you, you was nowhere on earth yet!'" her mother replies. "'Now that you're here, put this picture back where it belongs. Granny dear, don't you want to see it? Just one more time before it goes?' Granny waved it away.'"[9] What Beulah means is that it is good her daughter was not born before her mother married her father, but the phrase "back where it belongs," like Granny's waving the picture away, refusing a last look "before it goes," suggests that the photograph itself is about to undergo a burial.

If you move, you are a blur. If you attempt to fool the camera and double yourself, you still end up "putting [yourself] . . . into the face of oblivion." What saves one from oblivion is storytelling. Sam Dale Beecham is more present in the story- and memory-sharing of the family reunion than he can ever be in the double portrait of him at his sister's wedding.

A twenty-five-year-old photograph is scrutinized: its idiosyncrasies, its partial recovery of what was blurred or hidden or trying to self-amplify, of what "could not be mistaken" in the past. The past is what it is; it cannot be changed. Storytelling, like memory, can revisit and rescue the past.[10] The photograph itself is the face of oblivion unless it seeks out voicing. Otherwise, it is time's victim, stilled life.

What I have elsewhere called "the performance of ambivalence"[11] is portrayed here. An old wedding photograph seeks to make present what can't be literally preserved. It represents the absence, the pastness, of what was there in the moment of the photograph. When Aunt Beck tells Beulah that the picture is filling up with the dead, she paradoxically characterizes the photograph as a portrayal of deadness even as her language animates it. The family photograph is a *memento mori* that can be changed by time, love, imagination; it will fill up with the dead and, at the same time, preserve what fills it.[12] "'Feelings don't get old!' Aunt Beck said. . . . 'We do, but they don't. They go on.'"[13]

The failed attempt to discover who fathered Gloria Renfro had begun with a "brownish postcard" kept in Granny's Bible for many years after the death of her grandson. After Granny showed it for the first time to the family, Beulah "brought it to her eyes, picture side up." "'It's Sam Dale Beecham in his soldier suit!' she cried. 'I never saw him dressed in it except when we buried him.'"

Writing appears on the other side of the card, Uncle Curtis points out, but his sister "could not take her eyes from the picture." Everyone waits. Finally, Beulah turns the card over and reads aloud, haltingly:

> "Dear Rachel [Gloria's mother]. . . . Here is a—present for our—baby. . . ."—something—"*trust* it keeps good time. . . ." Something—"Sincerely your husband Sam Dale Beecham."

The difficulty Beulah experiences in making out the writing on the postcard is like her difficulty in making out the blur that turns out to be Gloria's mother in the wedding photograph. The "somethings" in Beulah's hesitant reading aloud suggest the effort involved in resurrecting the past.

This photo-postcard was never sent to Rachel. It arrived with the dead body of its subject and author, along with his other possessions and the watch he had bought for the baby. "'It's a likeness,'" Granny says. "'I can peep at it before I get my prayers said.'" For Granny, the picture of her grandson is what matters, not the writing. For Beulah, the situation is complicated. What she wishes to see is impossible:

> She turned the card first to the faded handwriting, then to the picture, turned it back and forth faster and faster, as if trying through her tears to make the two sides one, bind them.

Granny "frisked the postcard out of Miss Beulah's fingers, returned it to her Bible, and shut up the Bible. Elvie sprang up and went hauling off with it."[14] As with Beulah's wedding photograph, the removal of Sam Dale's photo-postcard is a kind of burial. A secret is being shut away, once again.

The faded handwriting of Sam Dale, like his faded double portrait in the family photograph, is unmistakable but also deceptive. (Sam Dale Beecham has not fathered the child of Rachel, whom he was simply trying to protect.) Later, gazing at her brother's image in her old wedding picture, Beulah will say, "'Look at that face—there's nothing in it but plain goodness, goodness personified.'"[15] Now, attempting to view simultaneously both sides of the photo-postcard, Beulah is caught between visual image and written text, "trying to make the two . . . one, bind them."

It is a stunning moment in the novel, as if Beulah stands in for Eudora Welty, the taker of snapshots and the writer of stories, and the need to choose one mode of vision over the other. The only way to "make the two . . . one" is to create visual images through writing.

The identity of Gloria's biological father will remain a minor mystery in the novel. "'Don't make an ell's worth of difference, does it? If you're not Sam Dale's [daughter],' said Granny, waving her away." Granny waves away Gloria's history just as she waved away the wedding photograph and returned Sam Dale's brownish postcard to her Bible. Earlier, Aunt Cleo whispers, "'Don't she [Granny] know the difference yet? Who's alive and who's dead?'" Beulah replies, "'She knows we're all part of it together, or ought to be!'"[16] The figures inside and outside the photographs, living and dead, are part of a story told and retold by a polyphony of voices that interact and compete. Welty's narrative wraps itself around and transforms a who-done-it moment, as if what we thought was the mystery to be solved hid itself inside a larger perspective, an even larger mystery.

When Welty was six or seven years old, she was diagnosed by a doctor as suffering from a "'fast-beating heart,'" taken out of school for several months, and placed in her parents' double bed upstairs to rest during the day. In *One Writer's Beginnings*, she recalls how her parents covered the lampshade in their bedroom with the daily paper and sat talking in their rocking chairs in the part of the room still lit. "What was thus dramatically made a present of to me was the secure sense of the hidden observer," Welty writes. "I don't remember that any secrets were revealed to me, nor do I remember any avid curiosity on my part to learn something I wasn't supposed to—perhaps I was too young to know what to listen for. But I was present in the room with the chief secret there was—the two of them, father and mother, sitting there as one."

> What I felt was not that I was excluded from them but that I was included, in—and because of—what I could hear of their voices and what I could see of their faces in the cone of yellow light under the brown-scorched shade.[17]

In a sense, all of Welty's work can find its origins in this memory of childhood, as she herself suggests: "A conscious act grew out of this by the time I began to write stories: getting my distance, a prerequisite of my understanding of human events, is the way I began work."

> In my first journalism job, I stumbled into making pictures with a camera. Frame, proportion, perspective, the values of light and shade all are determined by the distance of the observing eye.[18]

The "distance of the observing eye" informs not only the description of the wedding photo but also the gathering of the family in *Losing Battles*. Framing the composition of a scene, understanding the values of light and shadow, and exploring the uses of perspective "stumbled" from Welty's photography into her fiction. Her account of her beginnings discloses the "observing eye" of the photographer and "fast-beating heart" of the writer.

* * *

The Optimist's Daughter, Welty has said, "is a novel concerned with vision. Vision is central in all that transpires, its presence and its absence."[19] In this, her last novel, Welty records a double loss of vision.

Laurel McKelva Hand, a widow in her mid-forties, leaves her home and job in Chicago to travel to New Orleans, where her father, Judge Clinton McKelva, with his new wife, Fay, has gone to be examined by an eye specialist. When Dr. Courtland gives the news, "'Your right retina's slipped,'" Judge McKelva asks him how soon he can operate. Fay cries out, "'Just for a scratch?'" Dr. Courtland responds:

> "But this eye didn't get a scratch. What happened didn't happen to the outside of his eye, it happened to the inside. The flashes, too. To the part he sees with."

Welty focuses on the harrowing aftermath of the operation on the optimist's right eye. The "dislocated vision" that had brought him to the hospital eventually dwindles into less and less vision. Even when the left eye is uncovered, Judge McKelva "seemed inclined to still lower the lid over his good eye. Perhaps, open, it could see the other eye's bandage."[20] It is as if Welty is trying to understand the loss of vision from inside the eye itself.

In the hospital room where Laurel spends much of her time, the Venetian blind "was kept lowered to let in only a two-inch strip of March daylight at the window," light which fell onto the book in Laurel's lap as she read aloud to her father. Her father becomes less curious, more and more silent, never asking about his eye or his daughter. "What occupied his full mind was time itself; time passing; he was concentrating."[21] Vision has turned inward.

With the loss of sight comes the loss of words. Judge McKelva lies unmoving in his bed, "his good eye closed, or open on the ceiling, and had no words to spare." He speaks only when spoken to, and then only after a pause, "as if he had to catch up."[22] In *Losing Battles*, Judge Moody says, as an attempt is made to save his car from destruction, "We're all holding on here now by the skin of our teeth! Can't conversation ever cease?"[23] Not in *Losing Battles*, but in Judge McKelva's hospital room, where Laurel and her father are holding on by the skin of their teeth, conversation has nearly ceased.

The good eye, when it opens, opens "on" the ceiling, almost as if pressed up against it, preventing "the distance of the observing eye." In fact, Judge McKelva "lay more and more with both eyes closed." Welty is now imagining a refusal of the effort to see at all.

After three weeks, all Dr. Courtland can report to the optimist's daughter is that he thinks Judge McKelva "[has] got some vision coming, just a little bit around the edge."[24] For a photographer-writer with an acute sense of frame, perspective, and the values of light and shade, and for the woman who remembers herself as a child seeing loved faces in a cone of yellow light, the surgeon's version of the kind of vision that may be coming, "just a little bit around the edge," would be something like a death blow. And shortly after this, Judge McKelva is dead. In the hall outside her father's hospital room, Laurel overhears Dr. Courtland say to the nurse: "'I believe he's just plain sneaked out on us.'"[25]

After the funeral at Mount Salus, Mississippi, Laurel remains in her family home for three days where memory returns "like spring." She sets herself the task of cleaning and ordering the house. In her father's library, she notices the absence of a picture that once stood on his desk: "a photograph of her mother, who had been asked to stop what she was doing and sit on the garden bench—this was the strongly severe result; and the picture was gone."[26]

The photograph of Laurel's mother is not the sort Welty ever sought in her 1930s snapshots: "I would not have dared to interfere with the poses."[27] More significantly, it is missing.

In a 1950 snapshot Welty took in Jackson, Mississippi,[28] published more than two decades after her own mother's death, Chestina Andrews Welty sits on the ground, surrounded by a somewhat blurred background of the garden flowers and plants she loved. Her legs are hidden beneath her long dark dress, and her right hand falls outside the frame of the picture. The left hand lies casually over her slightly bent knees, the thumb and forefinger perhaps holding something she has picked from the garden. Her posture is relaxed, her head turned gracefully to her right, as if she has been caught by the eye of the camera in an undisturbed moment.

Above her open, white lace collar, her face in three-quarters profile is serene, her mouth just opening in a private smile. Her white hair, falling just below the

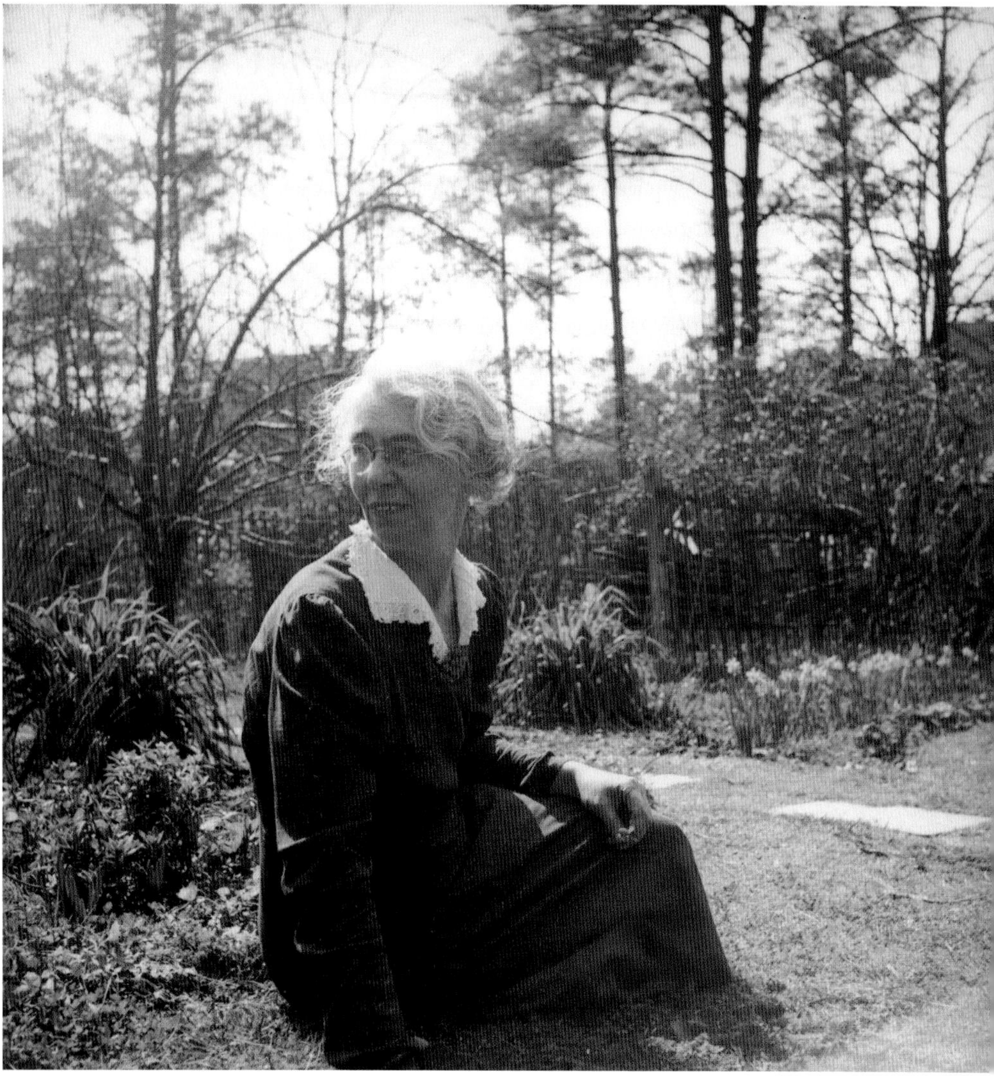

PLATE 11. Chestina Andrews Welty.

ear, seems ruffled a bit, either by wind or by exertion. Her brows are dark above thin-framed glasses that allow her eyes, meditative and focused elsewhere, to be fully visible. No matter how one turns the photograph, it is impossible to meet her glance, and yet the viewer is somehow "included" in the scene, like the child lying upstairs in her parents' double bed, watching the faces of her mother and father partly lit by a shaded lamp.

There are, in fact, what Welty calls "reverberations" of Chestina Andrews Welty in *The Optimist's Daughter*:

> [Becky Thurston McKelva] does not represent a portrait of my mother, nor was she intended to. All the same, there are in Becky qualities I came to know through knowing my mother—qualities that are at the heart of *The Optimist's Daughter*.[29]

Suzanne Marrs believes that this last novel "is one way Welty grieved for her mother's death."[30] Asked if writing *The Optimist's Daughter* helped her after the loss of her mother, Welty replied: "'I think it did; although, I did not undertake it for any therapeutic reasons, because I don't believe in that kind of thing. I believe in really trying to comprehend something. Comprehension is more important to me than healing.'"[31]

In *The Optimist's Daughter*, not only is the photograph of Laurel's mother missing but so are the letters Becky McKelva wrote her husband daily during the month she spent each summer of her married life, usually with Laurel, "'up home'" in West Virginia. Unlike Granny in *Losing Battles*, who holds on to the images and the writing of the dead, Judge McKelva seems to have made sure that "there was nothing of . . . [Laurel's] mother here for Fay to find, or for . . . [Laurel] to retrieve."[32]

On her last night in her father's house, during a raging storm, a chimney swift flies uncaught from one room to another, and Laurel seeks refuge from the bird in her mother's sewing room, where she had slept as an infant. She remembers her mother at her sewing machine and herself as a child collecting scraps of cloth that fell to the floor, transforming them into "stars, flowers, birds, people, . . . lining them up, spacing them out, making them into patterns, . . . with the shine of firelight, or the summer light, moving over mother and child and what they both were making."[33] Laurel, in shifting light, makes "scraps" into images, patterns.

In Becky's small writing desk Laurel finds the letters her father had written to her mother, "all she had received in her life, surely—there they were." She opens a single letter, reads its salutation, "'My darling Sweetheart,'" and "return[s] it to its place." Unlike Granny frisking away Sam Dale's postcard, which she had already looked at many times, Laurel leaves undisturbed and unread the letters her mother saved. It is photographs, not letters, that will bring forth memories of her mother's voice.

On the shelf above the pigeonholes of the desk, Laurel finds a record of her father's courtship of her mother in "a snapshot book":

> Still clinging to the first facing-pages were the pair of grayed and stippled home-printed snapshots: Clinton and Becky, . . . each taken by the other . . . , he

> slender as a wand, . . . swinging his straw hat; she with her hands full of the wildflowers they'd picked.[34]

Like Beulah's faded wedding photo in *Losing Battles*, the grayed and stippled images evoke family memories. What Laurel remembers most are voices, those of her grandmother and her six uncles, but especially the voice of her mother talking about the beautiful blouse she was wearing in the photograph, a blouse Becky herself had made. Laurel speculates that her mother "[had] developed the pictures too, for why couldn't she? And very likely she had made the paste that held them." The shifting roles of the author are represented by mother and daughter: Becky constructs a record of the past in home-printed snapshots; Laurel rescues voices from oblivion.[35]

Now Laurel remembers her mother's tormented years of failing vision and unsuccessful eye operations, how Becky had lashed out in anger at her husband and daughter, "out of her darkness of vision," "still . . . [holding] fast to their hands." "'*Liar*!'" she cried to her husband the optimist. To Laurel, her last words were, "'You could have saved your mother's life. But you stood by and wouldn't intervene. I despair for you.'" After a crippling stroke, Becky dies "without speaking a word."[36]

Laurel sits in the sewing room and thinks "of only one thing, of her mother holding and holding onto their hands, her own and her father's holding onto her mother's, long after there was nothing more to be said." Laurel could remember her mother's hands held before her eyes, "very close, so that she seemed to be seeing them, the empty, working fingers."[37] The empty, working fingers in front of Becky's eyes are not like the narrator's fingers that framed the world in "A Memory": all Laurel's mother can see is the frame. Welty says of Becky McKelva, who, like her own mother, was nearly blind by the time of her death: "Trust in others, in the world, in love, fails her. . . . Before she dies, everything fails her but her passion."[38] Non-therapeutic comprehension for Welty, in her last novel, has perhaps arrived.

Before she returns to Chicago, Laurel stands in the driveway of her family home, burning the letters her mother had kept, along with "saved little books and papers. . . . There was nothing she was leaving in the whole shining and quiet house now to show for her mother's life and her mother's happiness and suffering."[39]

This is the most quietly dramatic burning in Welty's fiction, itself so full of fires and fire imagery.[40] The fire seems to consume the snapshot book with the home-printed photographs of Laurel's parents.[41] Like Delilah in "The Burning," Laurel is both witness and survivor. Unlike Delilah, she takes nothing of the past with her on her journey: "The past is no more open to help or hurt than Father was in his coffin. The past is like him, impervious, and can never be awakened."

> It is memory that is the somnambulist. It will come back in its wounds from across the world.[42]

"To [Laurel]," Meg Gertmenian writes, "the past can never be reawakened, so it's sleeping, but memory the somnambulist can walk in that sleep."[43] Welty believes that memory should be given its due; throughout much of her fiction and perhaps most especially in her last novel, it is.

After I had written these words, I read a version of *The Optimist's Daughter* published as a story in the March 15, 1969, *New Yorker*. This earlier version of the novel was completed during what must have been a time of deep mourning: the year after the deaths, within the same week, of Welty's mother and her brother Edward, in January 1966.[44]

In the revised novel published in 1972, Welty omits the following explicit account of what Laurel preserves as mementos of the past: "Laurel stood in the driveway burning her mother's letters and little books and papers in the tall wire basket. . . . *Besides the book of snapshots—she could never give up a picture*—she had kept one thing. She had dropped the little stone boat . . . into her big Chicago handbag for her fingers to come upon some busy day" (italics mine).[45] Except for the first sentence of the quotation, none of this appears in the revised and expanded novel. The sentence declaring that the protagonist "could never give up a picture" is given up; the view that relinquishment of a photograph is impossible is relinquished. Welty's changing relationship to photography perhaps is reflected in the very different fates of the snapshot book—saved and burned—in the two published versions of the novel.

In a passage that only appears in the later, revised novel, the one thing Laurel wants to rescue from the burning is words:

> She saw the words "this morning?" with the uncompromising hook of her mother's question mark, on a little round scrap of paper that was slowly growing smaller in the smoke. She had a child's desire to reach for it, . . . by then it was consumed. All Laurel would have wanted with her mother's "this morning?" would have been to make it over, give her a new one in its place.[46]

Here, in her last novel, Welty privileges writing, even a scrap with two words, over snapshots. The words, if rescued, would have allowed Laurel to do what Welty as a writer does: "make it over," give a new "morning" in place of what is past.

"The greatest confluence of all is that which makes up the human memory—the individual human memory. My own is the treasure most dearly regarded by me, in my life and in my work as a writer. . . . The memory is a living thing—it too is in transit. But during its moment, all that is remembered joins, and lives—the old and the young, the past and the present, the living and the dead." It is after writing this that Welty ends *One Writer's Beginnings* with her famous statement:

> As you have seen, I am a writer who came of a sheltered life. A sheltered life can be a daring life as well. For all serious daring starts from within.[47]

At the conclusion of *The Optimist's Daughter*, Laurel McKelva Hand learns that "memory lived . . . in the freed hands, pardoned and freed, and in the heart that can empty but fill again, in the patterns restored by dreams."[48] Welty's "really trying to comprehend something" seems bestowed on, realized through, the protagonist of her last novel. As she says in her foreword to *The Optimist's Daughter*, "Laurel reaches the point of believing that it can never be, really, too late to begin to understand what has happened to you. . . . Clarity is born, or restored, in the mind's eye,"[49] in the visualizing mind.

Becky looked at her empty hands, the fingers no longer at work. Laurel, leaving her family home for the last time, her own hands newly freed and pardoned, sees "the twinkling of . . . hands, the many small and unknown hands"[50] of schoolchildren, waving goodbye. In the final moment of the novel, a multitude of young hands is twinkling. After the terrible darkening of vision, light returns, and we see what Laurel sees, not in the full blaze of sun or fire but in quick, intermittent flashes, like those of a camera or, with greater illumination, the visionary imagination. We see what Laurel sees by that light.

6

Rosamond Wolff Purcell

Beginnings

One day, . . . in St. Petersburg, in the pupil of a glass eye from the cabinet of Peter the Great, I saw the casement of the windows and the hall that the eye and I occupied. I saw that the eye was drinking in the light.

—Rosamond Purcell, *Owls Head*

"Since the age of nineteen or twenty," Rosamond Wolff Purcell told me, "I wanted to be a writer and have kept it up ever since. I wasn't really considered a writer until *Owls Head* [published in 2003]. . . . I stowed the writing for years. But, nevertheless, I write about photography. . . . My writing from high school and earlier was not remarkable. It was only interesting in that I wanted to *do* it."[1]

What Purcell has *done* in the years since she "stowed [her] writing" is extraordinary: over a dozen books, at least as many articles and essays, and over thirty one-woman shows of her photographs in addition to more than twenty group shows, in this country and abroad. A selected bibliography of her publications includes *A Matter of Time* (1975); *Half-Life: Photographs* (1980); *Illuminations: A Bestiary*, with Stephen Jay Gould (1986); *Finders, Keepers: Eight Collectors*, with Stephen Jay Gould (1992); *Suspended Animation: Six Essays on the Preservation of Bodily Parts*, with F. Gonzalez Crussi (1995); *Special Cases: Natural Anomalies and Historical Monsters* (1997); *Swift as a Shadow: Extinct and Endangered Animals, from the Collection of Naturalis, Nationaal Natuurhistorisch Museum of Leiden*, with museum staff (1999); *Crossing Over: Where Art and Science Meet*, with Stephen Jay Gould (2000); *Dice: Deception, Fate, and Rotten Luck*, with Ricky Jay (2002); *Owls Head* (2003); *Rosamond Purcell: Two Rooms* (2003); *Bookworm* (2006); *Egg & Nest*

(2008); and *Landscapes of the Passing Strange: Reflections from Shakespeare* (2010).[2]

"The main criticism [of my early writing] is that my transitions are not there," Purcell says. "The main transition is silence. . . . I'm really looking for my voice, . . . looking for it for years and years and years."[3]

Reynolds Price noted that Eudora Welty's "prime compulsion was to push beyond the silent voice of image" in her snapshots toward "the stronger but slower voice of words."[4] In contrast, Rosamond Purcell's prime compulsion was to push past the silent voice of her early writing to the arresting, visionary images of her photography. What these seemingly inverse journeys—photographer to writer, writer to photographer—share is a continuing dialogue between the observer's eye and the visualizing mind. Purcell says of her photographic work: "I continued to look *at* and *through* and *back at* the camera's subjects" (italics Purcell's). Welty, for her part, writes: "The fictional eye sees in, through, and around what is really there."[5]

In her mid-twenties, Purcell kept a log during a Greyhound bus trip from Boston to Santa Fe, New Mexico. These are notes, "taken as observed," she writes in a post-it attached to a xerox of a typescript with cross-outs and occasional letters cut off at the left or right margins.

The Greyhound log begins: "Journey itself immaterial—what matters is the log. If there is no log, then it is like peeling an apple for the sake of the [word x'd through] meat and finding there is nothing beneath the skin." Her log mentions "encounters" with other passengers, "amenities, jokes, confidences. . . . Confidences include snapshots: ('that's me at 97 pounds, sleeping . . . yah, the new Castro [a roll-away bed]. . . . That's the paneling Chester put up. That's Chester.')." The snapshots don't seem to be by, or of, Purcell. There is no further mention of photographs exchanged or taken.

Purcell continues to record conversations, sometimes mimicking the idiom and inflections of other voices, and includes observations during which, "in so far as [the] bus becomes environment, the scenery, places, become secondary. . . . [W]alk off bus and the mind still walks. . . . [M]ind goes around like a mouse on a wheel."

The notes in the log begin to take on more specific visual detail:

> Mother in silver-grey metallic furcoat, chemically reddened hair . . . elephantine. Black plastic "snakeskin" skirt, bulging white jersey—mammoth arms . . . red red mouth . . . —no front teeth.

On a page headed "Night," she writes about light and darkness: "Sun blurred like a half-cooked yolk dropping from bruised surface. . . . Sky tightens, darkens—. . . . Heads reflected in the driver's mirror—dark, dark, dark, lit—in layers back down the aisle. Shimmering, tissue paper heads. Silhouette, silhouette, then rosily lit, . . . chiaroscuro."[6]

Purcell's youthful log shows one photographer's beginnings just as Welty, in her memoir, reveals her beginnings as a writer by recording her response to the full moon. We see these beginnings in the visual images of the sun "blurred like a half-cooked yolk dropping"; the sky that "tightens, darkens"; heads reflected in a mirror, "dark, dark, dark, lit"; "shimmering, tissue paper heads"; the "silhouette, silhouette, then rosily lit." The reference to chiaroscuro anticipates the black-and-white photographs of Purcell's first book, *A Matter of Time*, published some seven years later.

At the same time, these images, as did Welty's "always seeing double,"[7] bring into view the writer's visualizing mind: the simile of the sun as a half-cooked egg dropping; the sky that tightens as it darkens (a tactile image yoked to a visual). The early log makes use of the rhetorical effect of reiterated language: (the Miltonic) "dark, dark, dark"; "silhouette, silhouette"; "red red mouth." The photographer's beginnings are experienced in, and as, writing. "Through writing, through the effort to visualize," Wright Morris has said, "I became a photographer, and through my experience as a photographer, I became more of a writer."[8] It is, for Purcell, a circular and unending process.

* * *

Almost four decades after writing her Greyhound bus log, Purcell published an essay on Mexican *ex-voto* paintings she had found in a San Francisco warehouse. *Ex-votos* ("from the vow made" or "in gratitude, devotion") present "a saint in action, intervening in a near-disaster, accident, or illness that befalls ordinary human beings or animals." These paintings on thin metal sheets hung behind church altars from the middle of the eighteenth to the middle of the twentieth century.[9]

"The text painted on or scratched into the surface [of the paintings] with a stylus is frequently faded to near-obscurity by the time I get my hands on it," Purcell writes. "The names, cryptified by dialect, effaced by rust, or painted over previous scenes, tell me little more than I can already surmise by studying the painted scenes. Yet, something about the scuffed and scratched surfaces of *ex-votos* conspires to increase their mysteries." Commenting on one of the paintings she has photographed, Purcell says: "The legend, though etched in an elegant hand, has vanished into a script as thin and ineffable as a spider-web."[10] For Welty, "the mystery lies in the use of language to express human life."[11] For Purcell, the scratched and worn surfaces of nearly obscured texts increase the mysteries of the *ex-votos*. The simile of the spider web, recalling some of Welty's own similes,[12] connects the vanishing words of a dead hand to the delicately woven creation of an insect, meant to entangle a living prey.

Purcell offers a detailed description of language disappearing in a photograph of three men who appear to have escaped from prison chains:

> The men are on their knees to two saints. . . . The inked inscription on paper is almost rubbed off, the story vanished, but we can see the iron has been broken—the men are freed.[13]

In her twenties what mattered was the log, the writing; otherwise, the visual scene was "nothing." In her sixties, Purcell observes words disappear; an inscription on paper is almost unreadable. "But," she adds, "we can see." What we see in the *ex-voto* is miraculous intervention. Welty finds mystery in writing itself. Purcell trusts the visual image to tell the story of the ineffable, even as her use of simile shares the telling.

7

Alchemy

I am interested in illusion, in camouflage, in spaces between shapes (and between photographs), in double portraiture, and in ambiguity.

—Rosamond Wolff Purcell, *A Matter of Time*

Like Eudora Welty's collections of snapshots in *One Place, One Time* but unlike most of Rosamond Purcell's later work, *A Matter of Time* includes black-and-white photographs of people. There are full-length and half portraits, faces (fully visible, partly concealed, in profile, shadowed, reflected in a mirror), isolated body parts (a torso, hands, and feet). Other images are not of people: the double, blurred head of a dog named Vanessa; the hind quarters of what seems to be a young deer; dolls; scraps in an auto yard; a rotten egg; and several haunting, unidentified shapes.

A Matter of Time contains one photograph that may recall the bus trip described in Purcell's Greyhound log. It is a double portrait: a white-haired man in a softly flowing white shirt with open collar is seated next to a woman wearing a dark, buttoned sweater over a collared blouse, earrings, and a wide-brimmed dark hat. The right side of each figure's face is in semi-shadow, the eyes fully visible but directed away from the camera. (An identical-looking couple is identified as Mique Kennedy and Marcia Ellery in a 1974 photograph.)[1] In response to my query, Purcell writes that "the title of the photo 'Greyhound' refers to [the] mood of [the] couple—reminiscent of people who travel by bus at night—adrift and exhausted."[2] Suzanne Marrs has suggested that Welty's "memories of . . . [certain] photographic occasions" inform her writing.[3] Purcell's *Greyhound* captures the state of mind of people who travel by bus at night, almost as if she is photographing a memory.

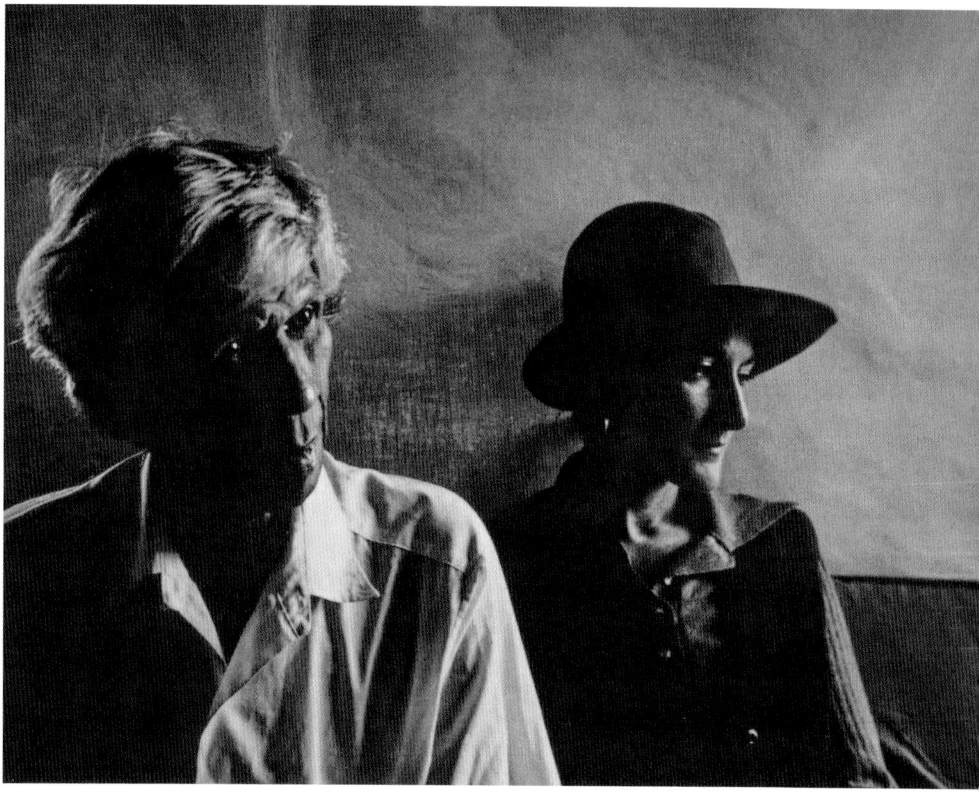

PLATE 12. Greyhound, 1973.

Courtesy of Rosamond Purcell.

The images in *A Matter of Time* are displayed on unnumbered pages with no captions.[4] Dated titles on the last page indicate that the photographs were taken between 1969 and 1974. In an afterword, Dennis W. Purcell notes that, in 1969, "Rosie was teaching in a high school and writing stories. . . . She had never studied design, nor had she any intention of becoming a photographer, yet within a few weeks of being casually lent a Polaroid camera, she had started a process of self-teaching[5] that was ultimately to reveal the real powers of her visual expressiveness."

> The elements of this self-teaching process were experimentation and rigorous self-criticism. . . . A year later, [she] took on the additional discipline of the studio view camera, working on more formal still lifes and portraits, and with the variables of perspective control and prearrangement of composition. . . .

> [P]rinting in the darkroom, . . . she can now control the image after the original picture-taking moment.[6]

Experimenting with variables in perspective and prearrangement of composition, enhanced by expertise in procedures that further control the image after the picture-taking moment, clearly has counterparts in the art of writing. The photographer's control of perspective corresponds to authorial choice of point(s) of view. Purcell's prearrangement of composition finds parallels in Welty's narrative configurations. As in other arts, control of the image in both photography and writing often involves a process of revision that follows the first "shot." The legendary photographer Ansel Adams, who originally intended to become a concert pianist, said: "The negative is the score, the print is the performance."[7]

John Szarkowski suggests that the central problem of the photographer is "a simple one: what shall he include, what shall he reject? The photographer edits the meanings and patterns of the world through an imaginary frame."[8] This "simple" problem is exactly that of the writer.

Adjustments in the tonal range of both black-and-white and color images parallel subtle or bold shifts of tone in a work of fiction. The photographer's achievement, or refusal, of depth of field corresponds to the writer's creation of vivid detail and clarity or intentional blurring and ambiguity. Underdeveloped or overdeveloped photographic images find intended or unintended counterparts in writing. Framing, as well as allowing subjects to escape the frame, is crucial to the work of both photographer and writer, among other artists, as is, of course, the contribution of creative inspiration. Finally, a process of self-teaching in modes of visual expressivity is much like the process of self-teaching through the sheer act of writing and rewriting and writing again: the practice of the art is its first teacher.

When a new medium offers a new challenge, practitioners make of it a new opportunity.[9] Rosamond Purcell tells me that she is "using digital photography completely now." She is also employing Photoshop, which, she says, "is this generation's version of the dark room." A gifted artist working with a new technology, she never loses her sense of wonder. Ansel Adams has said: "With all my analysis of photography, there is still something quite incomprehensible to me about the photographic process. The physics of the situation are fearfully complex, but the miracle of the image is a triumph of the imagination." Commenting on a recent project, photographing early twentieth-century apothecary jars, Purcell says: "It's alchemy."[10] Purcell's response as photographer to the transformative process of art-making echoes Welty's response as writer to the transfer of "vision . . . onto the pages of a novel . . . this alchemy . . . !"[11]

The sense of an alchemical process, a seemingly miraculous change of one thing into something else, links writer and photographer. "Think of a letter, Ralph Waldo Emerson urged his daughter, as 'a kind of picture of a voice.'"[12] If a text can be a picture of a voice, a photographic image can offer or invite voice, can even be a silent voicing of text, a kind of reverse ekphrasis. In this "silence" Purcell first finds her voice.

As photographers, Welty and Purcell certainly could not appear more different. Welty took black-and-white snapshots, developed initially in her kitchen. Purcell has produced both black-and-white and color prints, the latter now created digitally and edited with Photoshop. Welty focused on non-posed portraits of human figures and scenes in a particular region of the country. Purcell's early interest in human faces in *A Matter of Time* has been followed by carefully composed images of what is decaying, fossilized, illegible, often unrecognizable. Welty "always referred to [her] photographs as snapshots, herself as unskilled."[13] Purcell is a sophisticated, internationally acclaimed visual artist who continues to experiment with innovative photographic techniques.

On the other hand, both artists can, like John Donne, "make one little room an everywhere."[14] Shelley, in *Delta Wedding*, believes that if "Shellmound were a little bigger, it would be the same as the world entirely."[15] Welty has sought to defy and overturn the category of "regional writer," making the Mississippi of her stories and novels the whole world of human experience. Purcell has made her studio in Somerville, Massachusetts, into "a microcosm of the material world"[16] that challenges historical, geographical, and linguistic boundaries. For Welty, memory is the treasured somnambulist; Purcell's visual images walk in the sleep of history, waking it up. Both Welty and Purcell rescue and re-see the past so that it does not become the face of oblivion.

8

Double Vision

(and here I speak as a photographer)

—Rosamond Purcell, *Special Cases: Natural Anomalies and Historical Monsters*

Reynolds Price's description of the "yoking of disparate sights in a single image of startling freshness"[1] in Eudora Welty's fiction finds striking parallels in the visual work of Rosamond Purcell. In her photographs, Purcell creates what I have called, in chapter 4, visual convergence, in which two or more disparate sights are simultaneously present in a given image. Purcell continually offers in her photography a plurality of views, like that achieved by Welty's use of free indirect discourse in *Delta Wedding* and choric voices in *Losing Battles*.

In her 1997 book, *Special Cases: Natural Anomalies and Historical Monsters*, Purcell identifies herself (in a parenthesis) as a photographer offering commentary on her own image. On the page to the right of her photograph *Pangolin with two pinecones* [Museum of Comparative Zoology, Harvard University], she says: "Visually (and here I speak as a photographer), the pangolin is a changeling":

> its sharp-edged scales, formed of a kind of horn, looks like other things—a pinecone, over-lapping seashells, or an artichoke. But beyond all visual strangeness the creature possesses a metaphorical intensity.[2]

Purcell presents a liminal being, a creature that seems to defy clear boundaries and single identities. Here she demonstrates that same liminality; speaking as a photographer, she discovers her voice as a writer.

As I gaze again at the image of the pangolin after reading Purcell's text, I see what she sees. I notice, first, its resemblance to the larger of the two pinecones placed beneath its raised head and neck, the smaller pinecone seeming to receive

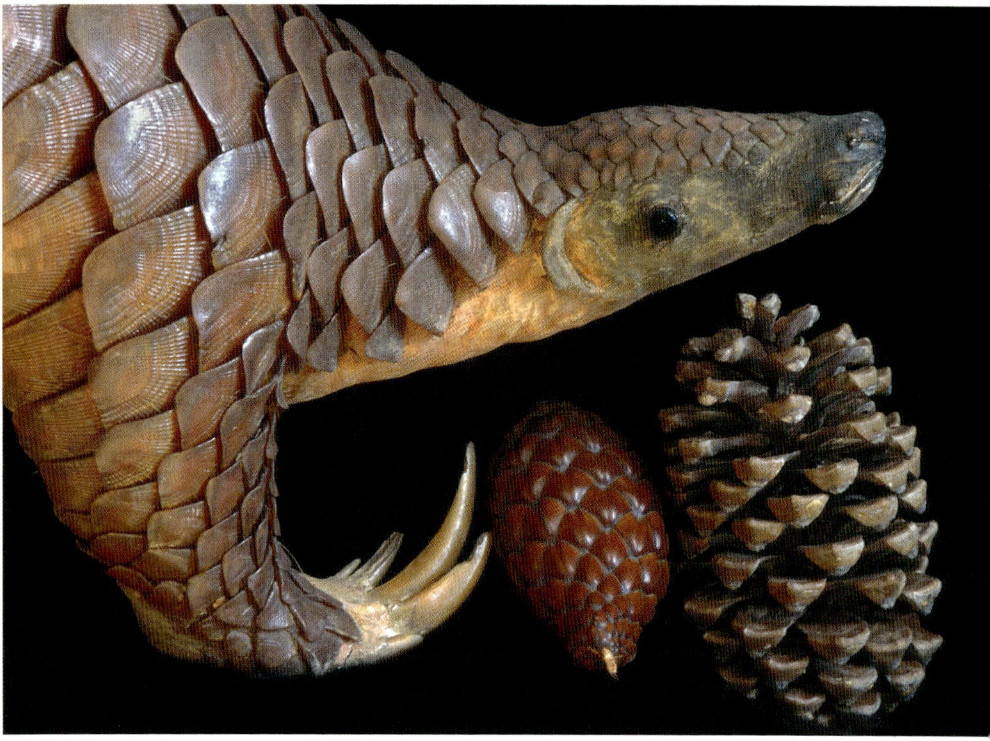

PLATE 13. Pangolin with two pinecones. c.1984.

Courtesy of Rosamond Purcell.

the slight pressure of the pangolin's gracefully elongated claws curving upward. Then, as my gaze shifts to the scaly body, I see various shapes and sizes of overlapping seashells; finally, the seashells become an appetizing artichoke.[3] In writing about her own work as a photographer, Purcell bestows image after image on a creature of visual strangeness. She finds a way back to writing through her photographic practice.

The cover photo of *Special Cases*, which also appears in the book itself, is titled *Hydrocephalic child whose skull has opened like a flower* [Universiteitsmuseum, Utrecht]. Purcell's arresting color image of a child's skeleton with its huge, blooming skull opened like a tulip is oddly beautiful. As with the photograph of the pangolin, we first see the image and then read the photographer's words. Purcell describes, in painful detail, the condition of hydrocephaly, which "allows the skull to fill repeatedly with fluid from the spinal column, fluid that . . . slowly pushes the skull outward until, without relief from a draining device, an enormous circumference is reached; the child—usually a child—dies with God knows what

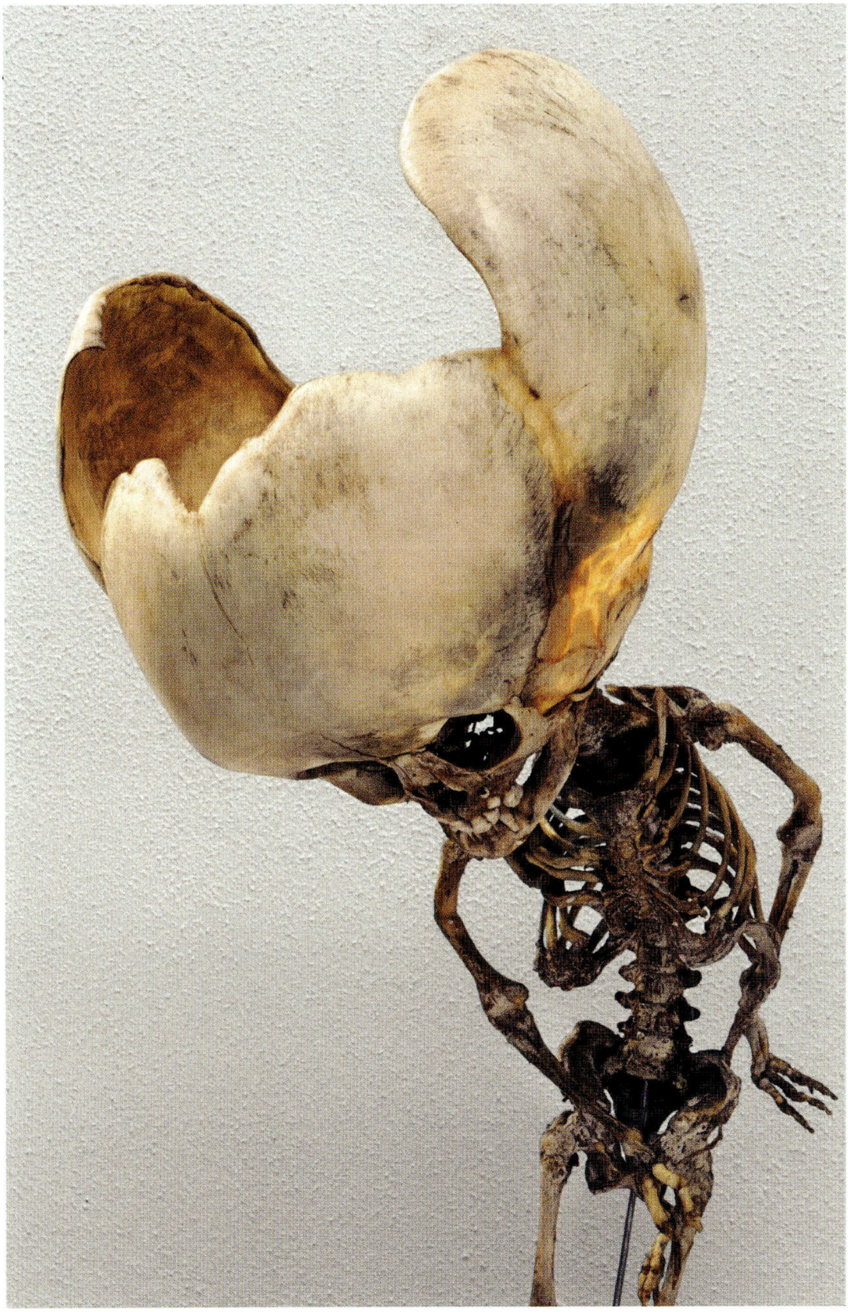

PLATE 14. Hydrocephalic child whose skull has opened like a flower. 1995.

Courtesy of Rosamond Purcell.]

sound of rushing water in his or her ears."[4] There is a disquieting disjunction for the viewer-reader who responds first to the otherworldly image and then to the author's presentation of the abnormal condition portrayed.

In one of her stories, Welty writes: "The most profound, the most moving sight in the whole world must be a face."[5] Purcell photographs a skeleton: there is no face. In the midst of a fairly clinical description of hydrocephaly, she tries to imagine the unimaginable state of a child who "dies with God knows what sound of rushing water in his or her ears." We become, in a variation on René Paul Barilleaux's portrayal of Welty's literary and visual art, the "compassionate observers" of what the "passionate image-maker"[6] has made. In Purcell's uncanny image, the skull has neither disintegrated nor collapsed. Instead, it has emerged, light-struck, into seeming life above a darker, tiny skeleton angled so as to throw focus on what blooms above it.

Purcell limits herself to a single simile in the caption for the hydrocephalic child. It is wise economy. What Purcell achieves, here as elsewhere, is a conversation between two artistic modes. Visual image and writing speak to each other.

For *Medea and Her Sisters: Leonard Baskin's Images of Women*, the catalogue of an exhibition at the Smith College Museum of Art, Purcell provided both photographs and commentary. Jessica Nicoll, director and chief curator at the museum, describes Purcell's contribution as "a beautifully resonant visual and verbal reflection on Baskin's life and work."[7] Here is part of Purcell's response to one of Baskin's etchings, printed in color on handmade paper:

> *Fanaticism* shows a woman with deep shrouded eyes and a hand like the claw of a bird. . . . I turn the etching upside down and detect a concealed image of a prone beaked bird stretched across her eyes, its "legs" bridging her right pupil. . . . She is in transition between worlds and in danger of losing both.[8]

Purcell's comments appear on a page without an accompanying visual image. Just before reading the words, "I turn the etching upside down," the reader must herself turn the page. Purcell's writing now appears side-by-side with the visual image. Unlike the photographs of the hydrocephalic child and the pangolin in *Special Cases*, both of which precede any commentary, a visual portrait is first created by Purcell's words alone. When the reader sees the image itself, it is already being presented as inverted and as concealing a second image.

The new sequence of reading, looking, reading and looking—whether intended or accidental—is significant. Purcell (who did not take this photograph) offers a written portrayal of another artist's image; once that is lodged in the reader's imagination, she capsizes this image just at the moment the reader turns the page and is able to look at both text and etching. This sudden perspectival shift creates not mystification but double vision, or rather a vision that doubles back on itself with questions left unresolved, much like the searching of Sam Dale's photo postcard in Welty's *Losing Battles*. Is Baskin's image human, bird, human-bird? Are we responding to absence of light, disfiguring scar, birthmark? Is liminality being portrayed as transition or loss?

First "reading" the etching, then "rereading" it, one's view of Baskin's image is sharpened, paradoxically, by seeing the ambiguity Purcell insists on. Purcell, like Welty, sees what is there and then what is also there. Like Welty, she offers arresting similes: the lower joint of a hand "is drawn like a thickened carapace"; "dark lines across the woman's face are like . . . coarse etched feathers"; "hair like that of a werewolf sprouts from the palm of her hand."[9] These images might seem overwrought before we look directly at *Fanaticism*, but, in fact, as in Welty's fiction, the similes teach us how (else) to see what we are seeing. For both Welty and Purcell, that sense of what else there is to see in what we see becomes itself a way of seeing.

What Welty achieves by means of verbal reflection, Purcell creates without the use of words in her exquisite color photographs. Using natural light and her own visual imagination, she creates compositions and juxtapositions that connect seemingly disparate phenomena and objects. Her images suggest diverse analogues that overlap, like the imbrications of the pangolin. In the haunting photograph of the hydrocephalic child, sunlight on the edges of a human skull preserved in a museum in Utrecht transforms it into a flower opening its petals.[10]

* * *

Writing on Aldwyth's *The World According to Zell*, a 79-by-76-inch collage created by separating images from the pages of *Zell's Popular Encyclopedia* of 1871, Purcell notes that "the literal meaning behind each image has been cut free. . . . The purpose of an encyclopedia has been overturned, its pictures confiscated as fodder for new life, almost as if natural forces have foraged into an artificial world to extract its nutrients."[11] Freeing the image from its literal meaning and extracting nutrients from an artificial world animate Purcell's own photographic practice.

When she asked Aldwyth what the text of *Zell's Popular Encyclopedia* looked like after the excision of its images, Purcell received "a translucent envelope of carefully clipped words, left over perhaps from trimming around the illustrations. This presentation of the cast-off materials, as careful as the work itself, revealed that she was a saver of details, because—well, you never know." In the exhibition catalogue of Aldwyth's work, there appears a photograph by Purcell entitled

Text Packet, the scraps of cast-off words seen indistinctly through the translucent envelope.[12] Purcell reveals her ambivalent relationship to text, writing, words themselves as artifacts even as she makes of them one more visual image. As demonstrated by decades of obsessive foraging in an eleven-acre Maine junkyard, Purcell's fascination with cast-off materials feeds her art.

9

Foraging and Reconfiguring

HAMLET Do you see yonder cloud that's almost in shape of a camel?
POLONIUS By th' mass, and 'tis: like a camel, indeed.
HAMLET Methinks it is like a weasel.
POLONIUS It is backed like a weasel.
HAMLET Or like a whale.
POLONIUS Very like a whale.

—William Shakespeare, *Hamlet*

What may appear as incongruous interests—a seventeenth-century cabinet of curiosities, a junkyard in Maine, paintings that record millennia of fossils—can be seen as alternative images of memoir, a place where you collect, organize, and revive what is random, damaged, petrified. Rosamond Purcell's photographic interest in museums, junkyards, and fossils anticipates, and perhaps leads to, the writing of her memoir, *Owls Head*, in which, as in all memoirs, the past is reconfigured and transfigured.

The narrator in Orhan Pamuk's *The Museum of Innocence* says, "Real museums are places where Time is transformed into Space." Reviewing Pamuk's novel, Rónán McDonald suggests that the "innocence" in its title has as one of its meanings the innocence that is "regained by having access to the sensuous particularity of things and moments. The secret of happiness, Kemal suggests, is dismembering the seeming coherence of a narrative whole, the idea of time as a continuum, into its discrete isolated moments."[1]

Rosamond Purcell: Two Rooms, an exhibition of Purcell's full-size reconstruction of Olaus Worm's private museum and the re-creation of her own Somerville, Massachusetts, studio, began to tour several museums in the spring of 2003. In a pattern resembling Eudora Welty's near-simultaneous appearance as photographer and writer in the spring of 1936, in 2003 Purcell also published her memoir, *Owls Head*, describing her relationship with William Buckminster and his vast Maine junkyard that for more than twenty years provided thousands of objects for her own cabinet of curiosities.[2]

Olaus Worm's seventeenth-century museum, like Purcell's contemporary studio, does make "one little room an everywhere."[3] Purcell's *Two Rooms* is the work of a collector inspired by a visual image: "I saw an engraving [of Worm's natural history cabinet] and became completely obsessed with what was in that room. I filled a room with everything I could find that was in that room."[4] It is not hard to see why the collection of this Danish natural historian and archaeologist would interest an artist who had been doing her own archaeological excavations at Owls Head, Maine, for decades.

Purcell saw in Copenhagen "a wall-sized reproduction of the drawing of Worm's room; . . . nearby, in three-dimensional glory, sat one of the only survivors from his collection, a horse jaw grown round by the branch of a tree."

> The actual jaw through the branch seemed richer, thicker, because it existed in the drawing as well. I circled this curiosity with the camera—something one cannot do with a drawing made from one perspective. It was as if something had been—figuratively—pulled up from the roots. . . . It takes a certain suspension of disbelief to dream one's way back into a picture. . . . To enter, I would have to become a schematic, two-dimensional figure.[5]

For Purcell, the actual artifact seems richer *because* it also existed in the two-dimensional drawing. With her camera, the photographer circles a curiosity that seems pulled up by the roots, out of the engraving. In a kind of Alice-in-Wonderland world, Purcell imagines herself becoming a two-dimensional figure, like those in the engraving, in order to close the gap between herself and what she observes. It is as if things and thing-ness become more substantial, "thicker," by having been presented in a visual image. The photographer with the camera fixes on a three-dimensional artifact only to render it once again as a picture. For full entry into the experience, the photographer herself would have to become part of the picture. This constellation of bold curiosity, suspension of disbelief, and testing of boundaries defines much of Purcell's work, both as photographer and as visualizing writer who tries, like Welty, to see into a particular time and place.

The objects in Worm's museum evoke a cacophony of interpretations. In a kind of parody of Hamlet's conversation with Polonius about the shape of a cloud, Purcell positions herself as a viewer among viewers: "I study the objects [in the drawing], convinced I recognize the genuine articles—fur leggings, an egg-like pod, and a skin mask—until I look again, or a friend looking closer says, 'No, it's

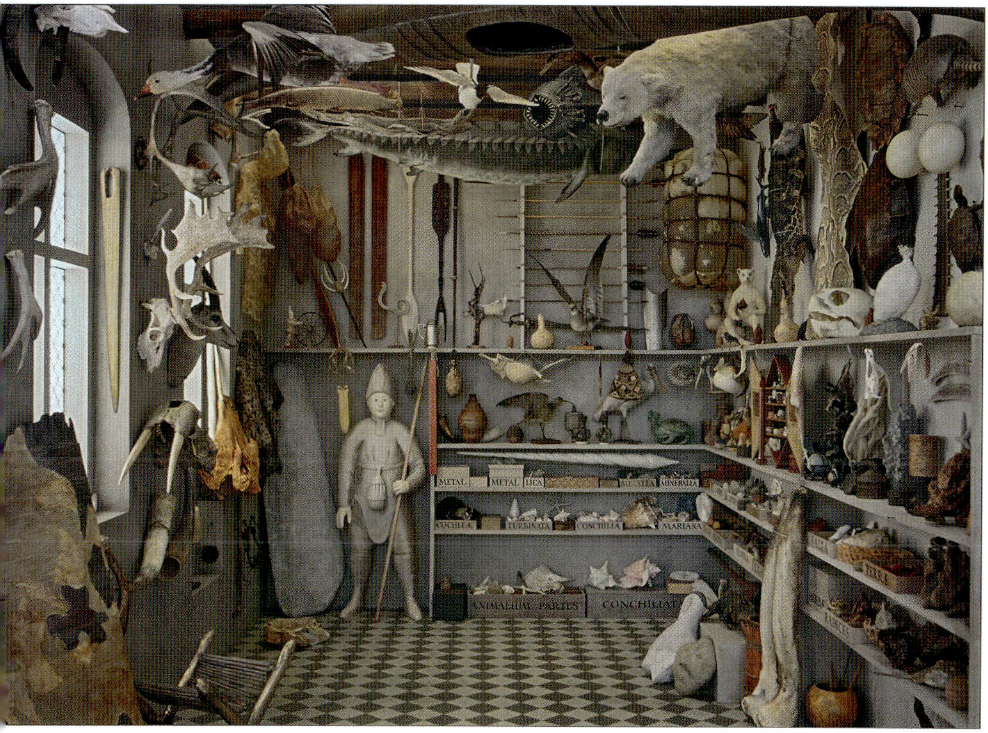

PLATE 15. Olaus Worm's Museum. c. 2000.

Courtesy of Rosamond Purcell.

not pants, it's a bag; not a seed pod, but an ostrich egg; not a mask, but a piece of driftwood with the impression of a human face.'"

> "That's a geode," says the paleontologist. . . . A second paleontologist calls it a paramudra, . . . and the expert on whales thinks it is ambergris. . . . The hollowed shape looks like all of these.[6]

This chorus of perspectives recalls the group ekphrasis of Beulah's wedding picture in Eudora Welty's *Losing Battles*. It can also stand for viewers' diverse responses to Purcell's own visual art.

A few years before the exhibition of *Two Rooms*, Purcell was asked to write a foreword for *Rock of Ages/Sands of Time*, a photographic presentation of Barbara Page's 544 contiguous panels of eleven-inch-square paintings, each panel representing the passage of a million years. The series of bas-relief panels functions, Page says, "as a visual metaphor for an immense period of time," nearly five hundred and fifty million years. Its eleven sections, which, when installed, stretch across five hundred feet, "represent the eleven geological periods between the dawn of the Paleozoic era 543 million years ago and today—Cambrian to Quaternary . . . a story written on rocks."[7] Purcell never saw the original works but responds to "snapshots of the paintings" sent to her by Page.[8]

Rejecting the frame of the painting as a firm boundary, Page allows panels to bleed into each other. Purcell's own testing of firm boundaries takes a different form:

> Under the right light, as a photographer, I believe I've witnessed signs of life in fossils where there are none. . . . I have the impression that these fossils are . . . beaks, footprints, fronds, bark, shell—still moving.

This world of shapes that come alive in the right light is described in a series of similes: "what looks like a fully extended and swimming ammonite (actually a tooth whorl of a shark) sails across its pale ground like a paper kite (271 mya [million years ago]). . . . And the bark of the giant clubmoss *Lepidodendron* (299–298 mya) looks like the coast of Africa."[9] These similes that intermingle the organic and the inorganic, the living and the dead, the manufactured and the natural, recall similes in Eudora Welty's *Losing Battles*:

> The mockingbird sat silent, all chest, like a zinc bucket filled to the top, all song contained. . . . It was a tobacco tin in the weeds that shone like a ruby; what crouched like a possum under the althea was somebody's lost apron. . . . The night-blooming cereus flowers looked like wrung chickens' necks.[10]

A missing apron, underneath a plant with tall spikes of showy flowers, looks like a possum; a tobacco tin is sea-changed into a precious stone. Welty mines the natural world in creating her imagined scenes of transformation; like Purcell, her photographer's eye catches the light that transfigures ordinary things (a tobacco tin in the weeds) into richness. In Welty's fiction, as we have seen, the living remember and wake up the dead past. In her photographic work, Purcell finds signs of life in fossils that, however fragmented, are "still moving."

* * *

Purcell's writing about the work of other artists is as evocative as her writing about her own. But it is in her memoir, *Owls Head,* that she emerges as a writer who has full possession of the voice she had sought "for years and years and years."[11] No longer commenting on Worm's seventeenth-century private museum or Page's millennia of fossils, Purcell becomes the memoirist of her foraging in a junkyard.

Welty's memoir, *One Writer's Beginnings*, contained black-and-white photographs of various sizes, collected together in the middle of the book, none taken by the author. In *Owls Head*, Purcell positions her own tiny black-and-white photographs as endnotes. The diminished size of her images and their location at the back of the book suggest the privileging of writing over photography that had occurred much earlier in Welty's career and is dramatically represented by the absence of any of her own snapshots in her celebrated memoir.

William Buckminster is often baffled by what Purcell takes away from his Owls Head junkyard. "'Let's face it,'" he says to one of her friends, "'the kind of thing she buys, I would take to the dump.'" Embracing what she calls the "category of the *sublimely diminished*," Purcell collects "objects notable for their exquisite reductions and patinas." As she closely observes "what happens between the ice and the inner tube, the sun and a glass plate negative, the rain and a roadmap," junk is sea-changed, given new life. For Purcell, "Owls Head is a place of tireless consumption, of active burial and renewal by mice, squirrels, bees, beetles, ants, and worms."[12]

Owls Head, in fact, opens with the tireless work of small creatures, imaged in its first photo-endnote: a small, black-and-white picture of part of one page of a termite-eaten book, found not in Buckminster's junkyard but in the basement of a Harvard building undergoing renovation. "The foraging by the insects had been most thorough," Purcell writes.

> Printed in French in eighteenth-century type, the lumps of uneaten matter stood high like islands on a relief map. Piles of sandy-orange termite leavings were packed throughout. I had never seen anything like it.[13]

A full-page color print of two pages from this termite-ridden book appeared earlier in *Half-Life*, Purcell's 1980 collection of both color and black-and-white photographs.[14] In the tiny black-and-white image at the back of the memoir, we do not see the sandy-orange termite leavings on the pages of the fully opened book. Even the words Purcell tells us have not been consumed by the termites ("*Moscou . . . villes anciennes . . . Si son père . . . fils*")[15] do not appear in the small photo-endnote; they can be found in the full-page color photograph of *Half-Life*. A list of twenty words, phrases, or parts of words is identified as "text from termite-eaten French book." Almost none of these are visible in the photo-endnote. In the memoir, photography lags behind as writing takes center stage.

Purcell begins to imagine the life of a typewriter she disinters at Owls Head: "At what point does a manufactured object turn into an organism? Do objects

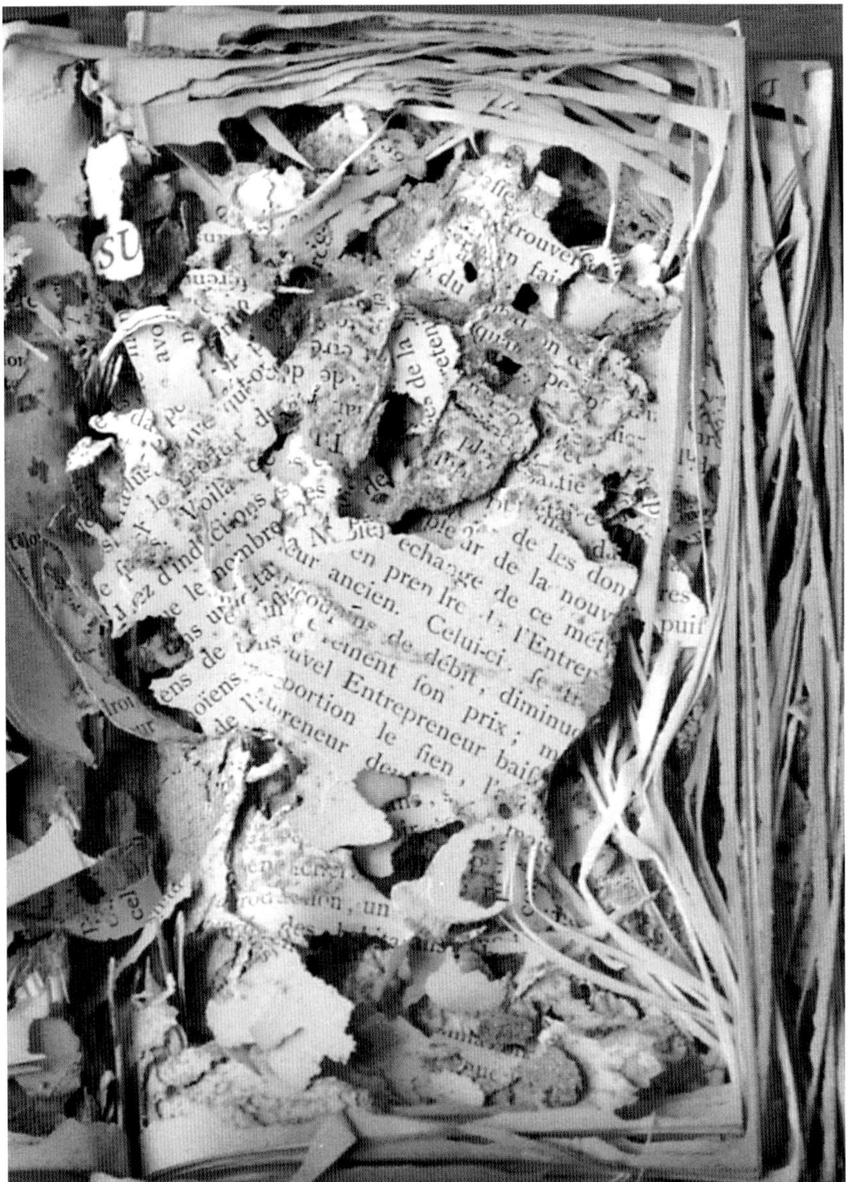

PLATE 16. Termite-eaten book. 2001.

Courtesy of Rosamond Purcell.

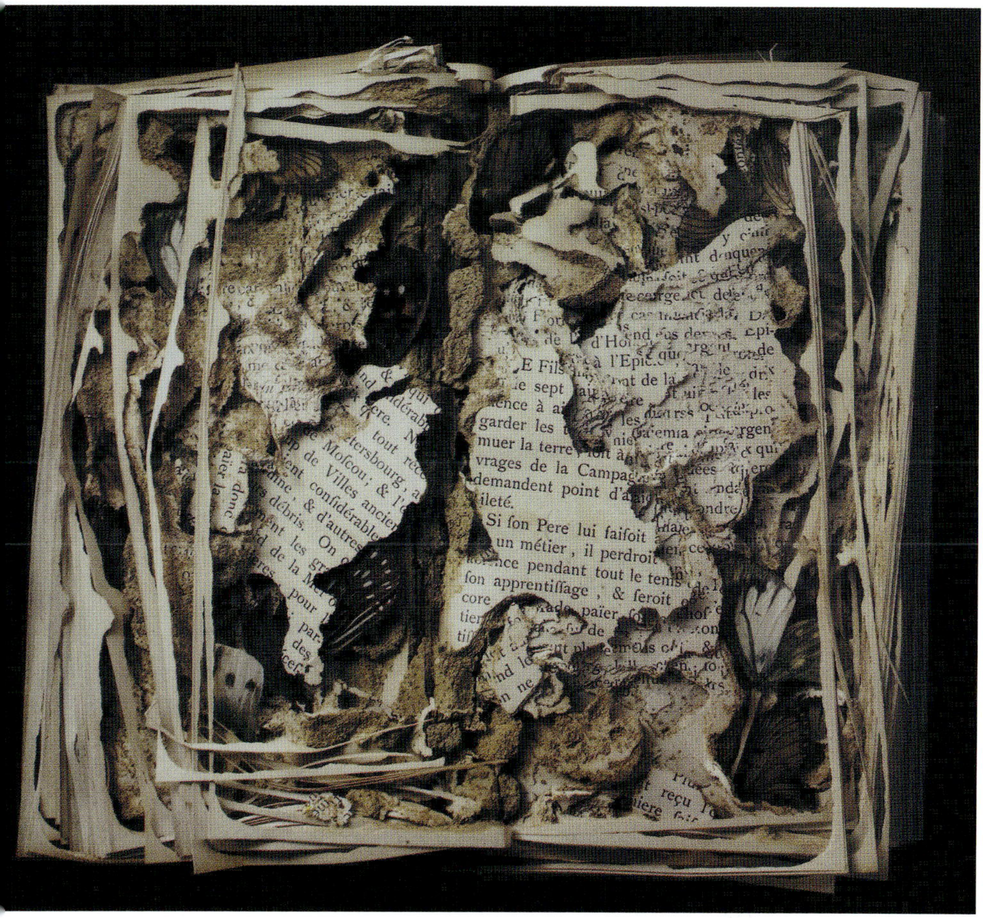

PLATE 17. Untitled. c. 1982.

Courtesy of Rosamond Purcell.

. . . ever possess a life . . . that might be taken away? Is an object transmuted into another substance ever, like a fossil, turned from flesh and bone to stone?" She names the typewriter "*Underwoodensis corrupta*, a close invertebrate cousin to an echinoid." "Its appeal," she writes, "is purely visual, of course."[16] The visual appeal of *Underwoodensis corrupta*, however, is partly eclipsed in the black-and-white endnoted image of the memoir. We see the typewriter's turquoise patina, shimmering like a sea beneath its rusty ribbings, only in the color print of a later volume, *Bookworm*.[17]

The books Purcell finds at Owls Head are damaged, dissolving, their language appearing in fragments. *Book-nest* is the first photo-endnote in a chapter headed "Disintegration":

> Two volumes, stuck together horizontally, had been converted into some kind of nest. The pages on one end remained more or less intact; at the other end lay the compact straw and paper nest, made, we decided, by a mouse. Interwoven in the straw were syllables and occasional words. By peeling back the fragments to a certain depth, we could read the title of the upper story of the nest as *Flying Hostess of the Air*. To read the title of the second book we would have had to destroy it.[18]

Only with the use of a magnifying glass, after the image has been turned upside down, are the following words legible in the endnoted version of the conjoined books: "and," "the," and, at a right angle and very faintly, the word "metal." A color

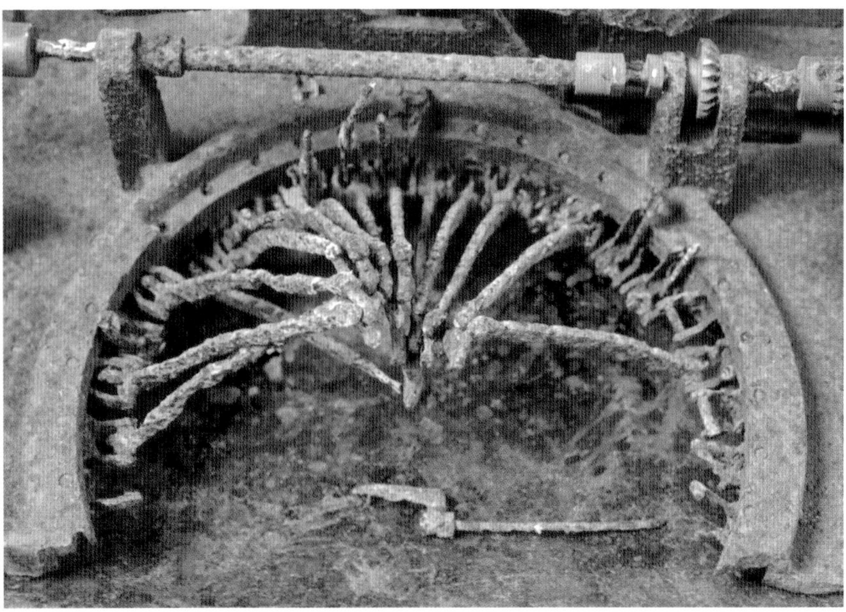

PLATE 18. Typewriter. Early 1990s.

Courtesy of Rosamond Purcell.

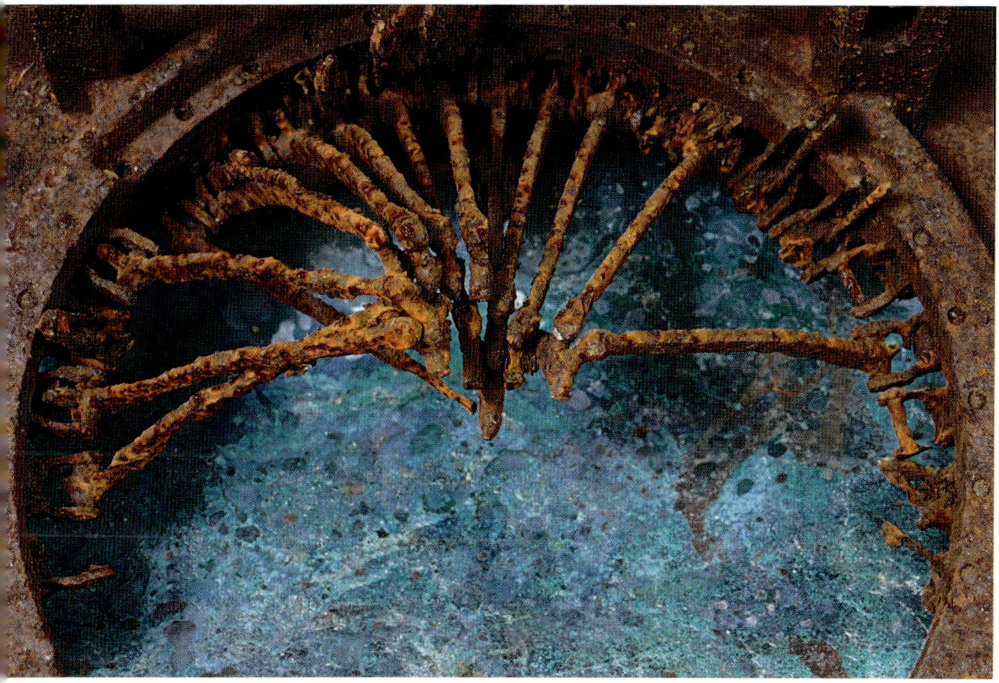

PLATE 19. Typewriter. Early 1900s.

Courtesy of Rosamond Purcell.

print of *Book-nest* appears with a subtle title change (*Book/nest*) in *Bookworm*,[19] its golden scraps of text blithely scattered about so that they cannot be read from a single perspective. Here, more words are visible and there is a sense of felt texture, an illusion of three-dimensionality, in the larger, stunning color image.

Looking at the photograph as it appears in *Bookworm*, Claire Sykes says: "Purcell does more than merely document an act of nature. Emphasizing their shapes, textures and colors against a dark, neutral background, she turns the books into a make-believe museum specimen. If you read 'Book/nest' like a sentence, from left to right, it tells the tale of the book's transformation in reverse (from nest to pages)."[20] In the tiny black-and-white photo-endnote of *Owls Head*, there are no textures and colors against a dark background. Even the title, which for Sykes forms a tale in reverse, has been altered, a slash replacing a hyphen. In *Owls Head*, the tale is textual.

In her memoir, Purcell describes the books she collects: "I have gathered up books in all phases of decay. They run the gamut from gently weather-beaten to hard-core metamorphosed, from faded volumes that can—more or less—be deciphered to books that resemble shells and rocks, and, beyond, to rocks that look like books. I find a poetry book unfurled to the rain. It has a clotted look, like wet wool, as words, letters, and syllables swell. Some words are now elongated, some lines swung around ninety degrees." There are "crooked Js and Ls, mushed Ms, Ts, and independent commas. Liberated letters gather like the limbs of insects . . . and as the book dries, real insects—silverfish, sow bugs, and very tiny ants—will join them."[21] Among the five photo-endnotes[22] of damaged or insect-altered books, none shows what Purcell describes. Writing replaces the photographic image of writing. The visualizing mind allows us to see the unshown.

Owls Head is the story of a search for artistic resources in a junkyard. It is also the portrait of a decades-long relationship with its owner, William Buckminster, who died as I was writing this chapter. Purcell's relationship with Buckminster, carefully portrayed in the text, is only hinted at in the images of him that appear as photo-endnotes.[23]

Photo-endnote 5 (chapter 3) shows two hands and a left forearm. Wrinkled fingers curl around coils of rubber stripped from wire. The rubber strips seem

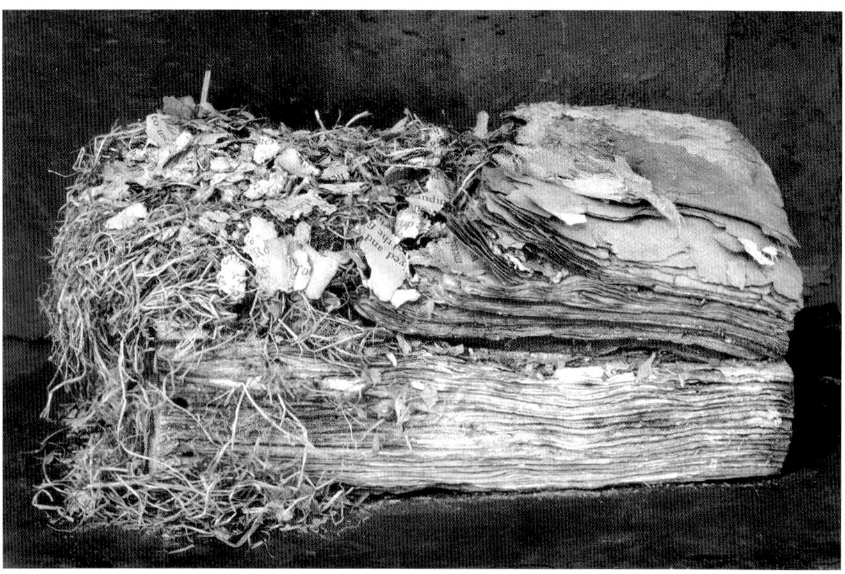

PLATE 20. Book-nest. Early 1990s.

Courtesy of Rosamond Purcell.

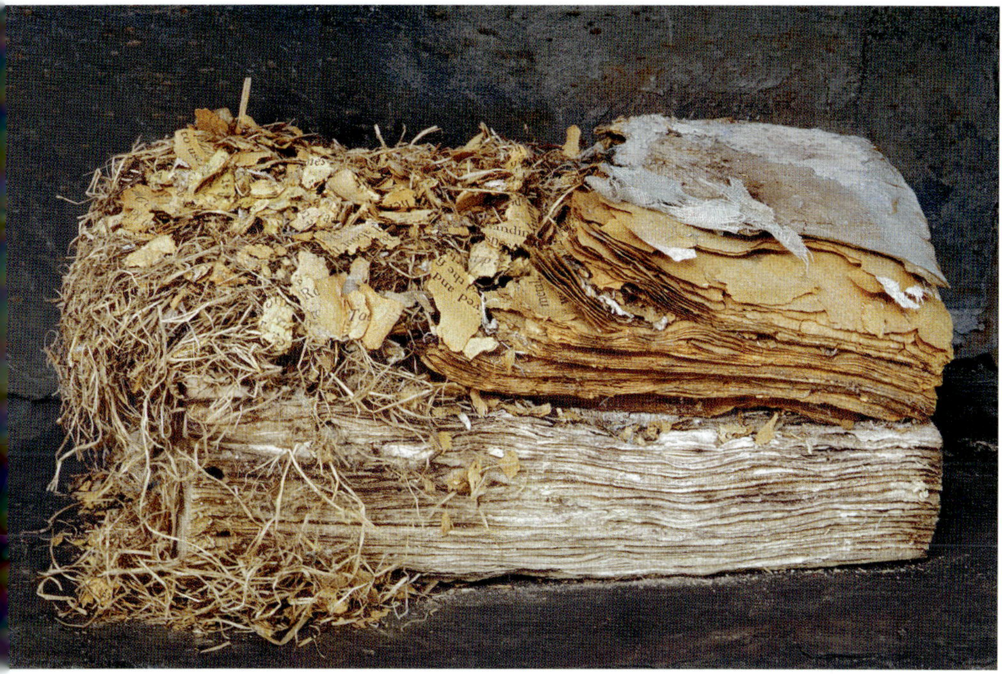

PLATE 21. Book/nest. Early 1990s.

Courtesy of Rosamond Purcell.

alive, worm-like, as they deploy themselves beneath the fingers of old, worn hands at work.

Photo-endnote 7 (chapter 4) presents only a left hand. The fingers with their broken, blackened nails press down on the open page of a small, spiral sales book.[24] Items are carefully handwritten on the left side, prices on the right. Turning the image sideways, I think I can make out the highest price ($30.00); the lowest is $2.00, or possibly $1.00. One item, just above the fourth finger with the widower's wedding band, is completely crossed out.

Photo-endnote 1 (chapter 6) shows Buckminster standing in the doorway of a house he had meant to inhabit with his wife, Helen, who died before they were able to move in. Leaning jauntily against the doorjamb, arms crossed over his chest, he wears a white T-shirt, dark slacks, and dark cap with a small brim. He is in the center foreground, his face clearly visible, his eyes gazing upward at something beyond the frame of the photograph. His mouth is open, as if in talk that escapes. It is the last image of Buckminster in *Owls Head*.[25]

Perhaps these tiny visual endnotes begin to tell the story of a life, like Welty's snapshot of a woman of the 1930s. "Once a photographer . . . always."[26]

* * *

In Welty's *One Writer's Beginnings*, a six-year-old child holds the moon in her mouth until it becomes a word. "It had the roundness of a Concord grape Grandpa took

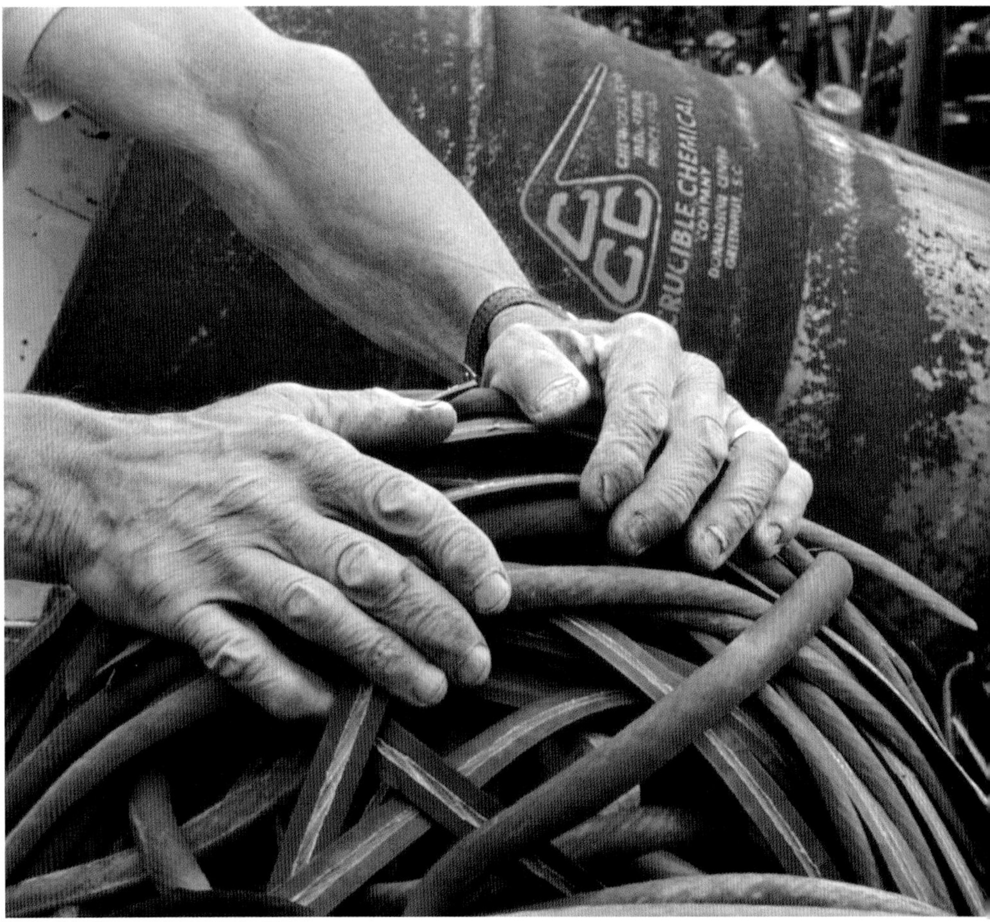

PLATE 22. Buckminster's hands on rubber stripped from wire. 1987–2002.

Courtesy of Rosamond Purcell.

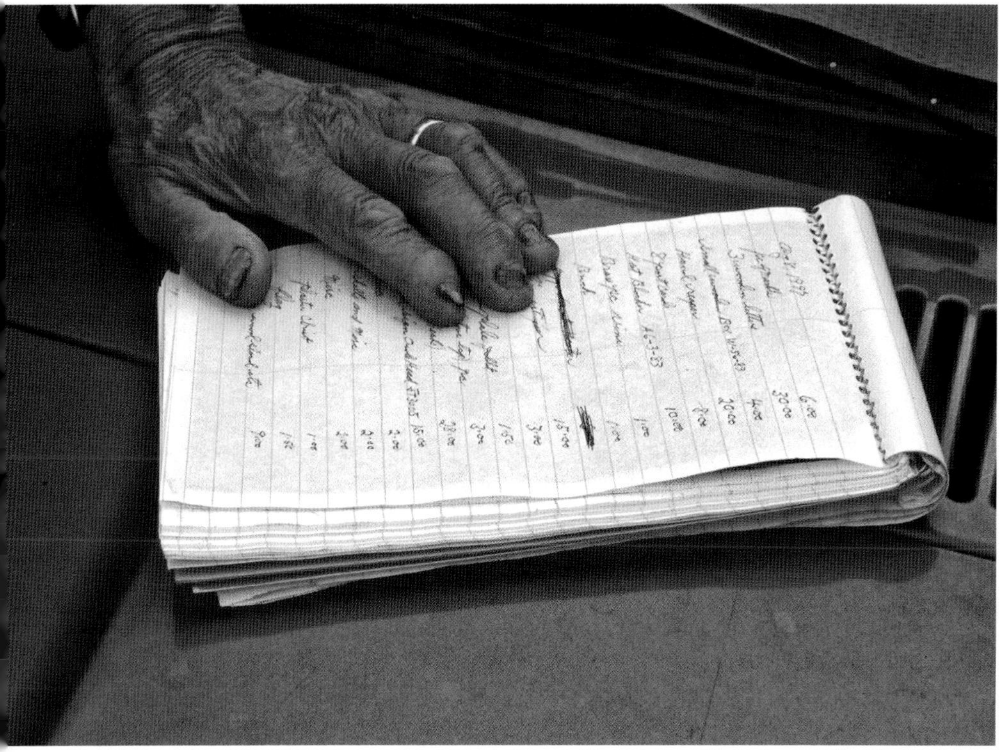

PLATE 23. Buckminster's sales book. 1987–2002.

Courtesy of Rosamond Purcell.]

off his vine and gave me to suck out of its skin and swallow whole, in Ohio." In the late 1940s, in Madison, Wisconsin, six-year-old Purcell receives a prize from the owners of a shoe store:

> a fabulous "all-day sucker," a ball of sugar candy made up of many layers. As each layer dissolved, not only the colors but the background would change from fields of polka dots to orbital circles or stripes. Flavors—lemon to raspberry to vanilla—rose ahead and then fell behind the geometric features. Unlike the fluoroscope [the X-ray machine in the shoe store], where everything was revealed at once, the candy unveiled its mysteries one layer at a time. I took the candy out of my mouth every few minutes . . . to study the changes, and in the sticky process something about the nature of time, past, present, and future, was sinking into my six-year-old mind.[27]We see two distinct "beginnings": Welty holding the moon as a word in her mouth, like the Concord grape ingested whole in Ohio;

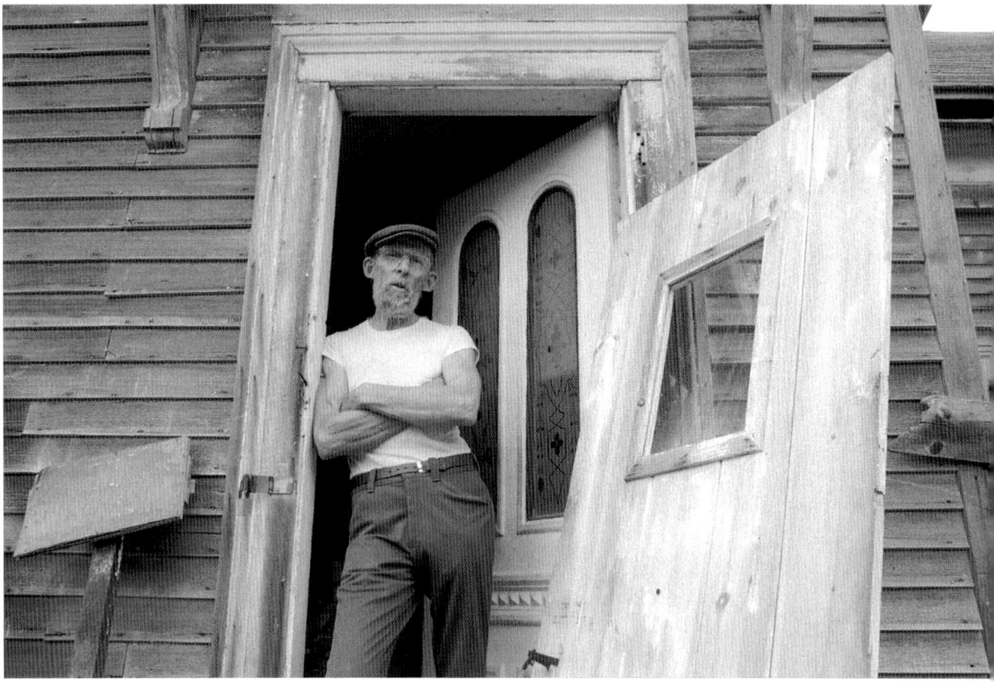

PLATE 24. **Buckminster in doorway of captain's house. 1987–2002.**

Courtesy of Rosamond Purcell.

Purcell, in Wisconsin, removing again and again the ball of sugar candy from her mouth to see its geometric features, its orbital circles or stripes ever-changing, its mysteries unveiled to the eye, layer by layer. And, at the same time, we also sense affinities between these two visionaries exploring the transformative mysteries of language and the dissolving layers of time.

10

Images Rich and Strange

> *Those are pearls that were his eyes;*
> *Nothing of him that doth fade*
> *But doth suffer a sea-change*
> *Into something rich and strange.*
>
> —William Shakespeare, *The Tempest*

What Laurel in *The Optimist's Daughter* wants, and fails, to do—that is, to save a fragment of text from burning and "make it over," make it new—Rosamond Purcell achieves in her strangely beautiful images of burned books and fragmented texts. If Eudora Welty's sense of the limitations of photography plays a part in her fiction, Purcell's ambivalent relation to writing informs her photographic work.

In William Buckminster's junkyard, nature was the first alchemist. The "trash-land"[1] of Owls Head was a treasure chest of castaway, sea-changed objects. Like the falling stars at the end of Welty's *Delta Wedding*, what falls onto, and then into, the earth is seen with wonder. *Bookworm*, published three years after *Owls Head*, returns photography to center stage even as it offers "rich and strange" images of texts, writing, and languages.

In the fall of 2008, I visited *First Doubt: Optical Confusion in Modern Photography* at the Yale University Art Gallery in New Haven, Connecticut, an exhibition of more than one hundred photographs selected mainly from the collection of Allan Chasanoff. The show was intended to reveal the gap between seeing and comprehending what we are seeing, that moment just before we find a known category for what we think we have perceived in a visual image.

Allan Chasanoff explains: "When an individual looks at the photographic image and—at the instant of perception—the image is visually confused or the subject matter's identity is compromised, that is what I call 'the optical.' . . . In some cases, the image, once deciphered, does not necessarily remain resolved, meaning that upon subsequent viewings, the observer will likely confront the visual disturbance again. It was 'the optical problem' as an endless quandary of vision that governed my major preoccupation with photography."

> "The optical" engenders the "failure" to see a photographic image correctly, allowing the viewer to attach doubt to reality itself.

Chasanoff adds, "I hope that throughout this exhibition . . . punishing doubt will be exercised."[2] This hope was fulfilled during each of my five visits. In his essay "It's Complicated," Joshua Chang notes: "As a society, we finally understand what photographers and picture editors have known all along: photographs can obfuscate and mislead as much as they reveal."[3] Standing next to two men looking at Gordon Matta-Clark's *Conical Intersect*, 1975, I overhear the following dialogue: "So this has to be the ceiling and this has to be a sprinkler and this *could* be a wall." "So this is up and [somewhat tentatively] this is down." "This could be the South Bronx. Does it say?" No. "It's really hard to know what is up and what is down." "Depends on the angle of the camera." "Gets your audience spinning."

In the presence of Purcell's images, too, even the trained eye experiences optical vertigo. Sven Birkerts describes his initial response to her photograph *Foucault's Pendulum*: "At first it was just the abstract beauty that slowed and then arrested my glance. I did not yet know what I was staring at. I was drawn by way of light, color, and sharply textured shapes into what seemed to be some kind of excavation site. . . . It took a moment for me to get the exhilarating double take: the mind's jarring shift from an abstract to a literal apprehension."

> Those marks on the bottom were, I suddenly realized, lines of print, parts of sentences, which meant, in turn, that the lit-up verticals on the left, straight as stalks of grain, were the edges of pages, that this jaggedly bit-into thing was a book.

Birkerts mentions the "echo-life of delayed recognition" that ultimately "isolates and heightens the idea of the book as material object."[4] *Foucault's Pendulum* is a photograph of a "paperback book eaten by termites in Bali, approx. 4 x 5½ inches. Somerville, Mass., 1996." This caption appears in small print in the list of illustrations at the back of *Bookworm*.[5] Most viewers will respond, as Birkerts did, first to the image itself.

Here is a perfect example of what Chasanoff calls "the optical problem." If one comes to *Bookworm* from *Owls Head*, it is likely that the clearly visible words, phrases, and near-sentences in the lower right quadrant of the image will be a clue to its subject, but the brilliant use of natural light together with the careful angling of the scooped-out portions of a succession of golden pages astonishes the eye. "Photography" derives from the Greek *phōs*, meaning "light," and *graphein*, "to write." Purcell writes with light,[6] and conventional categories of what constitutes writing fall away. Looking at *Foucault's Pendulum*, we don't automatically see paperback pages filled with readable print; we see a light-struck chasm with a repeating pattern of ridges hanging above golden sheaves. Ravaged, the book is ravishing.

In her introduction to *Bookworm*, Purcell says: "When glass or plastic mediates the effect of natural light, . . . I feel the atmosphere of a deeper place."[7] When asked if she can elaborate, Purcell describes this process in relation to both *Foucault's Pendulum* and *Grail*, an image of the same termite-eaten paperback, "with petrified egg yolk, refracted light."[8] In *Foucault's Pendulum*, she made use of "both natural light from skylights and [a] piece of plastic placed above the book that further softened the filtered sun. This plastic is a squarish block of translucent (but not transparent) industrial plastic . . . found at junkyard." In *Grail*, the picture of the "same termite-eaten book with petrified egg yolk . . . shows clearly the thick piece of plastic used to filter/soften the effect of the sun. If it looks like several pieces, that's because it is reflected or rather is reflecting itself as [the] sun hits it."[9]

This technical description does nothing to forestall an endless quandary of vision, especially when confronted with *Grail*. *Foucault's Pendulum* showed a multitude of left-hand, golden pages pressed closely together. *Grail* shows the right-hand pages, somewhat darkened, as if by burning.[10] Of the printed words and phrases, fewer are clearly legible. One sees at the very bottom of the image this phrase: "'You mean the Grail also comes into.'" At the center of the first page is an orange-red textured shape, like that of a halved peach, cradled within half of a broken gray shell.[11] Above it, the tops of termite-damaged pages look like the ridges of mountains or perhaps just a steep embankment gradually decomposing. In the upper half of the photograph, the thick piece of translucent plastic that has softened the sunlight is "reflecting itself" in an uncanny image of intersecting grayish, at times speckled, horizontal strips of varying widths; above these is a darker shaft narrowing and growing lighter as it slants downward from left to right. At the very top of the photograph, what looks like a roof of ice widens as it slopes down diagonally to meet the far-right edge of the dark shaft below it. Further down, to the far left, what appears to be the upper half of a yellowish-ivory (plastic?) ring, a demi-halo, peeks out from the top of the mountain-like page.[12] In both *Foucault's Pendulum* and *Grail*, the refracted light unveils mysteries of the tireless consumption of a text, one layer at a time.

Purcell's fascination with books and writing extends to foreign languages, including some she doesn't know.[13] Foreign-language texts or words appear in over a dozen images in *Bookworm*: French, German, Dutch, Italian, Latin, Chinese

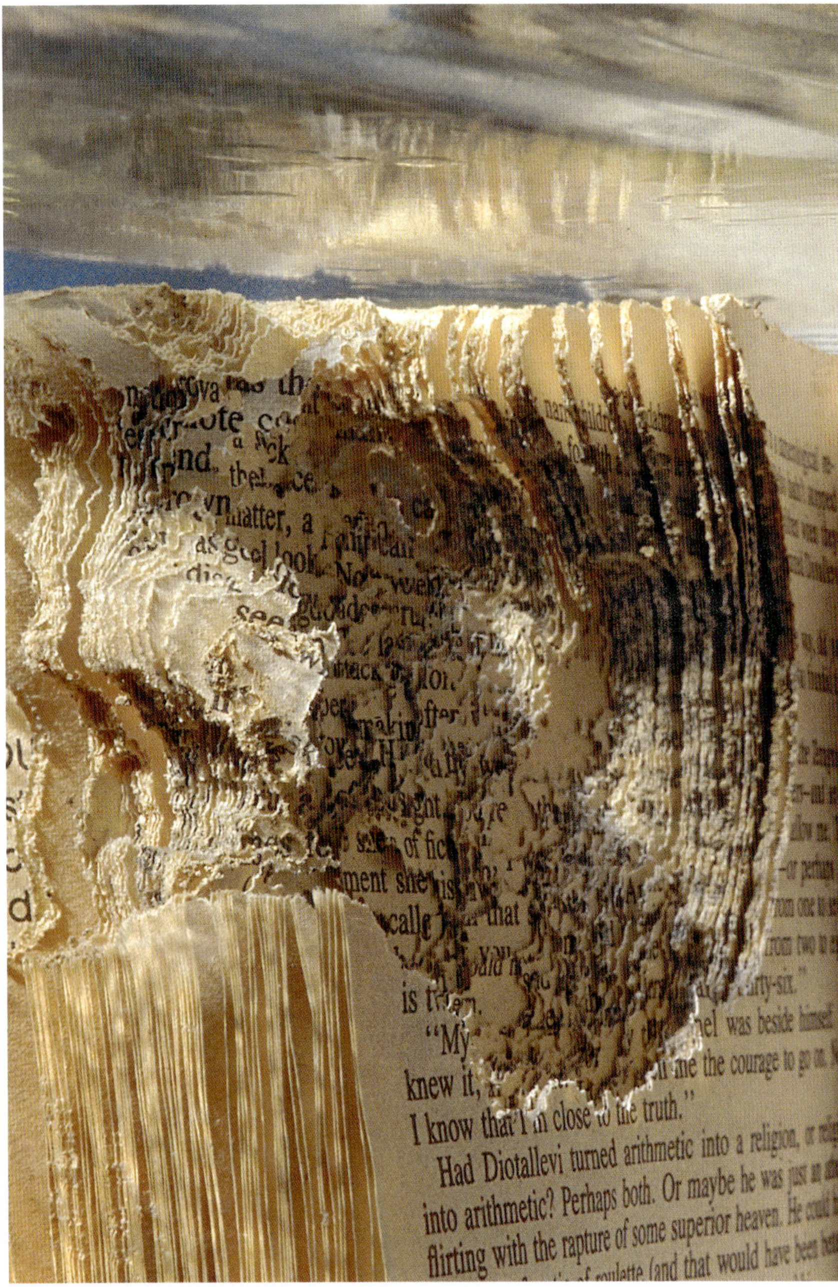

PLATE 25. Foucault's Pendulum. 1996.

Courtesy of Rosamond Purcell.

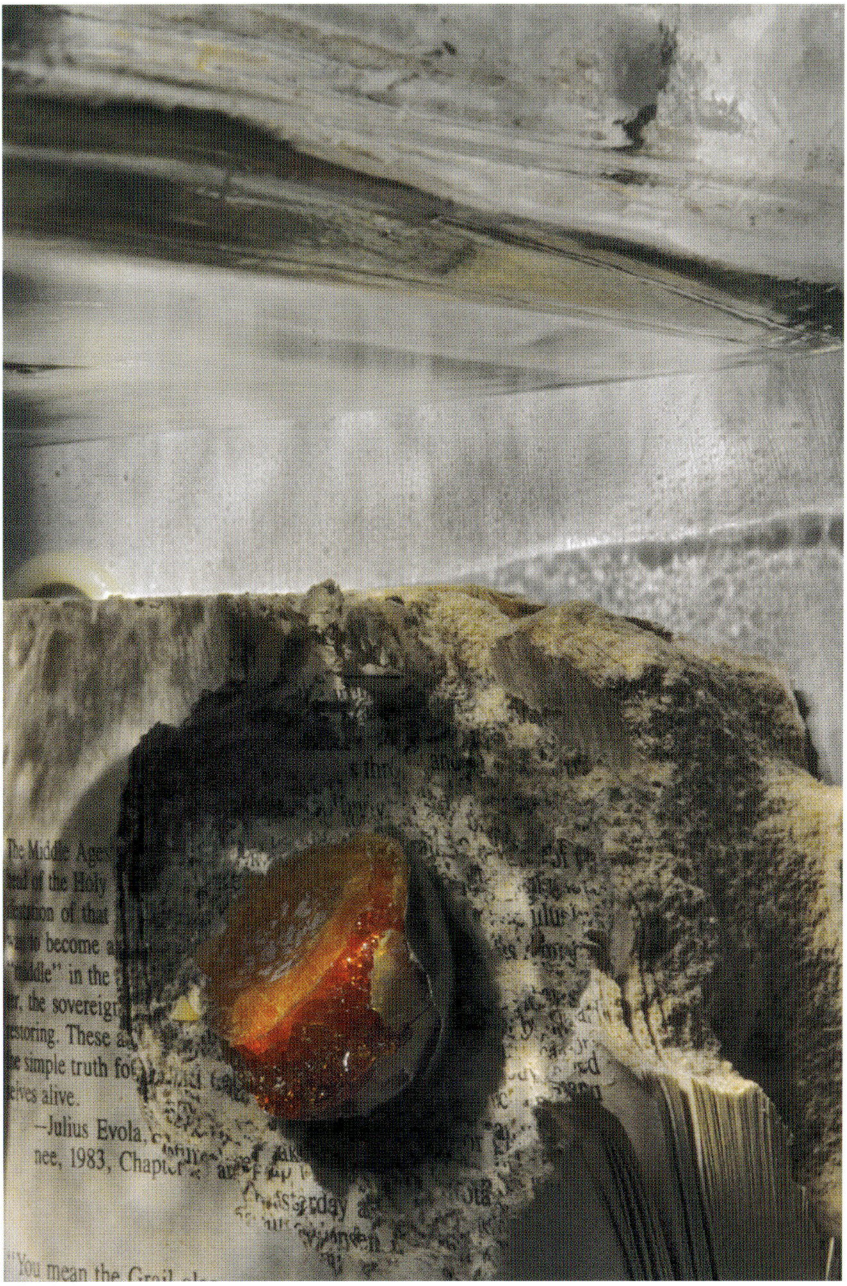

PLATE 26. Grail. 1996.

Courtesy of Rosamond Purcell.

ideograms (in six photographs), and Urdu.[14] The word "Anjil" is in a picture taken in Shalimar Gardens, Srinagar, India, which reminded Purcell of the phonetic spelling that George Herriman gave to "angel" in his comic strip, *Krazy Kat*.[15]

In *Bookworm*, there are images of titles of novels found at Owls Head (*The Frontiersman*, 41, and *The Lower Part of the Sky*, 61) as well as of books with titles known to the photographer but not visible to the viewer (Dante's *Inferno*, 87, and *Foucault's Pendulum*, 89, 141). There are other images of writing: fragments from a termite-eaten letter, layered on moistened birchwood and on advertising tin ("*Letter to Mr. Spalding*," 84, 92); and quotes from comic strips: "In the olden times, many, many millions of years ago—folks wrote on 'bricks.'" "'Bricks?'" (*Love Letters in Brick*, 31; quote from *Krazy Kat,* by George Herriman) and "I feel a tremendous pressure building up in my brain" (comic strip [Dagwood Bumstead] detail embedded in a cement slab from an Owls Head lobster pot, 56). We see writing on bars of 1920s olive oil soap (*Soap*, 54) and in columns of newspaper stock market reports, found on cement blocks at Owls Head (*Stock Market*, 64).

Creating a visual effect like that of Welty's shifting perspectives in *Losing Battles*, Purcell photographs a page of musical notes interspersed with words, some upside down, all legible if one changes one's angle of vision (*Bitter Store*, 79). Opposite the table of contents in *Bookworm* is a color photograph of a small figure with a bear-like face, dressed in a blue suit and blue hat, holding a small blue bag, surrounded by scraps of writing that can only be construed by revolving the image (*Traveler*, 6).

There is more straightforward writing. The handwritten legend in *Legend for piece of worm-eaten wood from original London Bridge* begins: "Wood from London clay bored by teredo [shipworm that feeds on wood]" (24). *Bread from World War One* (75) contains a poignant, handwritten label with its attached string curling over an insect-damaged piece of bread: "Bread given the prisoners at Saar Alben, and by one of them to me at Lunéville Nov. 19, 1918."

Of the 125 color images in *Bookworm*, well over half are of books, writing, texts. Only twenty photographs show heads or body parts of human figures, none living. There are faces on book covers (a man's head in profile and the head of a smaller figure, possibly a child, in *The Frontiersman*, 41) and the back of a man holding a cat in *By the author of "The Lower Part of the Sky,"* 61. Images of humans are often associated with animals. In a detail from a collage,[16] *Knight in chapel*, 120, a supine knight lies on a checkered floor, arms crossed over his chest, eyes open. Above him, at the end of a series of arches receding into the distance, is the face of a Golden Lion tamarin (a museum specimen). Creeping out from under the right shoulder of the knight is a tiny turbaned head. The disturbing face, in half shadow, with its pronounced brows, tightly shut mouth, and forbidding stare, seems to repel all further viewing of the image. Describing this and another collage, Purcell says that she is "*writing* [a visual scene] . . . in which animals corrupt imperial rooms."[17] In *Bookworm*, Purcell is "writing" scenes as settings for untold stories, like those escaped conversations in Welty's snapshots.

An explicit example of visual storytelling is *Descent of Man enters the woods*, 119, a detail from a collage titled *Traveling*, in which four upright figures evolving toward human form march across the lower half of the photograph. The title of the photograph foretells the story, as Purcell explains: "the iconic march of the smallest monkey evolving through the apes and early man to us is shown in reverse order . . . as if Homo sapiens came before the earlier forms and is now disappearing into the woods, consumed by the trees."[18]

There are also mysterious evocations of scenes in which shadowy figures appear. Apparent shadows of human forms are cast by artifacts: a somewhat mottled shadow of a tin man, seen in profile, seated on a handcart (*Irish Mail*, 108); the silhouette of a slender human figure on top of a huge, grayish, bulbous shape marked by a constellation of swirling lines, some of which extend over parts of the sleeping figure (*Sleep*, 152). Partly reminiscent of Welty's black-and-white snapshots is *Delivery*, 155, an image of the grayish shadow of a man seen in profile, his head thrust forward beneath the elongated brim of his puffed cap. Various appendages or parcels—vertical, horizontal, and at a jagged diagonal—stick out like projectiles above and to both sides of his torso. He wears a long jacket or coat that falls to his knees. A light gray triangle appears at his midriff. Burdened, Purcell's apparitional delivery man will continue on his way.

By contrast with Welty, there are no photographs of human conversation in *Bookworm*,[19] but there are images suggestive of voicing. *Public Domain*, on the title page of *Bookworm*, includes a flesh-colored face, with gaping mouth and eyes, lying near the bottom of what may be the frame of a box or a hollowed-out book with fragments of text visible. Outside the lower edge of the frame is a second, bluish-gray head with nostrils widened above lips cut off at midpoint. The mouth that could be forming words belongs to a severed head, below a barely readable text.[20]

Mount Rushmore with lips (140) offers fragmented images that give oddly moving expression to Jeff Wall's observation that talking escapes a picture.[21] Three distinct sets of lips, chins, and parts of nostrils appear to the right of center in the upper half of the photograph. In the lower set, the lips are closed, the upper lip very thin, the two lips together perhaps hazarding a thin smile. In the middle set, the very full lips are closed, with no indication of expression other than possibly an unintended pout. In the top set, the lips are open, with two teeth visible, as if speech is in progress or to follow. Purcell's different sets of lips are, in a sense, a visual image of Welty's use of free indirect discourse in *Delta Wedding*.

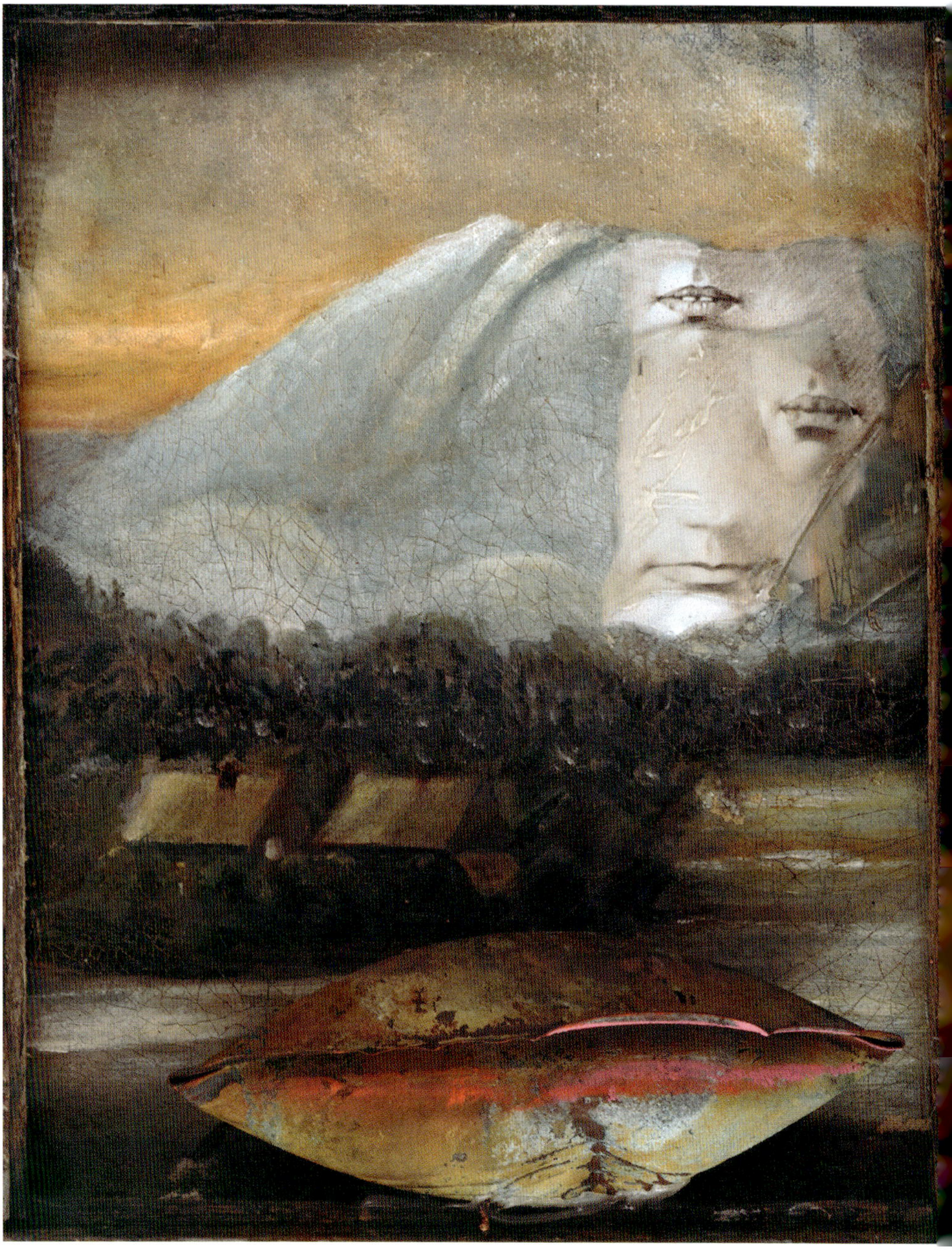

PLATE 27. Mount Rushmore with lips. 1989.

Courtesy of Rosamond Purcell.

As already suggested, Welty's attitude toward the photographers and photographs portrayed in her fiction is ambivalent. The itinerant photographers in *Delta Wedding* and "Kin" are hardly presented in an admirable light.[22] Photographic images are deceptive or marginal in "Music from Spain." Gloria Renfro's mother in *Losing Battles* is just a blur, someone she doesn't recognize. The photographic frame of the female narrator in "A Memory" is transcended by the visionary imagination of Delilah in "The Burning." Welty's own experience as a photographer, however, also finds positive expression in her marked attention to the subtle and changing effects of light in day and night; canny sense of the uses of the frame;[23] experiments with diverse angles of vision; extraordinary pictorial precision; images that make visible correspondences between the human and the natural world; creation of perspectives that, however disparate, converge. If she moved on from visual images to literary texts, she did not leave her photographic eye behind. The mystery of human life hinted at in Welty's snapshots is central to her fiction.

Like Welty's attitude toward photography, Purcell's attitude toward writing is also creatively ambivalent. Growing up, she had a complicated relation to books: "I read on two levels—for the words and again for the pictures. I preferred swinging along, negotiating the wide-open spaces of plot without illustrations, inventing these in a kind of simultaneous translation technique—reading and seeing—a two-ply trick. Distracted by whatever illustrations did appear, I would also read the book through for the pictures alone, and so formed two story lines." This two-ply trick of simultaneous translation foreshadows Purcell's two-ply career.

Of a short story she wrote in college, she was told by one professor, "This has no voice." A friend, reading her work, said, "This is a picture. You know, you should be a photographer." "So," Purcell said, "I took pictures, and at first they did not look anything like what I was thinking. The camera and I do not have a symbiotic relationship. I may care all I want to about what I see, but the camera is a machine and does not know how I feel."[24] The tension implied in the non-symbiotic relationship of camera and human sensibility finds eloquent expression in Purcell's haunting images of books. "I love books," she says. "I love them whole and unprovoked. . . . I pillage only those books already in an outlaw condition, those visited by termites, silverfish, mice, moths and beetles, damp, mold, rot, or fire. The tenacity of pages and bindings to survive such assaults seems miraculous." On the other hand, some of the books in her studio are "dried shut into pulp bricks, almost impossible to open, certainly to read." For Purcell, the daughter of a distinguished Harvard professor, this is strangely comforting:

> Owning them is restful because, as we were taught growing up, not to be "in a state of" reading . . . could be forgiven if there was nothing there to read. A book that is still a book but cannot be read imparts peace and promise.[25]

A book that is still a book but cannot be read is the paradoxical definition[26] of the texts imaged in *Bookworm*. It reflects the ironic trajectory of an artist who moved past writing to the photography that brought her back to writing "as a photographer."

In Purcell's memoir, small black-and-white images appeared as photo-endnotes, interspersed with conventional notes consisting only of text. In *Bookworm*, several images in similarly reduced form appear on the pages of the introductory essay, with captions located at the back of the book. Here, we replicate Purcell's own early reading experience ("I read on two levels—for the words and again for the pictures") in reverse: we "read" the pictures first and then again with the aid of words that may reconstruct our reading—or not. It is possible that Purcell's two-ply trick becomes three- or four-ply, because the more we look at Purcell's photographs, the more complicated looking becomes.

In the introduction to *Bookworm*, Purcell offers ekphrases of selected photographs, both small images that appear only on the pages of her essay and larger pictures to be found in the body of the book. Most readers will not turn immediately to the full-page color reproductions as they read the introduction. Two different experiences of reading/viewing are therefore possible.

On the one hand, written commentary occurs without benefit of an accompanying image. Brief, allusive, unable to stand on its own, it illuminates the full-page photograph once one views it. An example is Purcell's statement: "Although ritualistic book burning to annihilate history represents one of mankind's most heinous activities, I find the creatively burned book . . . a black chrysanthemum, unexpectedly beautiful." Only when we turn to page 87 and view the flower-like image of a burned copy of Dante's *Inferno*, found on a Boston street, do we see a ruined text bloom as visual art.[27]

A second kind of reading/viewing experience occurs when a small image is reproduced above, beside, or beneath the text. Directly above a photograph of several ruined buildings, Purcell describes what remains of an old gold-processing plant in Alaska:

> The staggered buildings . . . were collapsing into their interiors and into one another. Upright door and window frames were now oblique rectangles and squares, now ellipses creaking and twisting for a long time still.[28]

When asked about the word "ellipses," Purcell says that in her description of the picture, which is "usually seen as a print much bigger than [this] reduction of it," she was suggesting "how geometric shapes made by windows and vents appear when collapsing, . . . trying to reinforce the visceral response I felt to the off-kilter

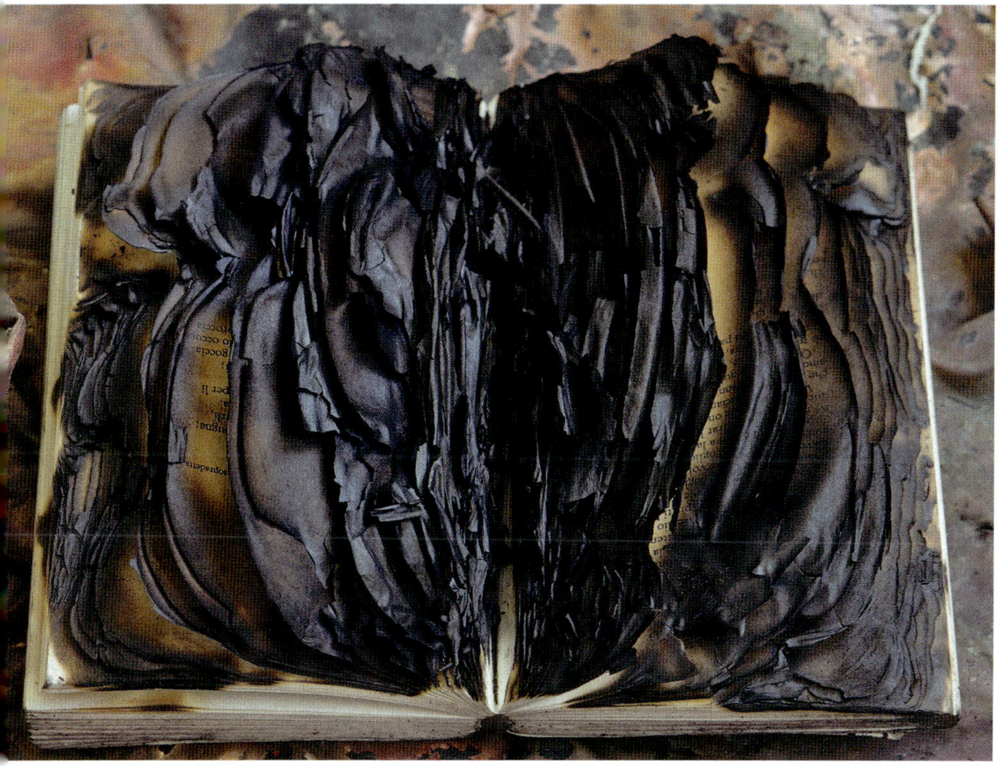

PLATE 28. Dante's *Inferno*. c. 1995.

Courtesy of Rosamond Purcell.

scene—of an abandoned building in the middle of very remote landscape."[29] In her phrase "ellipses creaking and twisting for a long time still," "still" may refer as much to the photographer's continuing visual and kinetic memory as to the still photo itself.

Here the two-ply trick is rapid and exhilaratingly circular. Text and image occupy nearly identical space on the same page, with the image at the bottom. Even as the eye reads the writing, there is a pressure to glance downward so that there seems to be an almost simultaneous reading of commentary and picture, a convergence of text and visual image. Purcell's Shakespeare-inflected musing that "all the world's an altered page"[30] links the photographer's eye with the writer's visualizing mind.

* * *

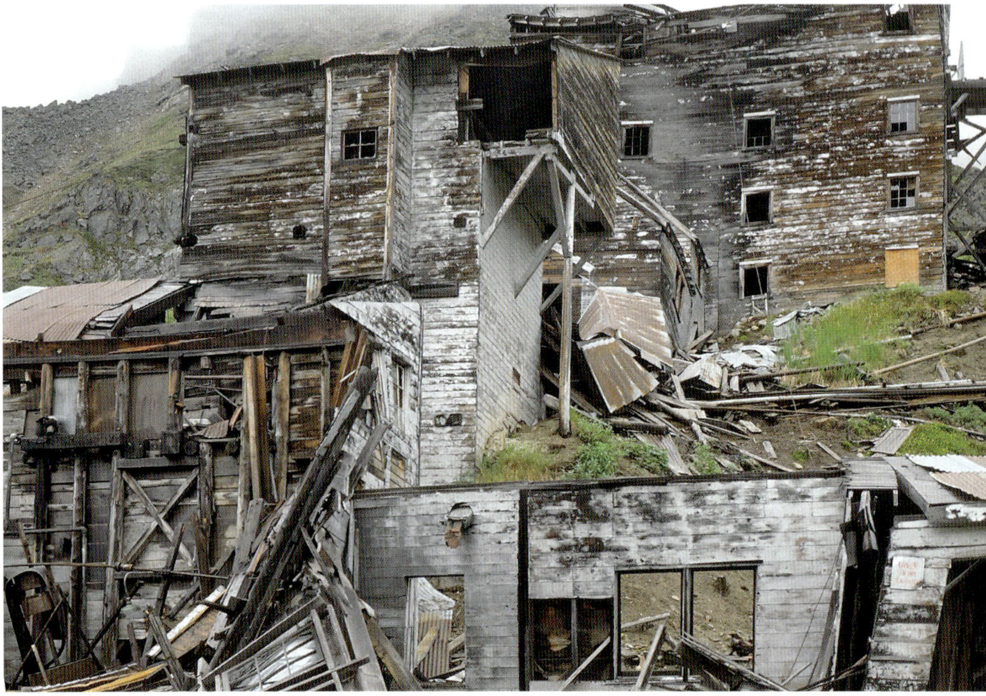

PLATE 29. Abandoned gold-processing plant, Alaska. 1995.

Courtesy of Rosamond Purcell.

The books beautifully imaged in *Bookworm* are decrepit, burned, or eaten by termites—termites at times "guided" (by Purcell and the proprietor of a university-sponsored termite colony) "in the foraging of carefully selected pages of text."[31] There is in Purcell's work a conscious seeking out of what is damaged or disfigured. "I'm interested in disintegration and metamorphosis," she says.

> Take six of the same flashlights, leave them outdoors . . . and over time, they will no longer resemble each other. . . . [They] are no longer functional; they've . . . gone their own ways, developed their own history of the afterlife.[32]

For Purcell a book that cannot be read and a flashlight dismissed from its function as a flashlight impart a sense of peacefulness. What is dismissed from one kind of identity is released into an individualized afterlife,[33] a sea-change like that of the typewriter, *Underwoodensis corrupta*, which then undergoes a second change from its reduced black-and-white image as endnote in *Owls Head* to its full-page glory as a color print in *Bookworm*. No longer functional as an instrument for writing, it is transformed in Purcell's visionary photography. In its afterlife, the typewriter retreats back into history: it is now like an ancient echinoid, a sea urchin reawakened from the past.

Welty took snapshots of cemeteries; Purcell's photographs resurrect the dead they record. What memory the somnambulist does in the fiction of Eudora Welty, the visual image performs in the work of Rosamond Purcell. Something magical has occurred: a new vitality has been made out of the dying or the dead. Transience and changefulness have been caught and preserved, forestalling final disintegration.

The photographs, the pages of the books that reproduce them, and the objects to which they have granted an afterlife, as Prospero tells us,

> shall dissolve;
> And, like this insubstantial pageant faded,
> Leave not a rack behind.[34]

But the alchemy of Purcell's art offers the paradoxical status promised in Edmund Spenser's *Epithalamion*: "for short time an endlesse moniment [monument]."[35] As for the collapsing remains of the Alaskan gold-processing plant, Purcell says:

> I feel uneasy and also grateful that there are buildings caving in, books on the verge of illegibility, . . . collapses that trigger growth. Then—for a very short time—only three things count: the light, the camera, and things, holding.[36]

11

Wonder

It is good work just to stare and wonder.

—Rosamond Purcell, "The Game of the Name"

Egg & Nest, published in 2008, was Rosamond Purcell's "first official foray onto the playing fields of digital photography."[1] Invited to photograph avian materials at the Western Foundation of Vertebrate Zoology (WFVZ) in Camarillo, California, Purcell produces extraordinary images of its eggs and nests, scenes of absence: "this immense collection of [avian] intentions—and I try not to refer too often to what has been suspended."[2]

Unlike the specimens in William Buckminster's Owls Head junkyard, the nests and eggs at WFVZ are kept in bags, boxes, and compartments, protected from parasites, weather, unauthorized human handling. Purcell says, "It is a struggle for me—moving beyond tens of thousands of glimpses to establish ways to *see*." Often she sees the background cloth for one of the specimens "*bent like a book opening sideways to the lens*" (italics mine).[3] No longer photographs, books become similes, Eudora Welty's characteristic figures of speech.

What Purcell sees is uncanny: "Make no mistake—over every egg and nest hover the ghosts of birds, plaiting straw, plastering crevices, punching holes in leaves."

> There is something about the empty egg of an extinct bird that is even more moving than the bird itself. A hollow shell is the ultimate symbol of the end of the line.[4]

Purcell speaks as a photographer, but at the same time she sees with the visualizing mind: background cloth has become a book opening; ghostly birds labor over their nest-building; unbroken eggs carefully emptied of their contents become symbols of finality.

The eggs are perfect subjects for Purcell's camera. "There is no 'best' view of an egg. It is endless. It has no front or back—no boundaries—and any number of possible horizons. Through the lens, it is like a planet rising." The boundary-testing—what she calls "elision of categories"—characteristic of Purcell's previous work is dramatically in play here. Cotton placed beneath an egg becomes a cloud; the egg becomes a moon. Like the aberrations on the surface of the mirrored jars that will become Purcell's stage in *Landscapes of the Passing Strange*, marks on the surface of a bird egg transform into hills or hollows, "change it into a landscape."[5]

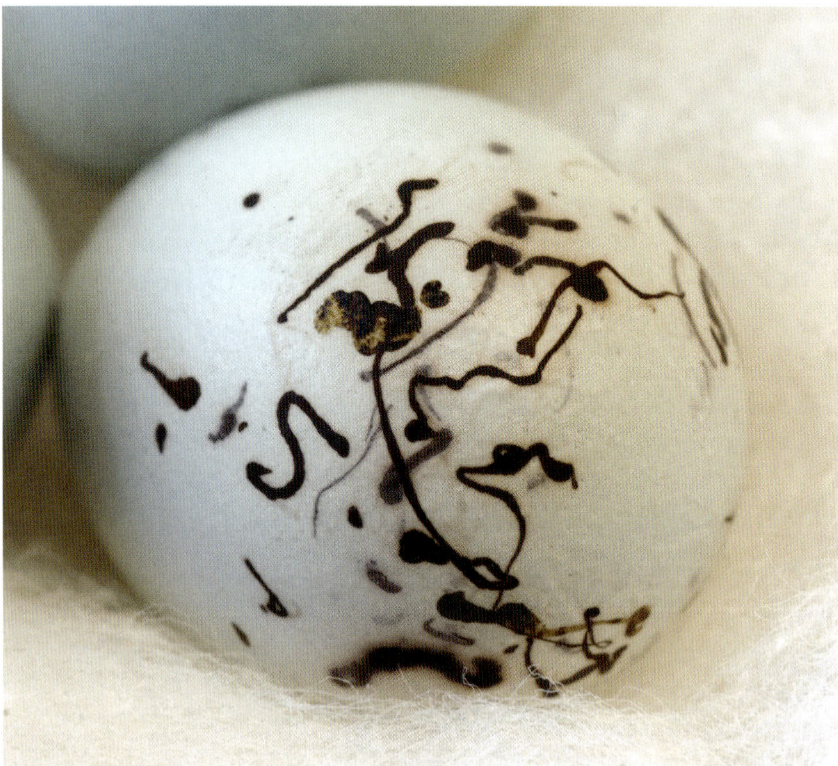

PLATE 30. Red-winged Blackbird (*Agelaius phoenicus*), close-up of egg. 2007.

Courtesy of Rosamond Purcell.

Purcell's never-abandoned fascination with language finds a new context in *Egg & Nest*. Writing, it seems, can be made out on the elongated shells of the eggs of the red-winged blackbird, "scribblings" that the bird never intended:

> the egg, moving down the birth canal, received its background color and the stains imprinted from broken blood cells. . . . As the albumen itself is applied in translucent coats, paler colors appear beneath one or more of these layers.[6]

Wonders arise from broken blood cells and albumen, a nutritive protein substance famously associated with the haunting albumen silver prints of Eugène Atget.[7] There are layers and layers of visible markings filled with possible untold stories on eggs of the blackbird and the common murre: "visual connections to other worlds," "lines reminiscent of Japanese writing," "intimations of human beings," apparitions.[8]

* * *

Purcell reads the calligraphy of birds through the camera's eye just as she reads the language of the bard in the allusive images of *Landscapes of the Passing Strange: Reflections from Shakespeare*.[9] Her "reflections" from Shakespeare's plays become a parallel universe, an offer of implications adjacent to Shakespeare's verbal and dramatic rendering of, at times, inexpressible human experience. In *Landscapes of the Passing Strange*, as in *Owls Head* and *Bookworm*, Purcell offers fragments of texts, but now her rebus-like pictures resonate with the life of Shakespearean drama. Her allusive visual images have their origins in—and return Purcell to her origins in—the art of writing.

Invited by the Russian director Konstantin Stanislavski to collaborate on a production of *Hamlet* for the Moscow Art Theatre, Edward Gordon Craig suggested that everything in the play be "conveyed without words, to which Stanislavski replied, presciently, 'Yes, but that would not be Shakespeare's *Hamlet*. It would be a new art founded on the theme of Shakespeare's *Hamlet*.'"[10] In approaching a work that is both a literary text and a script for performance—the dual status of the Shakespearean play—the visual artist must become director, actor, and critic,[11] making his or her viewers rethink the implications of writing that is to be seen, heard, read. How is this "new art" to be accomplished?

Purcell enters Shakespeare's text through a bottle. The early twentieth-century apothecary jars the photographer found one summer in an antique shop originally held fabric dyes and still retain "negative impressions of long-gone buttons and tacks pressed against the glass." Purcell purchased several of these jars, took some to a meadow in New Hampshire, and "turned them toward the light."

"Scarred by history and anamorphic in their reflecting properties," she says, "the bottles do not accommodate a single view without first changing it. Each is lined by two layers of close-set glass; the inner, a mirror, coated with silver in varying stages of . . . oxidation, the outer grimy or gleaming."[12] The bottles do not offer a single view without first changing it. How well this reflects the Shakespearean vision—or, indeed, Welty's "two pictures at once in [her] frame" as well as Purcell's own photographic art.

"I take these pictures," she tells me, "but I only see what I see in one layer of glass. . . . I don't know what I'm going to get ultimately—which is like being blindfolded at the same time you are visually aware. The glass—the doubleness—the transformation that occurs. . . . It's alchemy."[13] It is an alchemy not unlike that of the creation of Hamlet and Lear and Hermione. Especially in the theater, we are always seeing double, the actor and the character the actor portrays, one imperceptibly melding into the other.[14] This may be the theatrical version of what Allan Chasanoff has called optical confusion in viewing a photographic image: "at the instant of perception . . . the subject matter's identity is compromised."[15]

In "Eyed Awry," an essay that appears at the back of *Landscapes of the Passing Strange*, Purcell says: "When I began to work, the layers from inside cast unsteady shadows on the viewfinder and across the landscapes. Identification among reflected species grows uncertain as forms intermingle: animal becomes human; human, animal or vegetable."

> The wavering shapes begin to evoke the fluidity and multiple meanings found in speeches and verses of Shakespeare. Each element moves or dissolves if I shift the vantage point by so much as a millimeter. These come to be the shadows of the stage.[16]

The shadows and shadings, the fluidity of form and multiplicitous meanings, the effects of a shifting vantage point—all these relate as much to the art of Shakespeare as to the images whose stage is an empty bottle. Purcell's photographic work mirrors the work of visionary imagination.

We are no longer offered pictures of ravaged books, weather-beaten and dried shut, unreadable; nor do we see fragments of words, sentences with missing parts. The seeking out of what is disfigured, reconfigured, or unknowable has already been done: it is all there in the texts evoked by Purcell's pictures. Her reflections from Shakespeare are still, in a sense, fragments, parts of a whole, but they are also complete in themselves just as fragments of Shakespearean plays are resonant with meaning, like the repeated cry of Lear carrying his dead daughter in his arms: "Howl, howl, howl, howl!"[17] A world of terror arrives in four words.

Landscapes of the Passing Strange: Reflections from Shakespeare dramatically interlinks the resources and gifts of photographic eye and visualizing mind. In Welty's "The Burning," Delilah looks at reflections in a Venetian mirror and then becomes her own visionary seer. Purcell looks at reflections in the doubled-glass of abandoned apothecary jars, the inner glass a mirror, and with her camera records in natural light mysterious images, translated into allusions to Shakespearean texts that were never present to either jar or camera. Purcell has said that *Landscapes of the Passing Strange* "aspires to mystery."[18] In that, too, it is a reflection from Shakespeare. The secrets of Purcell's images, like the secrets at the heart of Shakespeare's greatest plays, abide.

It is time to enter, so far as one can, the stage of the mirrored bottle. We begin a look at seven of Purcell's photographs with *Heaven's Vault* (93),[19] the image of Lear's cry, "Howl, howl, howl, howl!" As he holds the body of his daughter, Cordelia, Lear says to those on stage, and perhaps also to the audience:

> Howl, howl, howl, howl! O, you are men of stones:
> Had I your tongues and eyes, I'd use them so
> That heaven's vault should crack. She's gone forever!
> I know when one is dead and when one lives;
> She's dead as earth.
> (Shakespeare, *King Lear*, 5.3.252–56)[20]

And despite Lear's later attempt to refute himself and see life returning, "Look on her, look, her lips, / Look there, look there!" (Shakespeare, *King Lear*, 5.3.308–9) —and in contrast to Shakespeare's source—Cordelia is "gone forever," "dead as earth."

Purcell's image speaks of a horror we, like Samuel Johnson in the eighteenth century,[21] can barely endure. The figure of the old king is erect. His hat and upper garment are blue; between them, a crumpled face. Lying horizontally across his chest, in the same pale, slightly bronzed color of the remainder of her father's body, is the figure of Cordelia, her head tilted backward, facing clouded skies. The body of Lear visible beneath the weight of his daughter looks as if it is itself turning to stone. In the lower left and right are what seem to be shadowy images of disembodied heads. With surprising fluidity, shapes blend into one another: Cordelia and Lear, skull-like faces and landscape, billowy clouds and geometric patterns. Horizontal lines streak stormy skies. Purcell's image has caught the moment between absolute despair ("She's gone forever! / . . . She's dead as earth.") and impossible hope ("look, her lips, / Look there, look there!"). In the background, heaven's vault is cracking. Purcell's images in *Landscapes of the Passing Strange* write scenes in the interstices of Shakespeare's own.

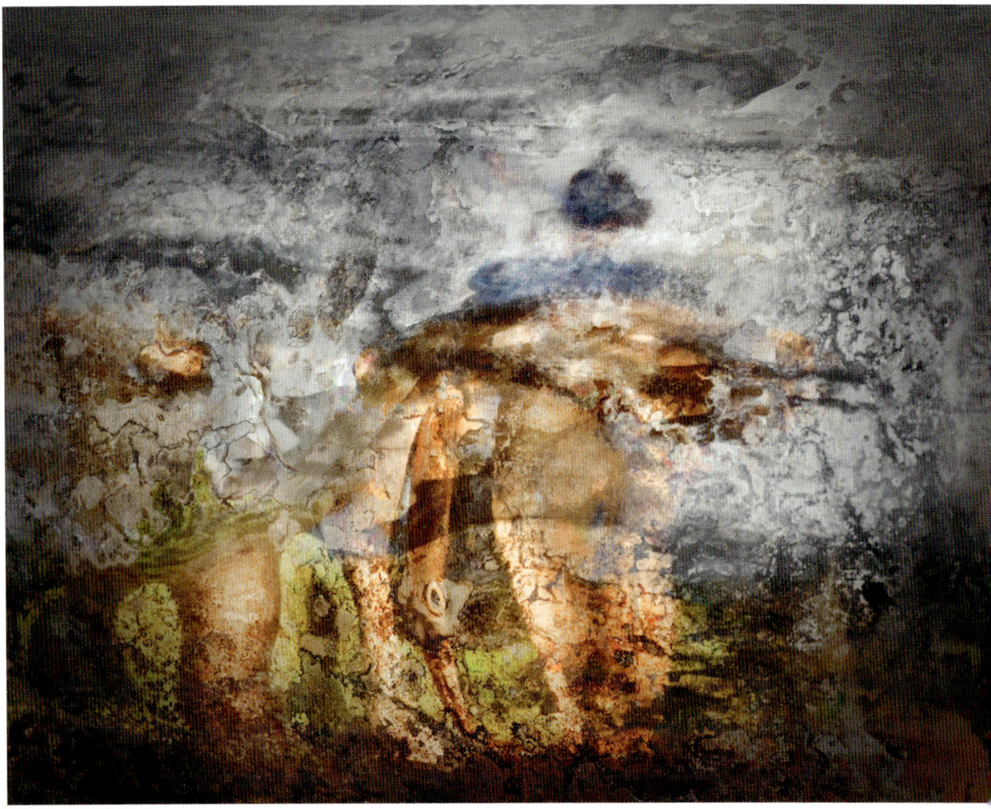

PLATE 31. Heaven's Vault. 2009–10.

Courtesy of Rosamond Purcell.

In the opening act of *Hamlet*, there is a return from the dead. A ghostly father visits his son, revealing fratricide and regicide, asking to be remembered. In a sense, Hamlet will carry his father in his arms for the rest of the play. *Remember Me* (32–33), Purcell's uncanny image of "leperous distilment" pouring into King Hamlet's skull, circumvents the leper-like effect of Claudius's poison on the king's body and goes straight to the bone. "Upon my secure hour," Hamlet's father tells his son,

> Thy uncle stole
> With juice of cursèd hebenon in a vial,
> And in the porches of mine ears did pour
> The leperous distilment [distillation causing the skin to become scaly]
> (Shakespeare, *Hamlet*, 1.5.61–64)

In Purcell's image, a skull lies on its side, its huge cave-like mouth open in pain below black nose and eye holes. The left eye, closely observed, may have within it a ghost-like face, perhaps that of the smiling poisoner. Above the skull is a blue skyscape topped by a greenish, ridged horizontal area; from its center a phallic funnel penetrates downward, picking up some of the blue of the sky as it explodes into nasty droppings falling into the ear hole of the king's skull.

Earlier in act 1, Hamlet's friend, Horatio, describes the ghost as wearing battle armor with his face guard up, revealing a "sable silvered" beard "as I have seen it in his life" (1.2.241–42). Later, Hamlet's father appears again "in his habit [dress and bearing] as he lived" (3.4.126). Purcell's *Remember Me* is, in a sense, a visualizing of Hamlet's own visualizing mind; as he listens to his father's narrative, he simultaneously "sees" its ending: the poison, the skull.

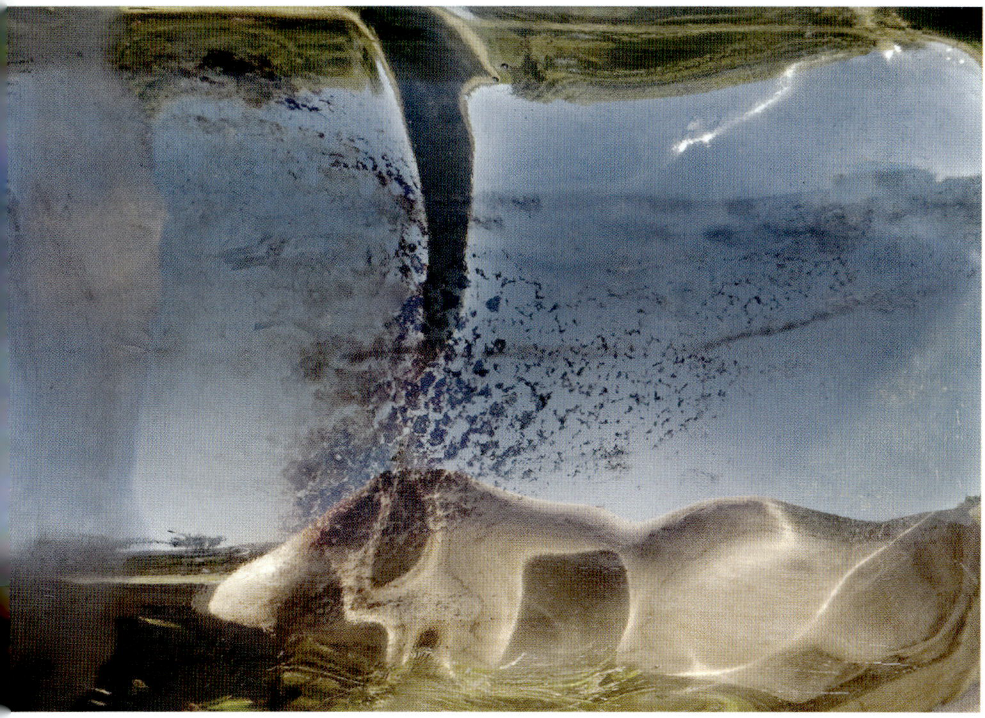

PLATE 32. Remember Me. 2009–10.

Courtesy of Rosamond Purcell.

Although the photographer cannot be said to have intended this, the image is also a possible linking of Hamlet's father's fate with that of Yorick, whom Hamlet talks to as if the court jester is still alive: "Where be your gibes now . . . ? Not one now to mock your own grinning?" Hamlet asks Yorick (5.1.175, 177). And, indeed, the wide, square, open mouth of the poisoned skull of the king, looked at again from another perspective, seems to be laughing. The doubleness and uncanniness of Purcell's image are Hamlet's own experience: a ghost appearing and speaking as in life tells a story of his death; a skull dug up in a cemetery, belonging to a jester at court, is addressed as if it could still smile. Purcell's rendering of the ghost's words, "Remember me" (1.5.91), reverberates endlessly from the dead to the living and back again.

The photograph titled *We Are Pictures* (94–95) takes on the perspective of another Shakespearean character, the new king Claudius, as he describes the daughter of the man Hamlet has just killed:

> poor Ophelia
> Divided from herself and her fair judgment,
> Without the which we are pictures or mere beasts.
> (Shakespeare, *Hamlet*, 4.5.80–82)

Purcell's image is a picture of many forms crowded together along the downstage edge of the frame. Ophelia herself stands far to the left, holding a basket,[22] perhaps the container of flowers she will distribute to the court in her next mad appearance. To her right are shadowy, often mud-colored shapes, "mere beasts," pressing her to the margin of the picture. The longer one looks at these figures—with their odd or missing appendages, fearsome postures, disembodied heads, blackened faces—the more one feels what Claudius calls "the poison of deep grief" (4.5.72) as it overtakes the bereaved Ophelia, the only character in the play permitted to express lament for a deceased father openly and directly to a king who represses and manipulates necessary rites of mourning.[23]

To the left of Ophelia is perhaps another female figure presented in profile, looking in the direction of—but not quite at—the mass of distorted figures. A transparent rectangular shape enclosing her head extends into a crumpled square, then funnels or billows diagonally upward, twisting into a downward slope where, with jagged edges, it becomes a disheveled, opaque version of the rectangle framing the head. It is as if "poor Ophelia / Divided from herself and her fair judgment" is now seen in two versions, one looking at a cloudy parody of her own face, visible within the transparent frame.

The doubleness in Purcell's image is not simply that implied by Claudius's either-or ("pictures or mere beasts"). Purcell complicates the picture Claudius presents: she offers a divided view of Ophelia rather than a divided Ophelia. Crowded to the margin, outnumbered by images of a frightening future, Ophelia stands erect, even as she undergoes transformation. The "mere beasts" are there, but so is she.

Purcell's *Twenty Shadows* (38) alludes to a speech in which Bushy, a follower of the doomed King Richard II, tries to comfort the grieving Queen, who fears, quite appropriately, for her husband's safety. Bushy's speech, like Purcell's images, offers a view of Shakespeare's perspective on perspective:

> Each substance of a grief hath twenty shadows
> Which shows like grief itself but is not so.
> For sorrow's eye, glazèd with blinding tears,
> Divides one thing entire to many objects—
> Like perspectives, which, rightly gazed upon,
> Show nothing but confusion; eyed awry,
> Distinguish form.
> (Shakespeare, *Richard II*, 2.2.14–20)

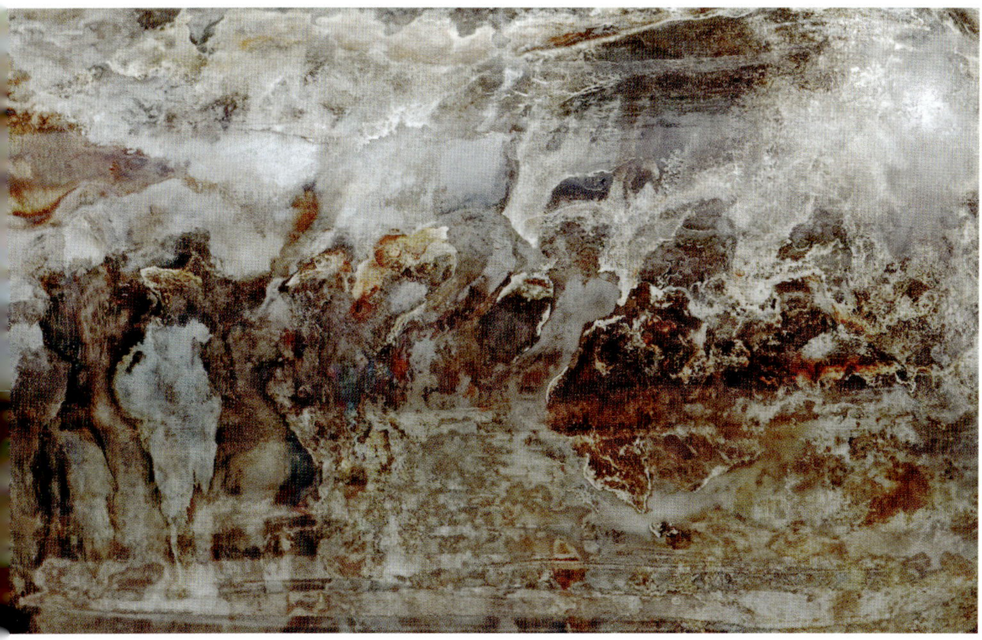

PLATE 33. We Are Pictures. 2009–10.

Courtesy of Rosamond Purcell.

Bushy suggests that the Queen's sorrowful eye, rather than simply dividing something from itself, multiplies a single entity into many objects or images. Then he compares this effect to that of a "perspective" or anamorphic picture that, gazed at head-on, will appear confused or distorted, its true form only becoming clear when viewed at a slant.

Twenty Shadows is described by Purcell in "Eyed Awry": "Against the light, . . . each of the threadlike oxidized figures casts a shadow as though at a different time of day. As if on gallows and lost in the glare, they hover, souls above a desiccated ground."[24] In this ekphrasis, we see Purcell as writer and Purcell as photographer in conversation. She writes her own dramatic scene, while at the same time keeping her photographer's eye on the effects of natural light. These shadows (which I count again and again, never arriving at the same number twice) are at once elongated dark threads angling upward and a congregation of slender human figures set beneath a bluish haze intersected by a whitish horizontal bar. They seem affiliated with one another in some indecipherable way and yet remain utterly distinct, each unique. A thick snake-like form curls across the lower edge of the photograph, its black markings possibly suggesting eyes, noses, and mouths. Purcell's *Twenty Shadows* is an image Bushy would not have shown the Queen.

Asked if any of the pictures in *Landscapes of the Passing Strange* are rendered in anamorphic perspective, Purcell replies: "The perspective has been altered by reflection but not in the classic sense—in the way that change of perspective would reveal some alternative 'truth.' That is not the purpose."[25] Purcell is speaking, as a photographer, of the effects of mirrored bottles and their mysterious reflections. In Shakespeare's plays, especially the late romances, change of perspective reveals some alternative "truth": in *The Tempest*, unorganized noise becomes music that beguiles and speaks; in *The Winter's Tale*, a statue, seen with the eyes of awakened faith, returns a woman who seemed, like Lear's Cordelia, to be gone forever.

Perspective thrown upon perspective is what Shakespearean drama, early and late, offers. The title of Michael Witmore's introductory essay in *Landscapes of the Passing Strange*, "More Strange than True," alludes to the skeptical speech of Theseus, who, in the last scene of Shakespeare's early comedy, *A Midsummer Night's Dream*, denies the existence of the whole middle of the play that the audience has been viewing with delight and wonder. He is contradicted by his wife, Hippolyta, who claims that "minds transfigured so together" (the four lovers' and also the audience's) may have witnessed "something of great constancy; / . . . howsoever, strange and admirable [wondrous]" (5.1.24–27). Theseus's wry eye is also contested, in theater's terms, by the appearance of Puck, representing the fairy world, alone on stage at the end of the play, speaking directly to the audience. There is no further perspective beyond the staging of this final speech in

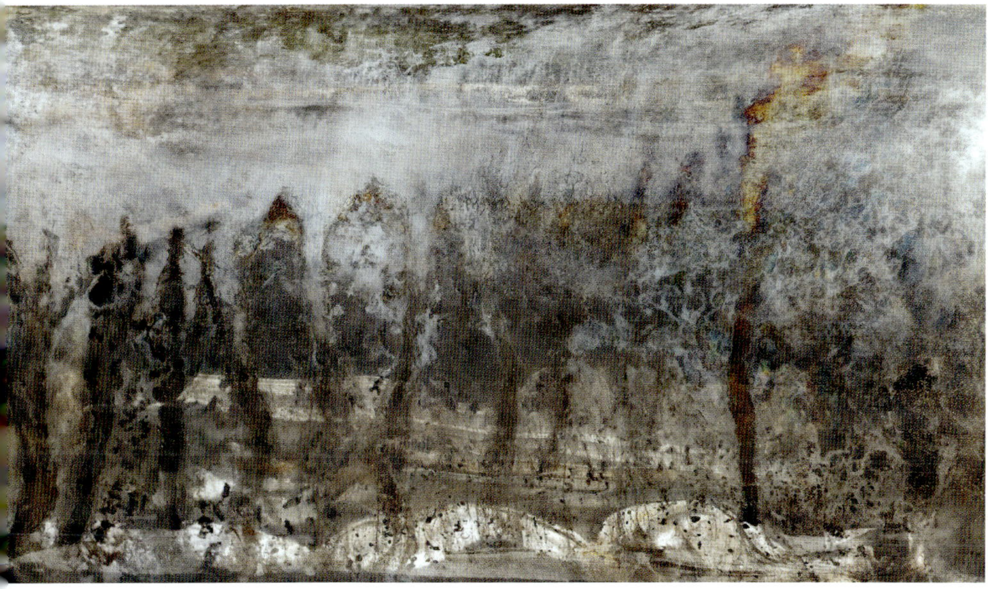

PLATE 34. Twenty Shadows. 2009–10.

Courtesy of Rosamond Purcell.

which Puck makes us reflect on the kind of reality theater offers. Purcell's images invite a plurality of perspectives that encourage us to reflect on photography's version of "reality" as well as our own. Warwick Wadlington, in his study of Faulknerian tragedy, argues quite convincingly that a work of fiction "defiantly solicits the reader's collaborative performance."[26] Wadlington's observation clearly applies to the viewers of visual images as well.

An Art That Nature Makes (16–17) foregrounds what Michael Witmore describes as "riotous buds of green and white," suggesting, he says, the way Shakespeare's own images "grow in tangles."[27] The title alludes to a debate between Perdita and her lover's father, Polixenes, over the suitability of "bastard" flowers, nature cultivated by the art of the gardener. Polixenes argues that "nature is made better by no mean / But nature makes that mean. So over that art / Which you say adds to nature is an art / That nature makes."

> This is an art
> Which does mend nature—change it rather; but
> The art itself is nature.
> (Shakespeare, *The Winter's Tale*, 4.4.89–92, 95–97)

This passage looks forward to the final scene in the play when a work of art, like many of Purcell's own images, not only mends nature but "change[s] it rather."

In Purcell's photograph, it is a little hard to see "buds of green and white," but it is easy to see tangles of enormous vegetation spreading over the landscape in the bottom half of the picture. These huge twisting forms evoke ancient sea creatures as much as they do the twisting tendrils or roots of giant plants. Tubular forms curve and wind, sometimes overlaying each other, becoming somewhat greener as they fade into the rolling meadows and hills in the middle distance.

Above is a bluish sky beneath a slightly ominous, dark horizontal blur extending from one side of the frame to the other. (When the photograph is turned sideways, this looming shape may suggest a human face in profile, with

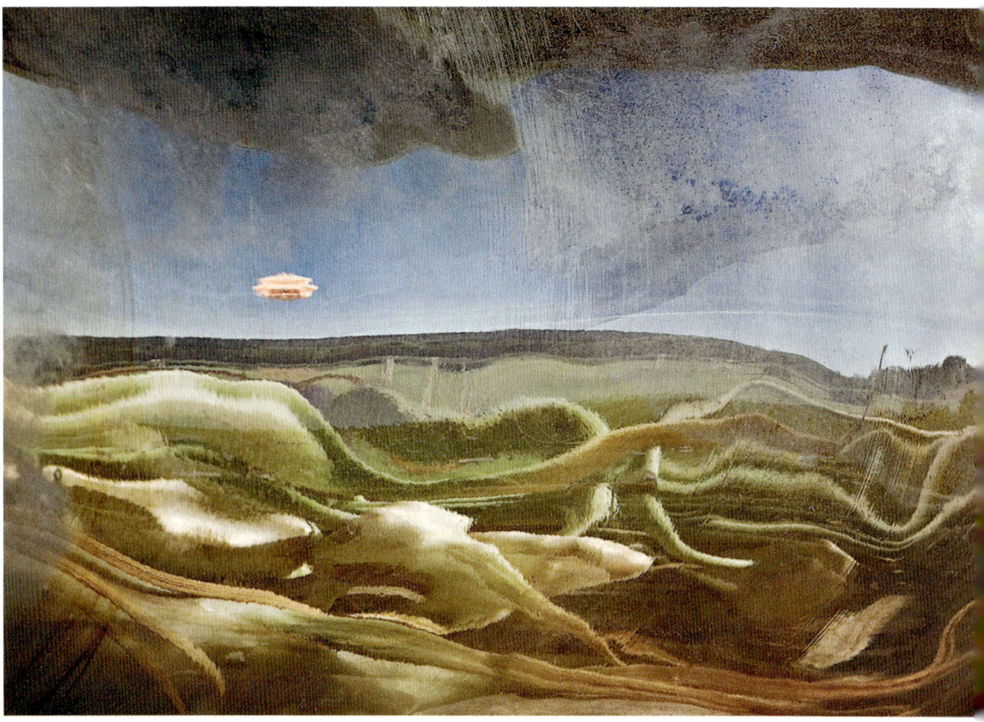

PLATE 35. An Art That Nature Makes. 2009–10.

Courtesy of Rosamond Purcell.

a long curved nose and one open blue eye.) A mysterious pink object appears in the sky, suggesting a sun-suffused cloud or a rising/setting sun, just to the left of center, as if offering a possible perspective from above on what appears at ground level to be an unsortable tangle of images in the natural world. The art that nature makes is problematic, as Purcell dramatizes in her own photographic art.

Two last images, both from *The Winter's Tale,* present, separately, a child and a "dead" parent. In the first, we see the baby Perdita, left to die on the famously non-existent seacoast of Bohemia at the command of her father, who believes her to be a bastard. There she is miraculously found and raised by an old shepherd. To his son, returning from the shipwreck of those who brought the infant to land, the shepherd says: "Thou metst with things dying, I with things new-born. Here's a sight for thee" (Shakespeare, *The Winter's Tale*, 3.3.104–5). It is the first hint in the play that dying and new birth may be connected.

In *Perdita's Landing* (26), Perdita ("the lost one") lies on a red chair or pillow, face aglow. Beside her are indistinct luminous images of gold artifacts, representing the treasure that has been left with her. Above the baby, the multicolored sky is a beautiful medley of blues, rusty browns, and off-whites. A darker background beneath poses no threat, or if it does, it is literally in the background of the child's destiny. Perdita herself is the treasure, and yet another treasure is waiting for her at the end of the play.

That treasure is imaged in Purcell's *Awake Your Faith* (23), a reflection of, and on, one of the most beautiful and mystifying moments of transformation in Shakespeare. Perdita's mother, Hermione, apparently driven to death sixteen years earlier by her husband's mistaken belief in her infidelity, returns in the form of a statue, a gift of Paulina to the reunited father and daughter. Paulina says to those who stand in wonder, "mocked with art" by Hermione's "dead likeness": "It is required / You do awake your faith."

> [To HERMIONE] 'Tis time. Descend. Be stone no more. Approach.
> Strike all that look upon with marvel. Come,
> I'll fill your grave up. Stir. Nay, come away.
> Bequeath to death your numbness, for from him
> Dear life redeems you.
> (Shakespeare, *The Winter's Tale*, 5.3. 68, 15, 94–95, 99–103)

This scene in which, contrary to Shakespeare's source, the dead mother returns is variously interpreted as a trick or a miracle, a female resurrection. The debate between Polixenes and Perdita, referred to earlier, is, in a sense, renewed and transfigured in the final scene of the play and in Purcell's image. The art that offers a dead likeness is replaced by the living form it represents.

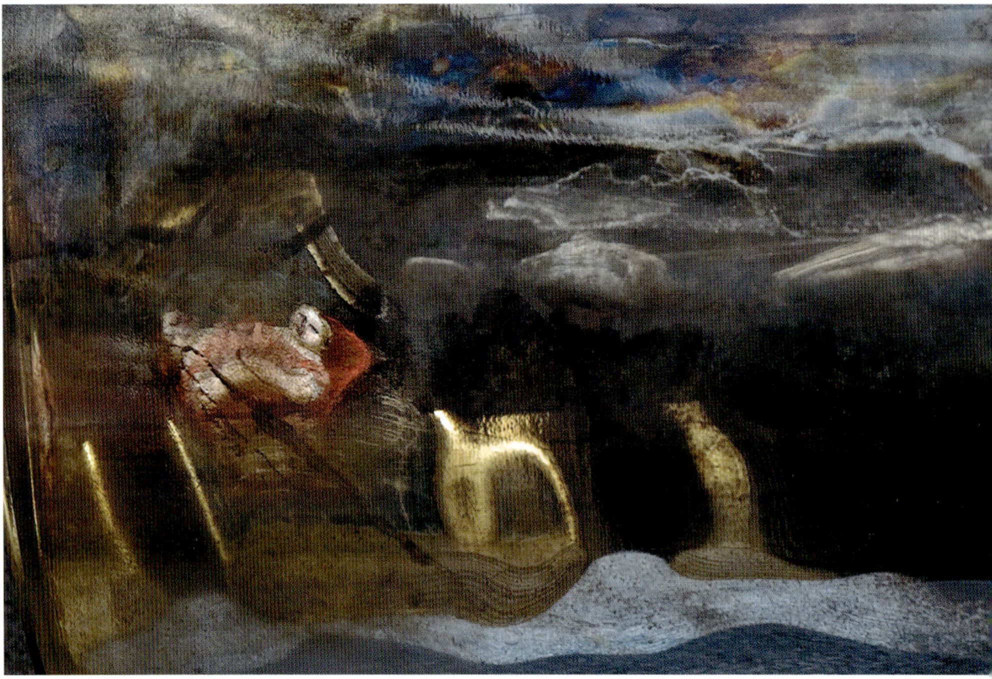

PLATE 36. Perdita's Landing. 2009–10.

Courtesy of Rosamond Purcell.

In *Awake Your Faith*, the perspective is from below the statue, as would be Perdita's, so that we too look up, and up, at the about-to-descend figure of Hermione returning from a statue to life. A transcendent moment arrives as we follow the camera's upward gaze. Eyed awry, Hermione is and is not Hermione. Unlike the ghost in *Hamlet*, the dead parent really returns; unlike Lear's looking futilely for possible signs of life on Cordelia's stilled lips, Hermione's finding her daughter alive is no less a miracle than her own reappearance:

> Tell me, mine own,
> Where hast thou been preserved?
> (Shakespeare, *The Winter's Tale*, 5.3.124–125)

This is precisely what we would wish to ask Hermione and precisely what the play will not tell us.

Paulina says of the statue, "look upon with marvel." Looking at Purcell's photograph may awaken the viewer's faith in miraculous transformation. The almost

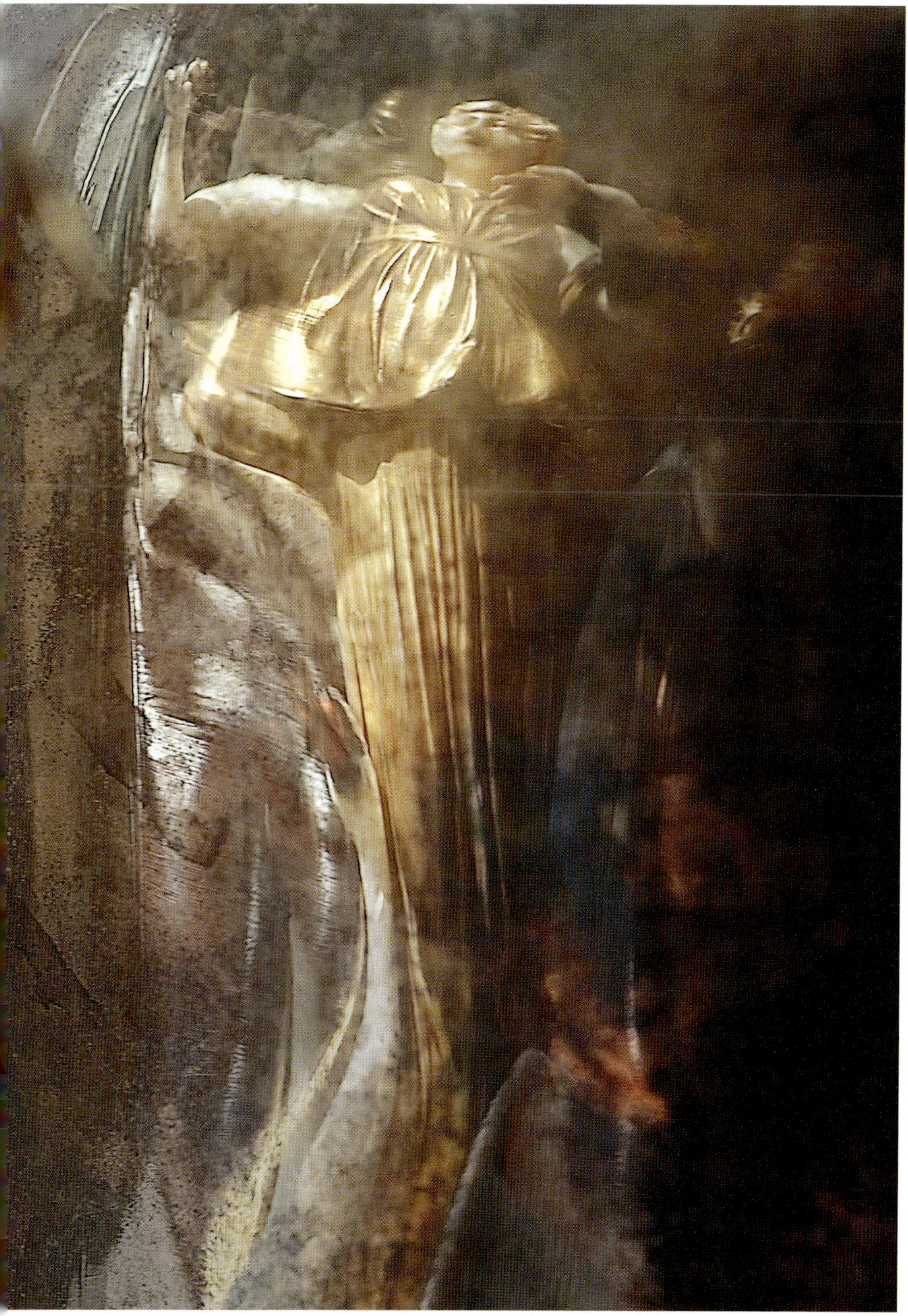

PLATE 37. Awake Your Faith. 2009–10.

Courtesy of Rosamond Purcell.

impossibly elongated figure of a woman, with foreshortened head, right arm upraised and left hand extended forward as if to begin an embrace of a missing daughter, is clothed in folds of gold, similar to the luminous golden treasures with which Purcell surrounds the infant Perdita in Bohemia. Hermione's mouth seems to hold a smile that would be fully visible only from a perspective above her head. Her raised eyes, slits of dark shadow, see what we cannot see. One breast is highlighted in a kind of golden-white radiance, as if dramatizing the maternal function her death forestalled. To the right and just below the partially extended left arm a tiny head appears. It seems to suggest the diminished state of any onlooker, especially Leontes, whose unawakened faith in Hermione caused the loss of unrecoverable life with her daughter and husband. This small pale face looks more ghostly than the statuesque Hermione, who seems to enter a life in which art and nature each play their part.

In the background of the golden Hermione are suggestions of vegetable life: in the upper left corner, a petal-like shaft of green; in the lower right, flower-like areas of color. In the lower left corner, a mysterious, speckled, triangular shape, possibly a remnant of the world Hermione has just left or of the world she will now enter, directs the eye upward toward a spiraling form that seems to partner the figure of Hermione—perhaps the discarded winding sheet of her burial or a phantasmagoric image of another realm.[28] If the photograph is turned on its side, one might see faintly, beneath Hermione's upraised right elbow, another tiny figure, perhaps that of her dead son, Mamillius, who is truly gone forever.

Like Delilah in "The Burning," a heroic female figure takes center stage; both statue-like and fluid, she seems to ascend even as the situation posits a descent. In her transformation from one form to another, Hermione emerges whole from the bottle.

Welty as writer seems to downplay and virtually abandon photography even while her fiction remains visual in texture. Purcell frees text/language from its moorings, reconstituting it in one arresting image after another, yet she herself is always writing—writing about the photographic art that does not displace or replace writing itself.

We feel the strangeness, the intricate layering, of a returning vision in Purcell's *Awake Your Faith*. The camera, that instrument of seeming transferal of "life" to page, like the play that transfers life to the stage, tells us only a secret about a secret, the final gift of art and nature. It is a gift offered by the photographic eyes and visualizing minds of both Eudora Welty and Rosamond Purcell—as well as by Shakespeare's vision of experience. Ultimately, the "story," for writer and photographer alike, for those who write with light, is the story of the ineffable.

Epilogue

It seems appropriate here to offer a brief recapitulation. My intention in *Serious Daring* has been to shed light on the paradoxical affinities between two visionary artists, Eudora Welty and Rosamond Purcell. In their inverse trajectories, Welty and Purcell abandon the art they first pursued, and yet the art seemingly left behind stubbornly accompanies the chosen art.

Welty, who early in her life seemed to give up her wish to be taken seriously as a photographer, became a celebrated short story writer, novelist, essayist, lecturer, memoirist—and, finally, photographer. Purcell, who initially wished to become a writer of fiction, has become an internationally acclaimed photographer as well as an author and memoirist. For both these photographer-writers, the tensions and ambivalence underlying their different journeys have become an integral part of their art.

During her long life, Welty consistently referred to her magnificent black-and-white photographs of small-town Mississippi and New York City life as "snapshots." She viewed photography and writing as "two unrelated things,"[1] believing that, unlike the click of her camera, "a fuller awareness of what I needed to find out about people and their lives had to be sought for through another way, through writing stories."[2] Welty's fiction is filled with abundant, suggestive traces of the seemingly abandoned art of photography. At the age of ninety, Welty was, in fact, considering publishing a new collection of photographs, *Country Churchyards*.[3]

Just as Welty's fiction is full of references to photographs, photographers, and photography, Purcell's photographic work is filled with images of books, texts, writing. Visual images and writing increasingly partner each other in Purcell's collections of photographs. In her memoir, *Owls Head*, writing takes pride of place while photographs—miniaturized and printed in black and white—are reduced to mere endnotes. For each artist, the recovery of what seemed left behind, gone forever, represents a refusal to turn her back on a past that becomes a haunting presence in her life and work.

Eudora Welty and Rosamond Purcell cross and re-cross, again and again, the boundary between literary and visual art, between writing and photography. They show that continuity and discontinuity in one's career can operate in complicated and productive ways; reluctant abandonment and dogged pursuit of one's artistic projects may not cancel each other out.

Welty began her illustrious literary career in the 1930s. Purcell began her career as a celebrated art photographer in the 1960s. Despite obvious differences in their generational, geographical, cultural, and familial worlds, the work of each artist is a mirror image of the other. Not only do the artistic journeys of these two writer-photographers converge, but they form a seemingly endless circle in which writing begets visual images and visual images beget writing.

In Purcell's photographs, as in Welty's extraordinary similes, there is a seemingly miraculous change of one thing into another, a kind of alchemy. Purcell animates what is decaying, damaged, burned, termite-eaten, "*sublimely diminished*" (italics Purcell's). For example, she gives a name to a rusty, discarded typewriter she disinterred in a Maine junkyard: *Underwoodensis corrupta*, reimagining its life "as a close invertebrate cousin to an echinoid."[4] No longer functioning as an instrument of writing, the typewriter is transformed in Purcell's visual image. Dismissed from one kind of identity, the typewriter is reawakened and given a new afterlife, much like the reawakening of Purcell's deferred vocation as a writer.

Like Purcell's visual images, Welty's fiction creates scenes of transformation. In *Losing Battles,* a lost apron crouches like a possum; a tobacco tin undergoes a sea-change, shining like a ruby.[5] The ultimate source of "resurrection" in Welty's fiction is the living memory that wakes the dead.

It is possible, therefore, to claim that in the visionary art of Eudora Welty and Rosamond Purcell something magical occurs. A new life is given to what seemed dying or dead. This is as true of their art as it is of their careers. Purcell has said that her recent book, *Landscapes of the Passing Strange: Reflections from Shakespeare*, "aspires to mystery."[6] It would be difficult to find a work of fiction by Eudora Welty that does not fulfill that aspiration. The mystery of human life hinted at in her snapshots is fully present in Welty's stories and novels.

Bold curiosity, suspension of disbelief, and testing of boundaries define the work of both these visionary artists. Eudora Welty and Rosamond Purcell make us see, in writing and in visual image, what else there is to see in what we are seeing—that is, they offer us a new way of seeing. In Welty's fiction, a vision of mystery is transacted in writing. In Purcell's photography, a vision of wonder is transacted through visual images.

In *Serious Daring*, I have placed Eudora Welty and Rosamond Purcell in unexpected juxtaposition and allowed that juxtaposition to throw light on each. Indeed, unexpected juxtaposition is the hallmark of each of these artists and creates a bond between them. Welty and Purcell are career-changing artists who raise questions (and answer some) about the relation between verbal and visual art; they represent successful pursuit (fiction for Welty and photography for Purcell) and seeming abandonment (photography for Welty and fiction for Purcell) of an artistic trajectory; both negotiate the experience of continuity and discontinuity in the making of art.

Beyond all such juxtapositions, I hope to have shown in *Serious Daring* the power of juxtaposition itself. For me, each artist continues to light up in the presence of the other and each continues to throw light on the other.

Notes

Preface

1. Roland Barthes, *Camera Lucida: Reflections on Photography*, trans. Richard Howard (New York: Farrar, Straus and Giroux, 1981), 87, 67, 73, 100. (It has been suggested that there is no Winter Garden photograph, but, in the absence of other evidence, I see no reason not to take Barthes at his word.) Cf. Barthes's famous statement: "The photographic image . . . *is a message without a code.*" Roland Barthes, *Image-Music-Text*, trans. Stephen Heath (New York: Hill and Wang, 1977), 17.
2. Eudora Welty, *One Writer's Beginnings* (Cambridge: Harvard University Press, 1984), 99.
3. Barthes, *Camera Lucida*, 9, 82; Susan Sontag, *On Photography* (New York: Doubleday, 1989), 15–16.
4. In the case of John Keats's "Ode on a Grecian Urn," we assume the urn is fictional.
5. W.J.T. Mitchell suggests that "in a certain sense all ekphrasis is notational, and seeks to create a specific image that is to be found only in the text as its 'resident alien,' and is to be found nowhere else. Even those forms of ekphrasis that occur in the presence of the described image disclose a tendency to alienate or displace the object, to make it disappear in favor of the total image being produced by the ekphrasis." W.J.T. Mitchell, *Picture Theory: Essays on Verbal and Visual Representation* (Chicago: University of Chicago Press, 1994), 157n19.

Introduction

1. Wright Morris, *Time Pieces: Photographs, Writing, and Memory* (New York: Aperture, 1989), 148, 26. (I assume Wright is alluding to William Blake's heroic version of Satan when he quotes from Book I of John Milton's *Paradise Lost*: "The mind is its own place, and in itself / Can make a Heav'n of Hell, a Hell of Heav'n." John Milton, *Paradise Lost, A Poem in Twelve Books*, ed. Merritt Y. Hughes (New York: Odyssey Press, 1962), ll. 254–55, p. 13.
2. Suzanne Marrs, *Eudora Welty: A Biography* (New York: Harcourt, 2005), 569, 571.
3. Rosamond Purcell, telephone conversation with author, October 18, 2009.
4. Rosamond Purcell, email correspondence with author, November 11, 2009.
5. Walter Benjamin, *Illuminations*, trans. Harry Zohn (New York: Schocken Books, 1969), 224.
6. Richard Wolin, *Walter Benjamin: An Aesthetic of Redemption* (New York: Columbia University Press, 1982), 237.
7. Benjamin, *Illuminations*, 188.
8. Wolin, 238. Benjamin notes that "the camera records our likeness without returning our gaze." Benjamin, *Illuminations*, 188, 187.
9. Benjamin, *Illuminations*, 200n17.

10. Mary Price, *The Photograph: A Strange Confined Space* (Stanford: Stanford University Press, 1994), 141.
11. Marianne Moore, *Complete Poems* (Harmondsworth, UK: Penguin, 1982), ll.1,4–5, p. 218.
12. Richard Howard, "Charles Baudelaire," in *Misgivings* (New York: Atheneum, 1979), 40.
13. Welty, *One Writer's Beginnings*, 10.
14. René Paul Barilleaux, foreword, in *Passionate Observer: Eudora Welty among Artists of the Thirties*, ed. René Paul Barilleaux (Jackson: Mississippi Museum of Art, 2002), 7.
15. Price, *The Photograph*, 75.
16. W.J.T. Mitchell, *What Do Pictures Want? The Lives and Loves of Images* (Chicago: University of Chicago Press, 2005), 10.
17. See Géraldine Chouard, *Eudora Welty et la photographie: Naissance d'une vision* (Paris: Michel Houdiard, 2012), on Welty's persistent engagement with photography.
18. Eudora Welty, *Photographs* (Jackson: University Press of Mississippi, 1989), xv.
19. Eudora Welty, "Place in Fiction," in *The Eye of the Story: Selected Essays and Reviews* (New York: Random House, 1970), 125.
20. Rosamond Purcell, phone conversation with author, April 6, 2010.

1. Eudora Welty: Nine Photographs of Talking

1. Jeff Wall's carefully constructed, extremely large color prints, often weeks or even months in the planning, are a far cry from Welty's black-and-white snapshots, but his sense of how "talking escapes, and so . . . is itself an image of what is both included and never included in a picture" would be shared by a writer whose mastery of talk in *Losing Battles* has few rivals. Jeff Wall, *Jeff Wall: Selected Essays and Interviews* (New York: Museum of Modern Art, 2007), 252.
2. Eudora Welty, "Looking Back at the First Story," in *Eudora Welty: Occasions, Selected Writings*, ed. Pearl Amelia McHaney (Jackson: University Press of Mississippi, 2009), 305n. The twenty-six-year-old Welty adds, "I did the job out of pure interest, but it broke me, so I hope a publisher here [in New York] will buy them" (ibid.).
3. Erskine Caldwell, quoted in Patti Carr Black, "Back Home in Jackson," in *Passionate Observer*, ed. René Paul Barilleaux, 35–36.
4. Eudora Welty, *One Time, One Place: Mississippi in the Depression, A Snapshot Album* (New York: Random House, 1971), 5.
5. "In 1934 or so she finished a story ["Acrobats in a Park"], which would not be published for forty-three years." Marrs, *Eudora Welty*, 43–44.
6. Black, "Back Home in Jackson," 35. Black notes: "It seems clear that [Welty] was seriously considering a career in photography" (ibid.).
7. Marrs, *Eudora Welty*, 50.
8. Welty, "Looking Back at the First Story," 299.
9. Marrs, *Eudora Welty*, 52.
10. Eudora Welty's subsequent three collections are *Photographs* (1989), *Country Churchyards* (2000), and *Eudora Welty as Photographer* (2009). (This last book was

conceived without the participation of Welty and published posthumously.) "Eudora Welty in New York: Photographs of the Early 1930s," organized by photography curator Sean Corcoran, was presented at the Museum of the City of New York from November 7, 2008, through February 16, 2009. This superb exhibit, which I saw on December 7, 2008, restaged Welty's 1936 photographic exhibition, complemented by a selection of pictures she took of New York City.

11. Marrs, *Eudora Welty*, 53–54. William Trevor writes of the amateur photographer Florian Kilderry: "It was a place he might have come to [with his camera] . . . , Florian thought. But memory would more tellingly preserve it." William Trevor, *Love and Summer* (New York: Viking, 2009), 137.
12. Alan Trachtenberg, *Reading American Photographs: Images as History, Matthew Brady to Walker Evans* (New York: Hill and Wang, 1989), 251.
13. The one possible exception is *Royal Street/New Orleans/1930s*.
14. Welty, *Photographs*, xxvi, xxviii.
15. Welty, *One Time, One Place*, 4–5. Asked later in an interview why she considered her pictures in *One Time, One Place* snapshots and not photographs, Welty replied: "Well, they were snapshots. It refers to the way they were taken, which gave meaning to the book. They were taken spontaneously—to catch something as I came upon it, something that spoke of the life going on around me. A snapshot's now or never." Welty, *Photographs*, xiii.
16. Timothy Dow Adams, *Light Writing & Life Writing: Photography in Autobiography* (Chapel Hill: University of North Carolina Press, 2000), 159.
17. Welty's snapshots are at times given different captions in different contexts, including publication and gallery shows.
18. The photographs described, with plate numbers, appear in Eudora Welty's 1989 collection, *Photographs*.
19. Eudora Welty, "Literature and the Lens," in *Eudora Welty: Occasions*, ed. McHaney, 71–72. Rosamond Purcell encountered strong resistance to her taking photographs of specimens in natural history museums. "To many curators of scientific collections," she writes, "a browser at the door, with a tripod and without calipers, tends, upon occasion, to raise eyebrows, not to mention blood pressure." Rosamond Purcell, "Afterword," in *Illuminations: A Bestiary*, by Rosamond Wolff Purcell and Stephen Jay Gould (New York: W. W. Norton, 1986), 117. In her memoir, she recounts one of those occasions: "Recently I asked a friendly curator why, some fifteen years earlier, he had refused to let me photograph one of his most splendid toads, crying as he did so, 'Not my Booby!' and clutching the jar in his arms. Because it was a *type specimen,* he said . . . ; of such intrinsic scientific value, he explained, that 'an artistic take is not worthy of it.'" Rosamond Purcell, *Owls Head* (New York: Quantuck Lane Press, 2003), 148.
20. Welty, *Photographs*, xxvii.
21. Jeff Wall, *Jeff Wall: Selected Essays*, 252.
22. Barthes, *Camera Lucida*, 26–27. Michael Fried notes that Barthes's *punctum* "is a pure artifact of the photographic event—'[the photographer] could not *not* photograph

the partial object at the same time as the total object,' is how Barthes phrases it—or perhaps more precisely it is an artifact of the encounter between the product of that event and one particular spectator or beholder." Michael Fried, *Why Photography Matters as Art as Never Before* (New Haven: Yale University Press, 2008), 100. The first spectator of the *punctum* may be the photographer who is beholding, developing, and editing the photograph in the darkroom or on the computer screen.

23. Welty, *One Time, One Place*, 7.

2. Photography in Fiction

1. Reynolds Price, foreword, in Eudora Welty, *Photographs*, viii.
2. Welty, *One Time, One Place*, 8.
3. Eudora Welty, "Hello and Good-Bye," in *Eudora Welty: Occasions*, ed. McHaney, 287, 289, 291.
4. Eudora Welty, "The Whistle," in *The Collected Stories of Eudora Welty* (New York: Harcourt Brace Jovanovich, 1980), 57, 58, 61.
5. Eudora Welty, *Delta Wedding* (New York: Harcourt, Brace and Company, 1945), 217, 218.
6. Eudora Welty, "Kin," in *The Collected Stories*, 552, 561, 564, 565.
7. Eudora Welty, "Words into Fiction," in *The Eye of the Story: Selected Essays and Reviews* (New York: Random House, 1970), 137.
8. Eudora Welty, "Going to Naples," in *The Collected Stories*, 577, 576, 574–75, 591–92, 595–96, 600.
9. For the backstory of Eugene Hudson MacLain and the relation of "Music from Spain" to other stories originally published in *The Golden Apples* (1949), see Michael Kreyling, *Eudora Welty's Achievement of Order* (Baton Rouge: Louisiana State University Press, 1980), 94–100.
10. Eudora Welty, "Music from Spain," in *The Collected Stories*, 397, 405, 422.
11. When asked in an interview to define a "pose-yourself photo," Eudora Welty says: "A man came through little towns and set up a make-shift studio in somebody's parlor and let it be known that he would be taking pictures all day in this place, and a stream of people came. He had backdrops—sepia trees and a stool—and then let them pose themselves. That was an itinerant livelihood during the Depression. Itinerants were welcome, bringing excitement like that, when towns were remote and nobody ever went anywhere." Welty, *Photographs*, xx.
12. Eudora Welty, "Why I Live at the P.O.," in *The Collected Stories*, 49.
13. Eudora Welty, "The Key," in *The Collected Stories*, 35, 36.
14. Eudora Welty, "The Winds," in *The Collected Stories*, 217.
15. Katherine Henninger, *Ordering the Façade: Photography and Contemporary Southern Women's Writing* (Chapel Hill: University of North Carolina Press, 2007), 43–44. For a discussion of Welty's concern with issues of race, see Harriet Pollack, ed., *Eudora Welty: Whiteness and Race* (Athens: University of Georgia Press, 2013).
16. Eudora Welty, "Livvie," in *The Collected Stories*, 228, 231, 238–239. In the story "At the Landing," Jenny comes to know "that a fragile mystery was in everyone and in herself" (Welty, *The Collected Stories*, 245).

17. See Henninger, *Ordering the Façade*, 188n11.
18. Eudora Welty, "Petrified Man," in *The Collected Stories*, 20, 27.
19. Eudora Welty, "At the Landing," in *The Collected Stories*, 242.
20. Eudora Welty, "The Bride of Innisfallen," in *The Collected Stories*, 516, 518.
21. Reynolds Price, foreword, in Welty, *Photographs*, viii.
22. Welty, *One Time, One Place*, 8.

3. The Visualizing Mind

1. Barthes, *Camera Lucida*, 55.
2. Welty, *Photographs*, xvi. When asked if a particular scene in *The Optimist's Daughter* might be "a subconscious reflection" of one of her photographs of Mardi Gras in New Orleans, Welty responds: "Not as a reflection; I've seen it directly in life. But I went back and looked up my photographs *after* I had written this" (italics mine). Ibid.
3. Welty, *Photographs*, xv.
4. Christopher Ricks, "Undermining Keats," *New York Review of Books* 54, no. 20 (December 17, 2009): 49. Ricks points out that "there isn't a counterpart to the word 'visualize' for any of the other senses. . . . [W]e don't audibilize, tactilize, gustalize, or olfactorize, any more than we have a counterpart in the other senses for what it is to picture something." Ibid.
5. Eudora Welty, "The Wanderers," in *The Collected Stories*, 428.
6. Welty, *Eudora Welty: Occasions*, 302.
7. For this insight, as well as for much else, I am indebted to David Cole.
8. Welty, *Photographs*, xvi.
9. *Death Comes to the Old Lady* (1969), a series of five black-and-white photographs by the American photographer Duane Michals, shows a sequence in which the setting remains the same but the figures appear and disappear. We first see an elderly woman seated near a hallway to an adjoining room. In the second shot, a blurry man appears in the adjoining room. In the third shot, the man, less blurry, has moved closer to the seated woman. In the fourth shot, the man is replaced by a large, formless shadow. In the final shot, the shadow has disappeared; the woman, rising from her chair, is disappearing in a blur. See John Szarkowski, *Looking at Photographs, 100 Pictures from the Collection of the Museum of Modern Art* (New York: Museum of Modern Art, 1973), 210–11.
10. Eudora Welty, "A Memory," in *The Collected Stories*, 75–76, 79, 80.
11. John P. Schaefer, *An Ansel Adams Guide: Basic Techniques of Photography, Book I* (New York: Little, Brown and Company, 1992), 66–67.
12. Henri Cartier-Bresson's quote appears above two untitled photographs by Robert Doisneau in John Szarkowski's *The Photographer's Eye* (New York: Museum of Modern Art, 1966), 112–13. The first of these two 1957–1958 photographs shows a photographer bent beneath a dark cloth as he focuses his camera on its tripod, preparing to take a wedding picture of five tiers of bridal party and guests. In the second photograph, there is the same scene, except that the photographer and all the people posed for his picture are absent. The camera on its tripod remains in front of empty bleachers.

13. See, for example, Eudora Welty's *Home abandoned, old Natchez Trace/near Clinton/1930s* (Plate 117); *House with bottle-trees/Simpson County/1941* (Plate 121); and *Ruins of Windsor/Port Gibson/1942* (Plate 119), with the shadow of the photographer in the foreground, in Welty, *Photographs*. See also *Eudora Welty, Ruins, Natchez, Mississippi, post-1936*, in *Eudora Welty as Photographer: Photographs by Eudora Welty*, ed. Pearl Amelia McHaney (Jackson: University Press of Mississippi, 2009), 29.
14. Cf., for example, "the sharp sword" of Revelations 2.12; the "pale horse" in 6.8; the "living fountains of waters" in 7.17; the fire burning in 8.5, 8.7, and 8.10; the locusts in 9.3; the horses and wings in 9.9; and "every unclean and hateful bird" in 18.2. In the final chapter of Revelations, "a pure river of water of life" and "whosoever will, let him take the water of life freely" (22.1, 22.17), along with 7.17, are possible contexts for Delilah's escape into the river at the end of "The Burning." Revelations, Authorized (King James) Version of the Bible (1611).
15. Eudora Welty, "The Burning," in *The Collected Stories*, 482–83, 486–87, 490, 491–93.
16. For example, in *Delta Wedding*, Welty writes: "Only bits of sunlight, bright as butterflies, came through the dark tree"; "something that . . . went to a law of his being, that came to it, like the butterfly to his sight. [George] could have lifted a finger and touched, held the butterfly, but he did not. The butterfly he loved, the knife not"; "[Dabney] saw Uncle George . . . on a picnic, . . . with a butterfly going across his gaze, a way to make her imagine all at once that in that moment he had erected an entire, complicated house for the butterfly inside his sleepy body"; "And there was that same wonderful butterfly, yellow with black markings, that [Ellen] had seen here yesterday. It was spending its whole life on this one abelia" (Welty, *Delta Wedding*, 37, 34, 225). (Abelias are shrubs in the honeysuckle family; flowering continues from late spring to fall.)
17. I am indebted to Meg Gertmenian for this reading of Welty's phrase, "one whale made of his own grave." Meg Gertmenian, email correspondence with author, October 21, 2009.
18. Ruth D. Weston sees Delilah as "the true protagonist of 'The Burning.'" Ruth D. Weston, *Gothic Traditions and Narrative Techniques in the Fiction of Eudora Welty* (Baton Rouge: Louisiana State University Press, 1994), 78.
19. Eudora Welty, "The Burning," in *Collected Stories*, 494.
20. *Eudora Welty*, ed. Harold Bloom (New York: Chelsea House Publishers, 1986), 6, 9.
21. Alfred, Lord Tennyson, "The Lady of Shalott," in *The Norton Anthology of English Literature*, vol. E, ed. Stephen Greenblatt et al., 8th ed. (New York: Norton, 2006), ll. 38, 65, 128, 130, pp. 1115, 1117.

4. Doubling

1. Reynolds Price, foreword, in Welty, *Photographs*, x.
2. See John F. Fleischauer's fine essay, "Focus of Mystery: Eudora Welty's Prose Style," *Southern Literary Journal* 5, no. 2 (Spring 1973): 65. See also Michael Kreyling,

"Words into Criticism: Eudora Welty's Essays and Reviews," in *Eudora Welty, Thirteen Essays: Selected from Eudora Welty, Critical Essays*, ed. Peggy Whitman Prenshaw (Jackson: University Press of Mississippi, 1983), 224–35; Harriet Pollack, "'Words Between Strangers': On Welty, Her Style, and Her Audience," in *Welty: A Life in Literature*, ed. Albert J. Devlin (Jackson: University Press of Mississippi, 1987), 54–81. Ruth D. Weston notes Gabriella Serto's "seeing double" in Welty's story "Going to Naples"; in *Delta Wedding*, Weston finds "pervasive comparisons of the family to the wilderness and its various manifestations," although she considers the latter "an extended metaphor." Weston, *Gothic Traditions and Narrative Techniques*, 86, 109. See also Barbara Harrell Carson, *Eudora Welty: Two Pictures at Once in Her Frame* (Troy, NY: Whitson, 1992).

3. Diane Arbus, quoted in Michael Sprinker, "Fictions of the Self: The End of Autobiography," in *Autobiography: Essays Theoretical and Critical*, ed. James Olney (Princeton: Princeton University Press, 1980), 321.
4. Eudora Welty, "Death of a Traveling Salesman," in *The Collected Stories*, 130.
5. Welty, *Delta Wedding*, 80.
6. Ross Murfin and Supryia M. Ray, *The Bedford Glossary of Critical and Literary Terms*, 3rd ed. (New York: Bedford/St. Martin's, 2009), 190–91.
7. Here is a sample of the multiple shifts of speaker in the free indirect discourse of *Delta Wedding*: "Laura found herself with a picture in her mind" (15); "How Ellen loved their wide and towering foreheads. . . . Dear Orrin, talking so seriously now" (22); India "held the little lamp. . . . It seemed filled with the mysterious and flowing air of night" (49); "Dabney could not help it if she . . . felt beautiful. Does happiness seek out . . . the ones it can humble when it comes at last to show itself?" (49); "Laura felt it wordlessly; the animation of the living generations in the house" (55); "By Aunt Shannon in particular, the members of the family were always looked on with . . . general tenderness and love" (63); "In Ellen's mind dimly was that poetic expression to *shed* beauty. Now she comprehended it [italics Welty's]" (71); Laura shifting to Ellen within a single short paragraph: "Laura almost knew. . . . Ellen saw it" (77); Laura shifting or blurring into Shelley: "Laura had thought. . . . Shelley would not be caught dead wearing any of them [pieces of jewelry]" (82); India and Aunt Tempe's double perspective: "India . . . gazed at her aunt. . . . India could read her mind. The table lamp provoked Aunt Tempe. . . . Aunt Tempe closed her eyes to see Mashula's dulcimer still hanging by that thin ribbon on the wall. . . . India followed her gaze" (97–98); Robbie and Ellen's perspectives converging: "Now for a moment it struck Robbie and also Ellen humbly to earth, for it implied a magnitude, a bounty, that could leave people helpless" (161); an abrupt shift to Ellen's point of view: "It seemed to Ellen at moments" (186); "[Aunt]Tempe . . . experienced not a thought exactly but a truer thing"(190); "the Fairchilds took you in circles, whirling delightedly about, [Robbie] thought, stirring up confusions" (190); "It seemed to Shelley all at once as if . . . [l]ife was too easy—too easily holy, too easily not" (193); "Ellen stood at her window . . . in which there was a touch, today perhaps the first touch, of fall. . . . [N]ow there was over them . . . the distance and clarity of fall, out

of which came a breath of cool. Ellen took it, the breath" (198). See later in chapter 4 my presentation of Ellen as representing both the photographer's eye and the possibility of visionary imagination in *Delta Wedding*.

8. Welty, *Delta Wedding*, 97–98.
9. Ibid., 161.
10. Reynolds Price, foreword, in Welty, *Photographs*, x.
11. Snapshots with blurred backgrounds, discussed in the first chapter, are *Tall story/Utica/1930s* (blurry trees and buildings); *Conversation/Granada/1935* (blurred city buildings); *Royal Street/New Orleans/1930s* (the facial expression of the white-haired woman standing on the balcony is a bit blurred, especially her mouth); *A woman of the 'thirties/Hinds County/1935* (several blurred buildings in the distance). In chapter 5, the snapshot of Welty's mother, *Chestina Andrews Welty/Jackson/1950*, has a somewhat blurred background of garden flowers and plants.
12. Welty, *Delta Wedding*, 82, 84.
13. Ibid., 247.
14. Eudora Welty, "Must the Novelist Crusade?," in *The Eye of the Story*, 158.
15. Eudora Welty, "'Is Phoenix Jackson's Grandson Really Dead?,'" in *The Eye of the Story*, 161.
16. *Delta Wedding*, 247.
17. Louise Westling, *Eudora Welty* (London: Macmillan, 1989), 126. See also Westling's discussion of Welty's use of classical myth, especially the figures of Demeter and Persephone, in *Delta Wedding* and elsewhere. Such allusions may be considered implicit similes. Westling, *Eudora Welty,* 85–126 et passim.
18. Welty, *Photographs*, xiii, xiv.
19. First told by Ellen and Battle's son, Orrin (19), it is retold or referred to by their children, India (58–61), Shelley (87–89), and Roy (115); by Aunt Tempe (115); by Robbie (146–48); by Ellen (157); in dialogue between Robbie and Ellen (162–63); by Battle (in one rhetorical question, "'He didn't do it for you, eh, Robbie?'") (186); by Robbie and George in dialogue (186–187); by Ellen (188); by Robbie (191); and by Ellen (221). Finally, there is a "reenactment" by Shelley (234). All page references are to Welty's *Delta Wedding*. Michael Kreyling discusses the multiple allusions to, and retellings of, the Yellow Dog episode that, "taken together, testify to Welty's self-conscious plan to negate realistic, progressive narrative." Michael Kreyling, *Understanding Eudora Welty* (Columbia: University of South Carolina Press, 1999), 7; see also 88–92.
20. Welty, *Delta Wedding*, 221.
21. Ibid., 191. Robbie adds that George "looked out at the world, at her, sometimes, . . . as if an old story had taken hold of him—entered his flesh." Ibid. This might have been how Welty herself looked out at the world.
22. Welty, *Delta Wedding*, 219–20.
23. Ibid., 104, 226, 227, 221.
24. Ibid., 198.
25. Welty's *Delta Wedding* was published in 1946; *Losing Battles* was published in 1970.

26. Christopher Benfey, *American Audacity: Literary Essays North and South* (Ann Arbor: University of Michigan Press, 2008), 193–94.
27. Welty, *Photographs*, xv, xvi. Suzanne Marrs notes that Welty wrote *Losing Battles* "in fits and starts over a fourteen or fifteen year period," producing "draft after draft," between 1955 and 1970. Suzanne Marrs, *One Writer's Imagination: The Fiction of Eudora Welty* (Baton Rouge: Louisiana State University Press, 2002), 218, 209, 226.
28. Eudora Welty, *Losing Battles* (New York: Vintage, 1978), 402.
29. Mikhail Bakhtin's term "dialogic text" is quoted in Murfin and Ray, *The Bedford Glossary of Critical and Literary Terms*, 392–93.
30. Another possible gloss on the meaning of the title is supplied by Uncle Curtis: "'There ain't no end, it looks like, to what you can lose and still go on living.'" Welty, *Losing Battles*, 309. The title is clearly alluded to when Julia Mortimer's letter to Judge Moody is read aloud at the reunion: "'All my life I've fought a hard war with ignorance. Except in those cases that you can count off your fingers, I lost every battle.'" Ibid., 287. Suzanne Marrs notes that "in the 1969 galleys of the novel, Julia Mortimer feels totally defeated" and says, "'I lost, they won.'" In the altered, published version of 1970, she says, "'Mostly I lost, they won.'" Marrs, *One Writer's Imagination*, 224; Welty, *Losing Battles*, 287.
31. Eudora Welty, "Characters in the Novel," in *Losing Battles*, unnumbered page opposite title page.
32. Welty, "Looking Back at the First Story," *Occasions*, 302.
33. Eudora Welty, "Place in Fiction," in *The Eye of the Story*, 129, 128.
34. Eudora Welty, "Writing and Analyzing a Story," in *The Eye of the Story*, 113.
35. Welty, *Losing Battles*, 118.
36. Ibid., 218, 344–45.
37. Broomsedge is tall, tufted grass found in the southeastern United States.
38. Welty, *Losing Battles*, 353. Cf. "the risen full moon" that the six-year-old Welty imagines herself swallowing. Welty, *One Writer's Beginnings*, 10.
39. Vaughn is the only member of the family who devotes energy to internal reflection.
40. Welty, *Losing Battles*, 350.
41. Ibid., 414.
42. Welty, *One Writer's Beginnings*, 104.
43. Welty, "'Is Phoenix Jackson's Grandson Really Dead?,'" in *The Eye of the Story,* 161.
44. Welty, *One Writer's Beginnings*, 85. Cf. Wallace Stevens: "Said words of the world are the life of the world." Wallace Stevens, "An Ordinary Evening in New Haven," in *The Collected Poems of Wallace Stevens* (New York: Knopf, 1969), Section XII, l.18, p. 474.

5. Reverberations

1. Welty, *Losing Battles,* 314.
2. Ibid., 314–15.
3. When Granny is first moved to the porch, "lights hard as pickaxe blows drove down from every ceiling," a simile that suggests Welty's tactile response to light. Welty, *Losing Battles*, 300.

4. Eudora Welty, "Going to Naples," in *The Collected Stories*, 595.
5. Welty, *Losing Battles*, 315; Welty, *Photographs*, xiv.
6. Welty, *Losing Battles*, 316.
7. Ibid., 317.
8. Suzanne Marrs notes Julia Mortimer's "commitment . . . to the world at large": "Free of family ties, Miss Julia can take the larger view, and she once urged Gloria to share this perspective, to refuse Jack's proposal of marriage, and to turn herself 'into a better teacher and do him and the world some good.'" Marrs, *One Writer's Imagination*, 206.
9. Welty, *Losing Battles*, 317.
10. For Laurel McKelva Hand, the protagonist in Welty's last published novel, *The Optimist's Daughter*, "the past is like . . . [the dead], impervious, and can never be awakened," except by memory, "the somnambulist." Eudora Welty, *The Optimist's Daughter* (New York: Vintage, 1978), 207.
11. See the theory of tragedy proposed in my book, Susan Letzler Cole, *The Absent One: Mourning Ritual, Tragedy, and the Performance of Ambivalence* (University Park: Pennsylvania State University Press, 1985).
12. Recall Roland Barthes's comment on "that rather terrible thing which is there in every photograph: the return of the dead. . . . Photography has something to do with resurrection," and Susan Sontag's declaration: "All photographs are *memento mori*." Barthes, *Camera Lucida*, 82; Sontag, *On Photography*, 16.
13. Welty, *Losing Battles*, 333.
14. Ibid., 257–58.
15. Ibid., 315.
16. Ibid., 332.
17. Welty, *One Writer's Beginnings*, 20–21. In *The Optimist's Daughter*, Laurel remembers that, when she was a child lying in her bed at night, her parents' "two voices reading to each other . . . combined into one unceasing voice . . . [that] wrapped her around as she listened, as still as if she were asleep." Welty, *The Optimist's Daughter*, 71.
18. Welty, *One Writer's Beginnings*, 21.
19. Eudora Welty, foreword, *The Optimist's Daughter*, in *Eudora Welty: Occasions*, ed. McHaney, 312. The novel was originally titled "Poor Eyes." Marrs, *Eudora Welty*, 330.
20. Welty, *The Optimist's Daughter*, 14, 23, 27.
21. Ibid., 29, 28.
22. Ibid., 30, 33.
23. Welty, *Losing Battles*, 372.
24. Welty, *The Optimist's Daughter*, 33, 34.
25. Ibid., 46. There is a strong implication in the novel, however, that Fay McKelva has caused her husband's death by her impatient, agitated attempt to pull him out of his hospital bed. The nurse tells Laurel, "'She taken ahold of him. She was abusing him.'" At the end of the novel, Laurel accuses Fay of hurting her father and hurrying his death: "'What were you trying to scare Father into—when you struck him?'" Welty, *The Optimist's Daughter*, 44, 202.

26. Welty, *The Optimist's Daughter*, 136, 143. One might recall Barthes's refusal, for very different reasons, to exhibit the photograph of his mother in *Camera Lucida*, 73.
27. Welty, *One Time, One Place*, 5.
28. Eudora Welty, *Chestina Andrews Welty/Jackson/1950*, Plate 225, in *Photographs*.
29. "It is also true that here and there in particles and bits and in deeper reverberations sometimes, my mother is diffused over other characters I've written about—very different characters—in other books; she is part of Ellen in *Delta Wedding*, and a rather large part of Miss Julia Mortimer of *Losing Battles*." Welty, foreword, *The Optimist's Daughter*, in *Occasions*, 311.
30. Marrs, *One Writer's Imagination*, 228. *The Optimist's Daughter* is dedicated to Welty's mother, Chestina Andrews Welty. It appeared in the *New Yorker* in 1969, a year before the publication of *Losing Battles*. After revision, *The Optimist's Daughter* was published "in an expanded, book form" in 1972. Ibid., 240.
31. Charlotte Capers, "An Interview with Eudora Welty," in *Conversations with Eudora Welty*, ed. Peggy W. Prenshaw (Jackson: University Press of Mississippi, 1984), 116. Quoted by Marrs, *One Writer's Imagination*, 228.
32. Welty, *The Optimist's Daughter*, 144, 145. There is one photograph in her father's library: a picture of Laurel and her husband, Philip, now deceased, "running down the steps of the Mount Salus Presbyterian Church after their wedding." The present participle, "running," seems to animate this still image of the dead past; nonetheless, there is no mention of Laurel's retrieving the photograph. Ibid., 143.
33. Welty, *The Optimist's Daughter*, 159.
34. Ibid., 160–62.
35. Ibid., 162. Laurel's finding letters of a dead parent but not reading them and her looking at photographs that bring back voices alive from the dead have powerful resonance for me in relation to my own memoir: Susan Letzler Cole, *Missing Alice: In Search of a Mother's Voice* (Syracuse: Syracuse University Press, 2007).
36. Welty, *The Optimist's Daughter*, 171, 174, 176, 177–78.
37. Ibid., 177.
38. Welty, foreword, *The Optimist's Daughter*, in *Occasions*, 309.
39. Welty, *The Optimist's Daughter*, 196, 197–98.
40. See, for example, Welty's "The Burning," 484–88, 492, 494; "The Whistle," 59–61; "Clytie," 83; "Old Mr. Marblehead," 95; "Death of a Traveling Salesman," 127, 129; "First Love," 156–60, 164; "The Wide Net," 183; "Asphodel," 202; "The Winds," 220; "Livvie," 230; "At the Landing," 247, 251–52, 255–58; "No Place for You, My Love," 479–80; "Circe," 534, 537; *The Robber Bridegroom*, 142–43, 148–49, 173; *The Ponder Heart*, 75, 87–89, 104–5; *Losing Battles*, 176–77, 183, 241, 247, 265, 311, 334, 345–46, 349, 350; *Delta Wedding*, 46, 133, 162, 163, 166–67, 191, 221, 233, 235, 238, 242; *The Optimist's Daughter*, 196.
41. Lending support to this view, Meg Gertmenian points out that, in describing what Laurel puts in her suitcase before leaving Mount Salus, "Welty would have mentioned the snapshot book if it were in there." Meg Gertmenian, email correspondence with author, October 8, 2009.

42. Welty, *The Optimist's Daughter*, 207.
43. Meg Gertmenian, email correspondence with author, October 21, 2009.
44. Marrs, *One Writer's Imagination*, 227.
45. Eudora Welty, "The Optimist's Daughter," *New Yorker*, March 15, 1969, 125–26. In the writing desk where Laurel had discovered her father's letters and the snapshots of her parents, she had found a tiny stone in the shape of a boat that her father had made and given to her mother. Welty, *The Optimist's Daughter*, 161.
46. Welty, *The Optimist's Daughter*, 196.
47. Welty, *One Writer's Beginnings*, 104.
48. Welty, *The Optimist's Daughter*, 207–8.
49. Welty, foreword, *The Optimist's Daughter*, in *Occasions*, 313.
50. Welty, *The Optimist's Daughter*, 208.

6. Rosamond Wolff Purcell: Beginnings

1. Rosamond Purcell, phone interview with author, October 18, 2009.
2. Rosamond Purcell exhibits and talks about her work in the recent documentary film *An Art That Nature Makes: The Work of Rosamond Purcell,* directed by Molly Bernstein and produced by Molly Bernstein, Philip Dolin, and Alan Epstein, with music by John Purcell. The cinematographers are Philip Dolin and Mead Hunt. *An Art That Nature Makes: The Work of Rosamond Purcell* had its world premiere at the School of Visual Arts Theatre in New York City on November 14, 2015. See http:/www.parti-cleproductions.com (accessed January 17, 2016).
3. Rosamond Purcell, phone interview with author, October 18, 2009.
4. Reynolds Price, foreword, in Welty, *Photographs*, viii.
5. Purcell, *Owls Head*, 238. Welty, *One Writer's Beginnings*, 85.
6. Rosamond Purcell, 1968 log, unnumbered pages, mailed to author, November 2, 2009.
7. Welty, *The Eye of the Story*, 124. See my discussion of Welty's use of similes in chapter 4.
8. Morris, *Time Pieces*, 26.
9. Rosamond Purcell, "The Stories of Strangers: Mexican *Ex-Voto* Paintings," *Virginia Quarterly Review* 84, no. 2 (Spring 2008): 81, 83, 84.
10. Ibid.
11. Welty, "Words into Fiction," 137.
12. "A female voice . . . thin as a moonbeam, strung itself out into the night. . . . Lightning branched and ran over the world with an insect lightness." Welty, *Losing Battles*, 345, 353.
13. Purcell, "The Stories of Strangers," 86.

7. Alchemy

1. Photographs of people in Purcell's *A Matter of Time* are Plates 1, 4, 5, 6, 8, 11, 14, 16, 17, 19, 20, 23, 24, 25, 26, 27, 28, 29, 30, 31, 32, 33, 34, 37, 38, 42, 44, 47, 48, 49, 50, 51, 52, 55, 56, 61, 67, and 69; images of dog, deer, dolls, auto yard, egg,

and unidentified shapes are Plates 29, 35, 12, 60, 39, 64, 66, and 68 (unnumbered pages).

2. Rosamond Purcell, email correspondence with author, November 8, 2009.
3. Marrs, *Eudora Welty*, 54.
4. "*A Matter of Time* was my first book. . . . The lack of captions with the pictures may well have to do with that 'pure' impulse of wanting to promote image over words. . . . In some cases, early on, words seemed like a completely different part of the forest—using words seemed to redefine if not limit the meaning of an image rather than to allow it to breathe and the viewer a bit more free-range roaming." Rosamond Purcell, email correspondence with author, October 11, 2015.
5. Compare Eudora Welty's "self-teaching" as both photographer and writer. For Welty's very early work, one might look at "The Glorious Apology," a small handmade book she wrote and illustrated at the age of twelve. See Patti Carr Black, *Early Escapades* (Jackson: University Press of Mississippi, 2005).
6. Dennis W. Purcell, afterword, in Rosamond Purcell, *A Matter of Time* (Boston: David R. Godine, 1975), 70–71.
7. Ansel Adams, quoted in Martin W. Sandler, *Photography: An Illustrated History* (New York: Oxford University Press, 2002), 47.
8. John Szarkowski, quoted in Vincent Miholic, "Photography: A Writer's Tool for Thinking, Rendering, and Revising." See also Miholic's own list of the "basic processes and creative acts associated with photography [that] parallel those of writing." Both at http://www.questia.com/googleScholar.qst?docId=5001408020 (accessed October 15, 2009). Szarkowski offers a useful perspective on Henri Cartier-Bresson's famous "decisive moment": "Seeing the momentary patterning of lines and shapes that had been previously concealed within the flux of movement, . . . Cartier-Bresson defined his commitment to this new beauty with the phrase, *the decisive moment*, but the phrase has been misunderstood; the thing that happens at the decisive moment is not a dramatic climax but a visual one. The result is not a story but a picture." Szarkowski, *The Photographer's Eye*, 10. Szarkowski, who has commented on, exhibited, and admired the photographs of Eudora Welty, has said that her photographs "show us only the rarest and most evanescent truths." See http://www.nps.gov/nhl/find//statelists/ms/Welty.pdf, (accessed, December 20, 2009). Seeing the "patterning of lines and shapes . . . previously concealed within the flux of movement" may not occur until after the photographer has developed the image or the writer has completed a first draft.
9. In his study of the relation of realism, photography, and Victorian fiction, Daniel A. Novak paraphrases Geoffrey Batchen's view: "photography is in no way epistemologically different from the digital image." Novak adds that "digital technology and internet culture have *returned* to a Victorian theory of the photographic." Daniel A. Novak, *Realism, Photography, and Nineteenth-Century Fiction* (Cambridge: Cambridge University Press, 2008), 147.
10. Rosamond Purcell, phone conversation with author, October 18, 2009. Ansel Adams, quoted in Schaefer, *An Ansel Adams Guide*, 5.

11. Welty, “Place in Fiction,” 128.
12. Ralph Waldo Emerson, quoted in Stacy Schiff, “Please Mr. Postman,” *New York Times Book Review*, November 29, 2009, 13.
13. McHaney, *Eudora Welty as Photographer*, 17. McHaney quotes Welty’s comment to Joseph Cornell in 1945: “The photographs I took I feel are not really good, the subjects themselves are wonderful, but I am an inept photographer, or was, I have stopped—I do know the feeling of finding things in the familiar streets or just off them that make you think they can never be expressed.” Ibid., 24n45.
14. John Donne, “The Good-Morrow,” in *The Norton Anthology of English Literature*, vol. B, ed. Greenblatt et al., l. 11, p. 1264.
15. Welty, *Delta Wedding*, 220.
16. This is Lisa Melandri’s phrase, referring to William Buckminster’s huge junkyard in Owls Head, Maine, from which Purcell had been collecting materials and transporting them to her studio. Lisa Melandri, “About Appearance: The Work of Rosamond Purcell,” in *Rosamond Purcell: Two Rooms,* by Rosamond Purcell (Santa Monica: Santa Monica Museum of Art, 2003), 13.

8. Double Vision

1. Reynolds Price, foreword, in Welty, *Photographs*, x.
2. Rosamond Purcell, *Special Cases: Natural Anomalies and Historical Monsters* (San Francisco: Chronicle Books, 1997), 139.
3. Cf. Marianne Moore’s poem “The Pangolin,” in which she describes this “armored animal—scale / lapping scale with spruce-cone regularity. . . . / This near artichoke with head and legs.” Moore, *Complete Poems*, ll. 1–2, 4, p. 117. In her poem “The End of March,” Elizabeth Bishop makes use of an artichoke to create a visual image of a beach house, “set up on pilings, shingled green, / a sort of artichoke of a house, but greener.” Elizabeth Bishop, *Geography III* (New York: Farrar, Straus and Giroux, 1978), ll. 26–27, p. 43.
4. Purcell, *Special Cases*, 88–89, 94.
5. Eudora Welty, “Clytie,” in *The Collected Stories*, 83.
6. René Paul Barilleaux, foreword, in *Passionate Observer*, ed. Barilleaux, 7.
7. Jessica Nicoll, preface, in Rosamond Purcell, *Medea and Her Sisters: Leonard Baskin’s Images of Women* (Northampton: Smith College Museum of Art, 2007), unnumbered page.
8. Purcell, *Medea and Her Sisters*, unnumbered page.
9. Ibid.
10. “Though this child must have died shortly after birth, the photograph transforms the tragedy into a lyrical metaphor, the infant’s head a tulip opening toward the sun.” Melandri, “About Appearance,” 10.
11. Rosamond Purcell, “Planets of Thought,” in *Aldwyth: work v./work n.: Collage and Assemblage 1991–2009*, catalogue for an exhibition organized by the Halsey Institute of Contemporary Art, College of Charleston, Charleston, South Carolina (Charleston: Halsey Institute of Contemporary Art, 2009), 83. Of interest in connection with Benjamin’s concept of “aura” is Aldwyth’s caption for one of her

large collages, *Casablanca (classic version)*: "*visualizing a flood of eyes looking back, as if the art were the observer.*" Purcell writes: "Most of the eyes in *Casablanca (classic version)* belong to, or were painted by, artists. Eyes rim separate scenes like beads around a frame. As we look at art, Aldwyth says, this art looks back at us. It is like having a conversation, this meeting with the Eye." Ibid., 26–27, 87. Cf. the kind of "conversation" that occurs in Eudora Welty's snapshot *A woman of the 'thirties/Hinds County/1935*, discussed at the end of chapter 1.

12. Purcell, "Planets of Thought," 85.

9. Foraging and Reconfiguring

1. Rónán McDonald, "Beloved Object," *Times Literary Supplement* (January 8, 2010), 19. McDonald notes further that Orhan Pamuk, author of *The Museum of Innocence*, "has bought a building in Istanbul to house an actual 'Museum of Innocence,' which is due to open in late 2010." I am indebted to Deborah Frattini for alerting me to McDonald's review.
2. Purcell writes of the collection of objects in her Somerville studio's thousand-square-foot room: "By nonmetaphorical weight, almost 100 percent of the holdings came from Buckminster's, and by actual number almost 80 percent." Purcell, *Owls Head*, 139, 141.
3. Donne, "The Good-Morrow," l. 11, p. 1264.
4. Rosamond Purcell, phone conversation with author, October 31, 2009. Her reconstruction of Worm's cabinet—ten feet high, twelve feet long, and nine and a half feet wide—is "currently in Denmark in boxes." Ibid. A somewhat similar project is Jeff Wall's photograph, "After *Invisible Man* by Ralph Ellison, the Prologue," almost six feet high and over eight feet wide, of his reconstruction of the basement room, with its 1,369 light bulbs, of Ellison's narrator: "Without light I am not only invisible, but formless as well." Ralph Ellison, *Invisible Man* (New York: New American Library, 1964), 10. John Roberts notes that Wall's "photograph is the result of the building of a set/artwork whose details are derived from another artwork, . . . which in turn depicts an artwork in the making. The point, then, seems to be that the claims for meaning, realism, affect, empathy in photography are not diminished by this chain of displacement." John Roberts, quoted in Jeff Wall, "Post-60s Photography and Its Modernist Context: A Conversation between Jeff Wall and John Roberts," in *Jeff Wall: Selected Essays*, 344–45.
5. Rosamond Purcell, "Enticing Shadow, Elusive Form," in *Rosamond Purcell: Two Rooms*, 31.
6. Ibid., 35.
7. Rosamond Purcell, "Artist's Introduction," in *Rock of Ages/Sands of Time*, paintings by Barbara Page and text by Warren Allmon, foreword by Rosamond Purcell (Chicago: University of Chicago Press, 2001), xxi.
8. Rosamond Purcell, email correspondence with author, November 2, 2009.
9. Purcell, "Artist's Introduction," vii, ix, xi.
10. Welty, *Losing Battles*, 359.
11. Asked if she feels that her photographs "have or give 'voice,'" Purcell responds: "Not

that I know of." Rosamond Purcell, email correspondence with author, September 17, 2009. As already quoted in chapter 6, Purcell said, in a telephone interview on October 18, 2009: "I'm really looking for my voice, . . . looking for it for years and years and years."

12. Purcell, *Owls Head*, 65, 63, 58.
13. Ibid., 9.
14. Rosamond Purcell, *Half-Life* (Boston: David R. Godine, 1980), 47. It is the only untitled photograph in this collection.
15. Purcell, *Owls Head*, 10, 193.
16. Ibid., 49, 51–52.
17. Rosamond Purcell, *Typewriter*, in *Bookworm* (New York: Quantuck Lane Press, 2006), 100.
18. Purcell, *Owls Head*, 19–20.
19. Purcell, *Bookworm*, 39, 157. In Stephen Jay Gould and Rosamond Purcell, *Crossing Over: Where Art and Science Meet* (New York: Three Rivers Press, 2000), the image was titled *The Book Nest* (154). Purcell notes that discrepancies in the title of this image were not intended. "I do know that 'Book/Nest' is the most likely to reoccur in shows and as reprinted in articles." Rosamond Purcell, email correspondence with author, February 15, 2010.
20. Claire Sykes, "Rosamond Wolff Purcell: Choice Meets Chance," *Photographer's Forum* (Winter 2008): 43.
21. Purcell, *Owls Head*, 63–64.
22. Ibid., 193, 200, 220, 221, 233.
23. Purcell, *Owls Head*, see chapter 2, endnote 13; chapter 3, endnote 5; chapter 4, endnote 7; chapter 6, endnote 1. Ibid., 199, 202, 206, 209. Unlike Welty, who does not include any snapshots taken by herself in her memoir, *One Writer's Beginnings,* Purcell does include her own photographs in her memoir, *Owls Head.*
24. Cf. Wittgenstein's provocative comment, "thinking is an activity of our writing hand." Ludwig Wittgenstein, *The Blue and Brown Books* (New York: Harper & Row, 1958), 16.
25. When Purcell and her husband visited William Buckminster over Thanksgiving in 2009, they found him in a nursing home. "There are three buildings standing," she tells me, "and the rest [of the eleven-acre junkyard in Owls Head] is plowed over. The barn has completely collapsed." Rosamond Purcell, phone conversation with author, December 4, 2009.
26. Rosamond Purcell, email correspondence with author, November 11, 2009, previously quoted in the introduction.
27. Welty, *One Writer's Beginnings*, 10; Purcell, *Owls Head*, 77.

10. Images Rich and Strange

1. Purcell, *Owls Head*, 51.
2. Allan Chasanoff, "Lux, et tu, Veritas?," in Joshua Chang, *First Doubt: Optical Confusion in Modern Photography* (New Haven: Yale University Press, 2008), 215.

3. Chang, *First Doubt*, 15.
4. Sven Birkerts, "The Trained Eye," in Purcell, *Bookworm*, 10. Purcell writes: "I do not expect unilateral agreement from viewers about what these pictures 'mean.' I prefer to show the pictures rather than talk too much about them. I will describe the contents and intentions behind a photograph to demystify its superficial strangeness." Purcell, afterword, *Crossing Over*, 156. In preferring to show the pictures rather than to talk too much about them, Purcell recalls the practice of Welty; however, Purcell actually offers exquisite ekphrases of her images while not talking too much about them.
5. Purcell, *Bookworm*, 158.
6. In her book of poems about her great-great-grandfather, Ruth Padel writes: "In June [1939] Louis Daguerre / receives full patent for a camera. The photograph: / a system, one understands, for writing with the sun." Ruth Padel, "Confinement/I/ Symptoms," in *Darwin: A Life in Poems* (New York: Knopf, 2009), ll. 7–9, p. 78.
7. Purcell, *Bookworm*, 37.
8. Ibid., 89, 141, 160. Unless otherwise indicated, all future references for photographs in this chapter are to Purcell, *Bookworm*.
9. Purcell, email correspondence with author, September 14, 2009.
10. "A friend lent me a copy of Umberto Eco's 'Foucault's Pendulum.' I very much admired the termite-gnawed text, forged by these insects into a three-dimensional sculpture of layers and hollows and isolated phrases like 'I am close to the truth' and 'the rapture of some superior heaven.' I placed the book on a shelf where sunlight spilled across the pages. *Grail* is a photograph of the same book in lower light. The word 'Grail' is visible in the text. The object, here set into a hollow left behind by the insects' consumption of pages, was the yolk of an egg that had never hatched and had become petrified within the shell. It looks like a rough but precious stone and has a beautiful glow implying an external source or containment of light." Rosamond Purcell, email correspondence with author, August 16, 2015.
11. "The crystallized egg yolk," Purcell writes, "glows with the fire of life. When it regenerates, however, it will emerge not as a chicken but as a mass of maggots, which, to the naked eye, seem to have magically appeared." Purcell, *Bookworm*, 23. Purcell's statement and my own reading of the crystallized egg yolk illustrate, in different ways, Allan Chasanoff's views of the "'optical' engender[ing] . . . the 'failure' to see a photographic image correctly, allowing the viewer to attach doubt to reality itself." Chasanoff, "Lux, et tu, Veritas?," 215.
12. "The half-circle is not meant to be showing in the picture," Purcell explains. The "same thick plastic block . . . supplying the top-light . . . in *Foucault's Pendulum* . . . seems to have been placed behind/under the book and crystallized egg, and the rim of one of the holes (regularly drilled into its thick surface) is obliquely seen by [the] camera as a freestanding half-ring." Rosamond Purcell, email correspondence with author, February 15, 2010.
13. Purcell, *Bookworm*, 81, 82, 83, 84, 85, 86, 87, 89, 90, 92, 93, 94, 95, 112, 115, 117, 123, 124, 125, 126, 127, 130, 131, 134, 138, 141, 142, 146, 148, 156.

14. *Karakoram* is an image of graffiti, first in Chinese and then in Urdu, superimposed on a rock by a highway through mountains in Pakistan. Purcell, *Bookworm*, 146. When asked about the translation of both languages, Purcell says, "A friend of my nephew's (who studied Urdu) thought it was an argument: 'This was our road. . . .' 'No, this was OUR road!,' but it turns out (can't remember how I know this) it just means 'bus stop' in two languages." (Karakoram is the name of the highway.) Rosamond Purcell, email correspondence with author, September 3 and 14, 2009.
15. Rosamond Purcell, phone conversation with author, January 29, 2010. She added, "I love the way English is tortured into phonetics in *Krazy Kat*." Ibid.
16. "Many 'collages' or 'constructions' I made in order that they BE PHOTOGRAPHED. I was after the appearance of (rather than the actuality of) a three-dimensional object on film. . . . Often, afterwards, the collages/constructions were put aside, destroyed or simply vanished because I used the photograph as the final 'object.' But, for [*Bookworm*] (and previously for slide talks), I did photograph collages made to be—well—collages. . . . [Several] are even smaller as objects than these photographs of them!—in some cases, only a couple of inches in height/across. Occasionally, I have shown both collage and photograph of it side by side. Differences between these (scale, texture, etc.) [are] remarkable." Rosamond Purcell, email correspondence with author, September 14, 2009.
17. Purcell, *Bookworm*, 28.
18. Ibid., 29.
19. There are photographs of fish "[seemingly] engaged in earnest conversation" in Purcell and Gould, *Illuminations: A Bestiary*, 46, 48, 50, 51.
20. In "Playing with Pictures: The Art of Victorian Photocollage," an exhibit at the Metropolitan Museum of Art in New York City, February 2–May 9, 2010, the caption for one page of Georgina Berkeley's album notes: "In [Victorian] photocollages, heads are often severed from bodies and inserted into fantastic scenes . . . , as in this image." The earlier use of photocollages that feature severed heads seems to anticipate Purcell's collage *Public Domain*, among others. The shifts in scale and the Queen of Hearts' threatened severing of heads in a more famous Victorian work, Lewis Carroll's *Alice's Adventures in Wonderland*, are also possible antecedents for some of Purcell's work. John Crowley has said that "Rosamond Purcell is an Alice in a wonderland she has herself sought out." John Crowley, "Metamorphosis: Rosamond Purcell's Natural History," *Boston Review*, May/June 2007, http://bostonreview.net/BR32.3/ crowley.php (accessed December 16, 2009).
21. Wall, *Jeff Wall: Selected Essays*, 252.
22. Interestingly, Welty's mother entrusted a cherished photograph of a two- or three-year-old Eudora in the arms of her grandmother to an itinerant photographer who said he "could 'permanently preserve' any photograph." It was eventually sent back "'stuck forever between 2 sheets of glass.'" Welty reproduced this photograph, which neither she nor the itinerant photographer had taken, as Christmas gifts to several friends in 1971. Writing to Mary Lou Aswell on December 16, 1971, she explained: "I wanted you to have it *because of the story* & because of her & me & everything" (italics mine). Marrs, *Eudora Welty*, 369–70.

23. "Photographers," Purcell notes, "are aware of the chaos that plays outside the frame." Purcell, *Bookworm*, 34. Welty as fiction writer is clearly aware of that which plays outside the frame(s).
24. Purcell, *Bookworm*, 16, 20. Cf. Eudora Welty: "The camera I focused in front of me . . . was an eye . . . —not quite mine, but a quicker and an unblinking one—and it couldn't see pain where it looked. . . . It was what I used, at any rate, and, like any tool, it used me." Welty, *One Time, One Place*, 7.
25. Purcell, *Bookworm*, 21–22, 33. In her memoir, Purcell recalls "sneak[ing] . . . past my father's study door in order to escape. . . . To this day, I see no summer house without planning an escape route. When I stare at important books, fondle, covet, even collect them, part of me wants to *get it over with*: get out of the house, find my friends." Purcell, *Owls Head*, 160.
26. Stephen Jay Gould, describing Purcell's *The Book Nest* (as captioned in *Crossing Over*), distinguishes between function and structure: "In functional terms, the book can no longer be read and has *therefore ceased to exist*; the object now works as a nest for a different species. . . . In structural terms, we can still know that this nest passed through a former life as a pair of books" (italics mine). Gould and Purcell, *Crossing Over*, 153–54.
27. Purcell, *Bookworm*, 33, 87,158. A more truly ruined version of Dante's *Inferno* might be "Dante's Inferno," a video game released by Electronic Art on February 9, 2009, with Dante as a muscular action hero wearing body armor, except on his bare chest and sword-wielding right arm. Dave Itzkoff, "Abandon All Poetry, but Enter Hell With an Attitude," *New York Times*, January 30, 2010, C1.
28. Purcell, *Bookworm*, 35.
29. Rosamond Purcell, email correspondence with author, September 15, 2009.
30. Purcell, *Bookworm*, 35. Jaques says, "All the world's a stage." William Shakespeare, *As You Like It*, 2.7.138. All Shakespeare references are to *The Norton Shakespeare, Based on the Oxford Edition*, ed. Stephen Greenblatt et al. (New York: W. W. Norton, 1997). Purcell writes: "As I have long followed the advice of the late Minor White, photographer and sage, to photograph things 'for what else they are,' I also collect things for what they may become." Purcell, *Rosamond Purcell: Two Rooms*, 37. Cf. Wallace Stevens: "seemings that are to be, / Seemings that it is possible may be." Wallace Stevens, "Description Without Place," in *Collected Poems* (New York: Knopf, 1969), Section III, ll. 31–32, p. 342.
31. Purcell, *Bookworm*, 24.
32. *Photographer's Forum* (Winter 2008): 43.
33. Ricky Jay, describing Purcell's exquisite images of his collection of decaying celluloid dice, begins by alluding to her photographs of "weather-beaten books that are transformed—by design, by vision, by respect—into objects of great beauty"; "Rosamond Purcell, doyenne of decaying objects, . . . has come to know my dice. . . . She has analyzed every nuance of shape and color. She has at once halted their disintegration and catalyzed their resurrection. The dice have never looked better." Ricky Jay, *Dice: Deception, Fate & Rotten Luck*, photography by Rosamond Purcell (New York: Quantuck Lane Press, 2003), 54.

34. William Shakespeare, *The Tempest*: 4.1.154–56. Cf. Claire Sykes: "Purcell's eggs and nests, bones and beat-up books—and her photographs of them—will one day disintegrate into nothingness, towed by that inescapable force called time. But meanwhile, for me, they are all aesthetic treasures." Claire Sykes, *Photographer's Forum* (Winter 2008): 47.
35. Edmund Spenser, "Epithalamion," in *The Norton Anthology of English Literature*, vol. B, ed. Stephen Greenblatt et al., l.433, p. 916.
36. Purcell, *Bookworm*, 35.

11. Wonder

1. Rosamond Purcell, acknowledgments, in Rosamond Purcell, Linnea S. Hall, and René Corado, *Egg & Nest* (Cambridge: Harvard University Press, 2008), 217.
2. Purcell, Hall, and Corado, *Egg & Nest*, 187.
3. Ibid., 188.
4. Ibid., 189.
5. Ibid., 195, 191.
6. Ibid., 205.
7. The albumen process was already becoming obsolete at the beginning of Eugène Atget's career. A dying process, used by Atget until he died, produced some of the world's most famous photographs. See Peter Barberie, *Looking at Atget* (New Haven, CT: Philadelphia Museum of Art in association with Yale University Press, 2005), 12, 14.
8. Purcell, Hall, and Corado, *Egg & Nest*, 206, 210.
9. The title *Landscapes of the Passing Strange* alludes to Desdemona's response to the story of Othello's life: "She swore in faith 'twas strange, 'twas passing strange, / 'Twas pitiful, 'twas wondrous pitiful." William Shakespeare, *Othello*: 1.3.159–60.
10. Laurence Senelick, "The Craig-Stanislavsky 'Hamlet' at the Moscow Art Theatre," *Theatre Quarterly* 6 (1976): 73, quoted by Marjorie Garber, "A Tale of Three *Hamlets* or Repetition and Revenge," *Shakespeare Quarterly* 61, no. 1 (Spring 2010): 37–38. Interesting in this connection is Diane Paulus's production, *The Donkey Show*, a radical version of *A Midsummer Night's Dream*, in which "not a single word of Shakespeare's dialogue is uttered, but the action is true to his characters and their relationships." Craig Lambert, "Theater As If It Matters," *Harvard Magazine* 112, no. 2 (November–December 2009): 18.
11. Garber notes that Craig Lambert, in his woodcuts for the 1930 Cranach Press edition of *Hamlet*, "takes center stage and center page: . . . he is actor, director, and critic in one." Garber, "A Tale of Three *Hamlets*," 55.
12. Rosamond Purcell, "Eyed Awry," in Rosamond Purcell and Michael Witmore, *Landscapes of the Passing Strange: Reflections from Shakespeare* (New York: Norton, 2010), 115. The beautiful moment in which Purcell took the mirrored jars to a meadow and "turned them toward natural light" might be seen as a photographer's reenactment of Hamlet's famous advice to the actors at Elsinore: "The purpose of playing . . . was and is to hold as 'twere the mirror up to nature." William Shakespeare, *Hamlet*: 3.2.18–20.

13. Rosamond Purcell, phone interview with author, October 18, 2009.
14. Reviewing Peter Hall's production of *A Midsummer Night's Dream* at the Rose Theatre, with Judi Dench "as a staggeringly compelling Titania," Juliet Fleming writes that Dench's performance "puts audiences in the presence of a great actor acting both her part, and herself in her part." Juliet Fleming, "Bad Dreams," *Times Literary Supplement*, March 5, 2010, 17.
15. Chasanoff, "Lux, et tu, Veritas?," 215.
16. Purcell, "Eyed Awry," 115–16.
17. William Shakespeare, *King Lear*: 5.3. 252. Michael Witmore notes that "Lear's monosyllables are one of the great terrors of the play." Michael Witmore, *Shakespearean Metaphysics* (New York: Continuum, 2008), 80. Michael Goldman, writing of "the accumulative pattern, the use of intensifying repetition," and "the histrionic problem set by lines like . . . 'Howl, howl, howl, howl,'" tells us: "In performance . . . [such lines] act out a tension between . . . the thrill of letting go, of crying out, and the labor of concentration, of finding a precise image for each exclamation in the series. Such lines long to be only a cry, but they must have a content or they go dead: they threaten to escape, as every audience and critic longs to escape, from the dreadful particularity of the play." Michael Goldman, *Acting and Action in Shakespearean Tragedy* (Princeton: Princeton University Press, 1985), 88–89.
18. Rosamond Purcell, email correspondence with author, April 15, 2010.
19. All page numbers in parentheses following titles of photographs are to Purcell and Witmore, *Landscapes of the Passing Strange*.
20. This and the following quotation from *King Lear* are from the conflated text of *King Lear* in the Norton edition: William Shakespeare, *The Norton Shakespeare, Based on the Oxford Edition*, ed. Stephen Greenblatt et al. (New York: Norton, 1997).
21. Samuel Johnson writes: "I was many years ago so shocked by Cordelia's death, that I know not whether I ever endured to read again the last scenes of the play till I undertook to revise them as an editor." Samuel Johnson, "The Preface to Shakespeare," in *The Norton Anthology of English Literature*, vol. C, ed. Stephen Greenblatt et al., 2766.
22. In response to my question, "Is Ophelia holding a basket in the photo 'We Are Pictures?,' Purcell says: "I see 'Ophelia' with a basket, yes, and a hat, and with what looks like one big bird leg." Rosamond Purcell, email correspondence with author, April 25 and 26, 2010. Note the photographer's own careful phrasing: "I see . . . what looks like." The image of the bird leg may relate to one of Ophelia's mad speeches in this scene: "They say the owl was a baker's daughter," an allusion to a folktale about a baker's daughter who was turned into an owl after begrudging bread to Christ (Shakespeare, *Hamlet*: 4.5.41–42).
23. See Susan Letzler Cole, "'Maimèd Rites': Shakespeare's *Hamlet*," in *The Absent One*, 41–60 (especially 56–58).
24. Purcell, "Eyed Awry," 116.
25. Rosamond Purcell, email correspondence with author, April 12, 2010.
26. Warwick Wadlington, *Reading Faulknerian Tragedy* (Ithaca, NY: Cornell University Press, 1987), 7. See also the chapter on reading and performance, 26–49.

27. Michael Witmore, "More Strange Than True," in Purcell and Witmore, *Landscapes of the Passing Strange*, 7.
28. Rosamond Purcell and Michael Witmore each see in the lower part of the spiraling form the image of a swan. Private communications with author, December 18, 2012.

Epilogue

1. Welty, *Photographs*, xv.
2. Welty, *One Time, One Place*, 8.
3. Eudora Welty, *Country Churchyards* (Jackson: University Press of Mississippi, 2001).
4. Purcell, *Owls Head*, 63, 51.
5. Welty, *Losing Battles*, 359.
6. Rosamond Purcell, email correspondence with author, April 15, 2010.

Bibliography

Adams, Timothy Dow. *Light Writing & Life Writing: Photography in Autobiography*. Chapel Hill: University of North Carolina Press, 2000.

Barberie, Peter. *Looking at Atget*. New Haven, CT: Philadelphia Museum of Art in Association with Yale University Press, 2005.

Barilleaux, René Paul, ed. *Passionate Observer: Eudora Welty among Artists of the Thirties*. Jackson: Mississippi Museum of Art, 2007.

Barthes, Roland. *Camera Lucida: Reflections on Photography*. Translated by Richard Howard. New York: Farrar, Straus and Giroux, 1981.

———. *Image-Music-Text*. Translated by Stephen Heath. New York: Hill and Wang, 1977.

Benfey, Christopher. *American Audacity: Literary Essays North and South*. Ann Arbor: University of Michigan Press, 2008.

Benjamin, Walter. *Illuminations*. Translated by Harry Zohn. New York: Schocken Books, 1969.

Bernstein, Molly (producer/director). *An Art That Nature Makes: The Work of Rosamond Purcell*. New York: Hopscotch Films/Particle Productions, 2015.

Birkerts, Sven. "The Trained Eye." Introduction to *Bookworm* by Rosamond Purcell. New York: Norton, Quantuck Lane Press, 2006.

Bishop, Elizabeth. *Geography III*. New York: Farrar, Straus and Giroux, 1978.

Black, Patti Carr. *Early Escapades*. Jackson: University Press of Mississippi, 2005.

———, ed. *Eudora*. Jackson: Mississippi Department of Archives and History, 1984.

Bloom, Harold, ed. *Eudora Welty*. New York: Chelsea House Publishers, 1986.

Carson, Barbara Harrell. *Eudora Welty: Two Pictures at Once in Her Frame*. Troy, NY: Whitson, 1992.

Chang, Joshua. *First Doubt: Optical Confusion in Modern Photography*. New Haven: Yale University Press, 2008.

Chasanoff, Allan. "Lux, et tu, Veritas?" Catalogue essay in *First Doubt: Optical Confusion in Modern Photography*, by Joshua Chang, 213–16. New Haven: Yale University Press, 2008.

Chouard, Géraldine. *Eudora Welty et la photographie: Naissance d'une vision*. Paris: Michel Houdiard, 2012.

Cole, Susan Letzler. *The Absent One: Mourning Ritual, Tragedy, and the Performance of Ambivalence*. University Park: Pennsylvania State University Press, 1985.

———. *Missing Alice: In Search of a Mother's Voice*. Syracuse, NY: Syracuse University Press, 2007.

Crowley, John. "Metamorphosis: Rosamond Purcell's Natural History." *Boston Review*, May/June 2007. http:/bostonreview.net/BR32.3/crowley.php. Accessed December 16, 2009.

Ellison, Ralph. *Invisible Man*. New York: New American Library, 1964.

Fleischauer, John F. "The Focus of Mystery: Eudora Welty's Prose Style." *Southern Literary Journal* 5, no. 2 (Spring 1973): 64–79.

Fried, Michael. *Why Photography Matters as Art as Never Before*. New Haven: Yale University Press, 2008.

Garber, Marjorie. "A Tale of Three *Hamlets* or Repetition and Revenge." *Shakespeare Quarterly* 61, no. 1 (Spring 2010): 28–55.

Goldman, Michael. *Acting and Action in Shakespearean Tragedy*. Princeton: Princeton University Press, 1985.

Gould, Stephen Jay, and Rosamond Purcell. *Crossing Over: Where Art and Science Meet*. New York: Three Rivers Press, 2000.

Henninger, Katherine. *Ordering the Façade: Photography and Contemporary Southern Women's Writing*. Chapel Hill: University of North Carolina Press, 2007.

Howard, Richard. *Misgivings*. New York: Atheneum, 1979.

Itzkoff, Dave. "Abandon All Poetry, but Enter Hell with an Attitude." *New York Times*, January 30, 2010, C1.

Jay, Ricky. *Dice: Deception, Fate & Rotten Luck*. Photography by Rosamond Purcell. New York: Norton, Quantuck Lane Press, 2003.

Kreyling, Michael. *Eudora Welty's Achievement of Order*. Baton Rouge: Louisiana State University Press, 1980.

———. *Understanding Eudora Welty*. Columbia: University of South Carolina Press, 1999.

———. "Words into Criticism: Eudora Welty's Essays and Reviews." In *Eudora Welty, Thirteen Essays: Selected from Eudora Welty, Critical Essays*, edited by Peggy Whitman Prenshaw, 224–35. Jackson: University of Mississippi Press, 1983.

Lambert, Craig. "Theater As If It Matters." *Harvard Magazine* 112, no. 2 (November–December 2009): 18.

Marrs, Suzanne. *Eudora Welty: A Biography*. New York: Harcourt, 2005.

———. *One Writer's Imagination: The Fiction of Eudora Welty*. Baton Rouge: Louisiana State University Press, 2002.

McDonald, Rónán. "Beloved Object." *Times Literary Supplement*, January 8, 2010, 19–20.

McHaney, Pearl Amelia, ed. *Eudora Welty as Photographer: Photographs by Eudora Welty*. Jackson: University Press of Mississippi, 2009.

———, ed. *Eudora Welty: Occasions, Selected Writings*. Jackson: University Press of Mississippi, 2009.

Melandri, Lisa, "About Appearance: The Work of Rosamond Purcell." In *Rosamond Purcell: Two Rooms*, by Rosamond Purcell, 7–15. Santa Monica, CA: Santa Monica Museum of Art, 2003.

Miholic, Vincent. "Photography: A Writer's Tool for Thinking, Rendering, and Revising." http://www.questia.com/googleScholar.qst?docId=5001408020. Accessed October 15, 2009.

Mitchell, W.J.T. *Picture Theory: Essays on Verbal and Visual Representation*. Chicago: University of Chicago Press, 1994.

———. *What Do Pictures Want? The Lives and Loves of Images*. Chicago: University of Chicago Press, 2005.

Moore, Marianne. *Complete Poems*. Harmondsworth, UK: Penguin, 1982.

Morris, Wright. *Time Pieces: Photographs, Writing, and Memory*. New York: Aperture, 1989.

Murfin, Ross, and Supryia M. Roy. *The Bedford Glossary of Critical and Literary Terms*. 3rd ed. New York: Bedford/St. Martin's, 2009.

Novak, Daniel A. *Realism, Photography, and Nineteenth-Century Fiction*. Cambridge: Cambridge University Press, 2008.

Olney, James, ed. *Autobiography: Essays Theoretical and Critical*. Princeton: Princeton University Press, 1980.

Padel, Ruth. *Darwin: A Life in Poems*. New York: Knopf, 2009.

Page, Barbara, and Warren Allmon. *Rock of Ages/Sands of Time*. Chicago: University of Chicago Press, 2001.

Pollack, Harriet, ed. *Eudora Welty: Whiteness and Race*. Athens: University of Georgia Press, 2013.

———. "'Words between Strangers': On Welty, Her Style, and Her Audience." In *Welty: A Life in Literature*, edited by Albert J. Devlin. Jackson: University of Mississippi, 1987.

Prenshaw, Peggy W., ed. *Conversations with Eudora Welty*. Jackson: University Press of Mississippi, 1984.

Price, Mary. *The Photograph: A Strange Confined Space*. Stanford: Stanford University Press, 1994.

Purcell, Rosamond. *Bookworm*. New York: Norton, Quantuck Lane Press, 2006.

———. Foreword to *Rock of Ages/Sands of Time*, by Barbara Page and Warren Allmon. Chicago: University of Chicago Press, 2001.

———. "The Game of the Name." *Art Bulletin*, June 1995, 182.

———. *Half-Life*. Boston: David R. Godine, 1980.

———. *A Matter of Time*. Boston: David R. Godine, 1975.

———. *Medea and Her Sisters: Leonard Baskin's Images of Women*. Northampton: Smith College Museum of Art, 2007.

———. *Owls Head*. New York: Norton, Quantuck Lane Press, 2003.

———. "Planets of Thought." In *Aldwyth: work v./work n.: Collage and Assemblage 1991–2009*, edited by Mark Sloan, 78–91. Charleston: Halsey Institute of Contemporary Art, 2009.

———. *Rosamond Purcell: Two Rooms*. Santa Monica: Santa Monica Museum of Art, 2003.

———. *Special Cases: Natural Anomalies and Historical Monsters*. San Francisco: Chronicle Books, 1997.

———. "The Stories of Strangers: Mexican *Ex-Voto* Paintings." *Virginia Quarterly Review* 84, no. 2 (Spring 2008): 81–91.

Purcell, Rosamond, Linnea S. Hall, and René Corodo. *Egg & Nest*. Cambridge: Harvard University Press, 2008.

Purcell, Rosamond Wolff, and Stephen Jay Gould. *Illuminations: A Bestiary*. New York: Norton, 1986.

Purcell, Rosamond, and Michael Witmore. *Landscapes of the Passing Strange: Reflections from Shakespeare*. New York: Norton, 2010.

Ricks, Christopher. "Undermining Keats." *New York Review of Books*, December 17, 2009, 48.

Sandler, Martin W. *Photography: An Illustrated History*. New York: Oxford University Press, 2002.

Schaefer, John P. *An Ansel Adams Guide*. New York: Little, Brown and Co., 1992.

Shakespeare, William. *The Norton Shakespeare, Based on the Oxford Edition*. Edited by Stephen Greenblatt et al. New York: Norton, 1997.

Sontag, Susan. *On Photography*. New York: Doubleday, 1989.

Sprinker, Michael. "Fictions of the Self: The End of Autobiography." In *Autobiography: Essays Theoretical and Critical*, edited by James Olney, 321–42. Princeton: Princeton University Press, 1980.

Stevens, Wallace. *Collected Poems*. New York: Knopf, 1969.

Sykes, Claire. "Rosamond Wolff Purcell: Choice Meets Chance." *Photographer's Forum* (Winter 2008): 38–47.

Szarkowski, John. *Looking at Photographs*. New York: Museum of Modern Art, 1973.

———. *The Photographer's Eye*. New York: Museum of Modern Art, 1966.

Trachtenberg, Alan. *Reading American Photographs: Images as History, Matthew Brady to Walker Evans*. New York: Hill and Wang, 1989.

Trevor, William. *Love and Summer*. New York: Viking, 2009.

Wadlington, Warwick. *Reading Faulknerian Tragedy*. Ithaca, NY: Cornell University Press, 1987.

Wall, Jeff. *Jeff Wall: Selected Essays and Interviews*. New York: Museum of Modern Art, 2007.

Welty, Eudora. *Collected Stories*. New York: Harcourt Brace Jovanovich, 1980.

———. *Country Churchyards*. Jackson: University Press of Mississippi, 2001.

———. *Delta Wedding*. New York: Harcourt, Brace and Co., 1945.

———. *The Eye of the Story: Selected Essays and Reviews*. New York: Random House, 1970.

———. *Losing Battles*. New York: Vintage, 1978.

———. *One Time, One Place: Mississippi in the Depression, A Snapshot Album*. New York: Random House, 1971.

———. *One Writer's Beginnings*. Cambridge: Harvard University Press, 1984.

———. "The Optimist's Daughter." *New Yorker*, March 15, 1969.

———. *The Optimist's Daughter*. New York: Vintage, 1978.

———. *Photographs*. Jackson: University Press of Mississippi, 1989.

———. *The Ponder Heart*. New York: Harcourt, Brace, 1954.

———. *The Robber Bridegroom*. New York: Doubleday, Doran & Co., 1942.

Westling, Louise. *Eudora Welty*. London: Macmillan, 1989.

Weston, Ruth D. *Gothic Traditions and Narrative Techniques in the Fiction of Eudora Welty*. Baton Rouge: Louisiana State University Press, 1994.

Wolin, Richard. *Walter Benjamin: An Aesthetic of Redemption*. New York: Columbia University Press, 1982.

Susan Letzler Cole is professor of English and director of the Concentrations in Creative Writing and Dramatic Studies at Albertus Magnus College. She is the author of *The Absent One: Mourning Ritual, Tragedy, and the Performance of Ambivalence*; *Directors in Rehearsal: A Hidden World*; *Playwrights in Rehearsal: The Seduction of Company*; and *Missing Alice: In Search of a Mother's Voice*.